Ramchandra Gandhi

RAMCHANDRA GANDHI

Talks and Writings

Edited by

A. Raghuramaraju

With a Foreword by

Daniel Raveh

Orient BlackSwan

RAMCHANDRA GANDHI: TALKS AND WRITINGS

ORIENT BLACKSWAN PRIVATE LIMITED

Registered Office
3-6-752 Himayatnagar, Hyderabad 500 029, Telangana, India
e-mail: centraloffice@orientblackswan.com

Other Offices
Bengaluru, Bhopal, Chennai, Guwahati,
Hyderabad, Jaipur, Kolkata, Lucknow, Mumbai,
New Delhi, Noida, Patna, Visakhapatnam

First published by Orient Blackswan Private Limited 2020

ISBN 978-93-90122-53-0

Typeset in
Dante MT Std 11/13
by Le Studio Graphique, Gurgaon 122 001

032375

Printed in India at
Glorious Printers, Delhi

Published by
Orient Blackswan Private Limited
3-6-752 Himayatnagar, Hyderabad 500 029, Telangana, India
e-mail: info@orientblackswan.com

Contents

Part III
Self and Politics

List of Ramchandra Gandhi's Works

Books

1. *Two Essays on Whitehead's Philosophic Approach*, Indian Institute of Advanced Study, Shimla, 1973.
2. *Presuppositions of Human Communication*, Oxford University Press, New Delhi, 1974.
3. *The Availability of Religious Ideas*, MacMillan Press Ltd, London, 1976.
4. *Language, Tradition and Modern Civilisation* (ed.), Indian Philosophical Quarterly, Pune, 1983.
5. *I Am Thou: Meditations on the Truth of India*, Indian Philosophical Quarterly, Pune, 1984. Reissued by Academy of Fine Arts and Literature, Delhi, 2011.
6. *Svaraj In Ideas* (eds K. J. Shah, Ramchandra Gandhi and Probol Dasgupta), Indian Philosophical Quarterly, Pune, 1984.
7. *Sita's Kitchen: A Testimony of Faith and Inquiry*, State University of New York Press, Albany, 1992.
8. *Svaraj: A Journey with Tyeb Mehta's 'Shantiniketan Triptych'*, Vadehra Art Gallery, New Delhi, 2002.
9. *Muniya's Light: A Narrative of Truth and Myth*, IndiaInk, Roli Books, New Delhi, 2005.

Essays

1. 'Whitehead on the Distrust of Speculative Philosophy', *International Philosophical Quarterly* 12 (3), September 1972: pp. 389–414.
2. 'A False Lead in the Philosophy of Language', *Philosophical Studies* 24, 1973: pp. 38–44.
3. 'Injury, Harm, Damage, Pain, etc.', *Philosophy and Phenomenological Research* 34 (2), December 1973: pp. 266–69.
4. 'Self-consciousness', *Indian Philosophical Quarterly* 1 (3), April 1974: pp. 167–81.
5. 'On Meriting Death', *Philosophy East and West* 31 (3), July 1981: pp. 337–53.
6. 'Brahmacarya', *Contributions to Indian Sociology* (new series) 15 (1–2), January–December 1981: pp. 205–21.
7. 'Numbers or Standards?: The Dilemma of Higher Education in India', *Indian Philosophical Quarterly* 9 (4), July 1982: pp. 405–09.
8. 'Earthquake in Bihar: The Transfiguration of Karma', in Ramchandra Gandhi (ed.), *Language, Tradition and Modern Civilisation*, pp. 125–51, Indian Philosophical Quarterly, Pune, 1983.
9. 'What We Do and Say in Saying and Doing Something: An Exploratory and Experimental Move from Austin to Advaita', *Indian Philosophical Quarterly* 11 (2), April 1984: pp. 145–60.
10. 'The Svaraj of India', *Indian Philosophical Quarterly* 11 (4), October 1984: pp. 461–71.
11. 'The Adoration of Form and Formlessness', *Indian International Centre Quarterly* 13 (1), March 1986: pp. 130–38.
12. 'The Peacock and the Sage: Reflections on the Advaita of Architecture', *India International Centre Quarterly* 15 (2), Summer 1988: pp. 27–30.
13. 'Two Cheers for Tolerance', *Seminar* 435, November 1995: pp. 146–51.
14. 'The Firefly's Prayer: A Parable of Sri Ramakrishna Paramahansa', *First City*, April 2002, p. 37.
15. 'Is Our Heart On the Right Side?', *First City*, January 2003, pp. 36–39. Reprinted in *Postcolonial Studies* 6 (1), 2003: pp. 57–64.

Talks

1. 'Modern Indian Spirituality: Sri Ramakrishna, Sri Sarada Devi, Swami Vivekananda, Sri Ramana Maharshi, Alagamma, Sri Aurobindo, The Mother Mirra, Sri J. Krishnamurti and Mahatma Gandhi', Sound Photosynthesis, California Institute of Integral Studies, California, July 1988.
2. 'Moksha and Martyrdom', National Institute of Advanced Studies, Bangalore, 14 November 2003.
3. 'Nirmal Smriti Vyakhyan', India International Centre, New Delhi, 3 April 2007.

Interviews

1. 'Ethics, Ecology and Enlightenment', interview by Chandan Gowda, *The Hindu*, 18 November 2007. Originally published in *Lankesh Patrike*, 21 September 2003.
2. 'In Conversation with Ramchandra Gandhi', interview by Rajiv Mehrotra, *Doordarshan*, New Delhi, date unknown.

Newspaper Articles and Short Pieces

1. 'An Easter Tribute: Meeting Mother Teresa', *Himmat* 15 (24), 13 April 1979: p. 16.
2. 'Chikmagalur Recalled', *Swarajya*, 23 December 1979, pp. 38–41.
3. 'Confusion and Communication', *Swarajya*, 30 December 1979, pp. 35–37.
4. 'A Sense of Rumour', *Himmat* 17 (14), 15 June 1981: p. 47.
5. 'Private Knives, Hives', *Himmat* 17 (23), 1 November 1981: p. 40.
6. 'Himalaya Betrayed', *Indian Express*, 20 January 1989.
7. 'A Prayer for Fantasy', *Indian Express*, 18 January 1993.
8. 'Gandhi's Prophecy Came True', *Indian Express*, 30 January 2003.
9. 'Foreword', in C. B. Dalal (2007), *Harilal Gandhi: A Life*, trans. Tridip Suhrud, Orient Longman, Chennai, pp. *xi–xii*.
10. 'Stephen Lila', *The Stephanian*, St Stephen's College, date unknown.

Unpublished Manuscripts

1. '"God is Truth" and "Truth is God": An Incomplete Exploration', May 1980.
2. 'Non-violence is the Law of Our Being', June 1980.
3. 'Notes Towards a Coherent Iconography of Christ, Buddha and Krishna', July 1980.
4. 'Philosophical Scepticism and Theistic Faith', July 1980.
5. 'Inner/Outer: A Largely Advaitic Metaphysical Meditation', December 1980.
6. 'Testing Times', undated.
7. 'Towards Nuclear Non-violence', 10 September 1996.

[Manuscripts #1–5 are with Gurveen K. Singh and #6–7 are with Chandan Gowda.]

Tapes of Lectures/Scripts for Dramatic Performances

1. Talks on the Upanishads, particularly on the Kena Upanishad, Hyderabad, undated.
2. Talk at Rotary Club on Nuclear Weapons and Peace, Hyderabad/Secunderabad, undated.
3. Ramchandra Gandhi along with Richard Gombrich at Nehru Centre, London, 5 June 1993.
4. Talk at BBC Urdu Service, 14 August 1993.
5. Scripts for Shovana Narayan's dramatic performances in *The Clown of Assisi* (1993), *The Sadhu and the Sage* (1993), *Mohan and Rambha* (1994), *The Temptation of Vivekananda* (1995) and *The Unmasking of Death* (1995).
6. Ramchandra Gandhi archive prepared by Suresh Sharma and Tridip Suhrud.

[Tapes #1–2 are with Gurveen Singh; #3 is with Gopal Krishna Gandhi; #6 is with Suresh Sharma and Tridip Suhrud. I have not seen #4–6.)

FOREWORD

On Hospitality: A Dialogue with Ramchandra Gandhi

Ramchandra Gandhi (henceforth, Ramu) is a unique thinker. In the following paragraphs, I attempt to unpack his uniqueness, in content and style. I will introduce his work as I read it, with special emphasis on his later work, namely *I Am Thou: Meditations on the Truth of India* (2011 [1984]), *Sita's Kitchen: A Testimony of Faith and Inquiry* (1992) and *Svaraj: A Journey with Tyeb Mehta's 'Shantiniketan Triptych'* (2002). For me, these books comprise Ramu's *prasthanatrayi* (textual trinity). Here, his lucid voice finds expression in the fullest. I will not summarise his personal and academic biography. Instead, I hope to provide the readers with several keys with which to 'open' the treasure-box of Ramu's materials that this volume consists. My present dialogue with Ramu focuses on death and life in the face of death, his original inquiry into the notions of *ahimsa* (non-injury) and *advaita* (non-duality), the possibilities and impossibilities of language, and finally, hospitality. These are the main themes that define his later thinking, including the talks and writings collected here.

'With a good deal of associative thinking, which is no fancy'

At the very beginning of his talk, 'Moksha and Martyrdom' (2003), Ramu explains his method of inquiry:

> My training is philosophical and mythological, and increasingly devotional. But I don't by this mean that I have retreated from the demands of rigour. There are many ways of being rigorous. I will try to be rigorous, but not in the sort of premise to conclusion way, but often conclusion to premise, often premise to premise, and often conclusion to conclusion; and with a good deal of associative thinking, which is no fancy, but which is more of the nature of exploring the atmosphere, which always surrounds the subject. There is more to the subject than one notes.

I read this initial statement as an outline of creative thinking, consisting of interdisciplinarity and a sense of freedom, which finds expression in associative thinking. Rigour, Ramu pleads here, is of many shades, and associations, albeit non-linear, have a 'logic' of their own. Associations, he further implies, have the special capacity of revealing new aspects of the subject at hand. In 'Moksha and Martyrdom', as in many of Ramu's writings, the subject to be explored is death, as question and presence, and even as a teacher. I will come back to Ramu on Death as we move on.

Another clue for Ramu's working method, I find in the subtitle of *Sita's Kitchen* (1992): 'A Testimony of Faith and Inquiry'. Each of these notions is interesting. When I read Ramu, I often think that he writes in English but thinks through Sanskrit concepts. *Sita's Kitchen* is a philosophical reflection in the first person—all of Ramu's later writings are written in the first person, in the 'present personal'—on the political-religious saga over the Babri Masjid in Ayodhya. Incidentally, Ramu visited Ayodhya about a year before the demolition of the mosque in December 1992, when the heat was already in the air. A 'specialist' of violence and conflict—'speciality' that he 'inherited' from his grandfather, the famous Mahatma—Ramu travelled to Ayodhya, in search of a quantum of ahimsa in the midst of the boiling violence. 'I had to go to Ayodhya', he writes (1992: 13). He searched for a new angle, through which 'partition'—not as the name of the 1947 historical event, but as a state of consciousness, what Salman Rushdie wittily refers to (in *The Moor's Last Sigh*, 1995) as 'cuttofication', his antonym of 'unification'—can be transformed into what Ramu pertains to as advaita. For him, advaita is not the antonym, but the remedy of 'partition'. When Ramu speaks of 'testimony', this is not just to say that the essay is based on his visit to Ayodhya and is a first-hand report. It is rather to suggest (and here I take a cue from 'Moksha and Martyrdom') that he aims for nothing less than the position of a *sakshin* (witness). Testimony is *sakshitvam*, and sakshitvam, witness-hood, is a matter of transcending the limitations of 'I' and 'my'. This articulation draws on the Bhagavadgita, dear to Ramu as much as to the Mahatma. 'Having abandoned all his desires', the text famously says, 'roaming about without desires, without "my" and without "I", one approaches the sublime' (*vihaya kaman yah sarvan, pumamsh carati nihsprhah, nirmamo nirahankarah, sa shantim adhigacchati*) (Bhagavadgita 2.71). Am I not exaggerating when I ascribe to Ramu ideal aspirations such as sakshitvam? I do not think so. His charm (or one of Ramu's many charms) is that he speaks, and writes, and thinks through these great ideals expounded in the scriptures. His 'testimony' is a spiritual-philosophical experiment, an 'experiment with truth' if you wish, apropos the title of the Mahatma's autobiography.

The other ingredients of the subtitle of *Sita's Kitchen* are 'faith' and 'inquiry', two notions that seem to have little in common if the latter pertains to rational investigation, and the former is about religiosity which allows insight into realms unreachable by the latter. In his prologue (1992: 3), Ramu speaks in place of faith and inquiry, of the mutuality of *bhakti* (devotion) and *vichara* (inquiry). Bhakti, or devotion, is related to, but is not a synonym of faith. Faith alludes to the Sanskrit notion of *shraddha*; and shraddha takes us to the Katha-Upanishad, retold in brief by Ramu in his talk 'Modern Indian Spiritualism' (Chapter 1) and in the second Nirmal Smriti lecture (Chapter 4), both available in the present volume. In the Upanishadic tale, Nachiketa (Ramu imagines that he is a 16-year-old boy, of the same age as Ramana Maharshi when he left home for Arunachala), finds himself (like Ramana) face to face with death, or with Yama as the personification of death. The meaning of his name, Nachiketa is 'one who does not know and therefore seeks to know' (Radhakrishnan 2005: 595). His foremost characteristic is shraddha, faith, or rather, the Upanishadic author suggests that faith 'took hold of him', or 'possessed him' (*avivesha*), opened his eyes and empowered him to face death (or Death). For Ramu, looking death in the eye, without shying away, is the heart of the matter. This unique capacity he sees in each of his protagonists, from Nachiketa to contemporary figures like Ramana Maharshi, Ramakrishna Paramahansa, Sri Aurobindo, Jiddu Krishnamurti, Mahatma Gandhi and others. Ramu does not only discuss and interpret the life and teaching, or life as teaching, of each of these figures, but moreover creates an animate dialogue between them. If one dares to look death straight in the eye, without fear, the tables can suddenly, amazingly, turn, as in the Katha-Upanishad (1.21) when Death begs Nachiketa, 'Do not press me, release me from this' (*ma moparotsir ati ma srjainam*). Such is the power of shraddha. It is Death who asks the young boy to be released, and not vice versa. Death and this turning of tables, 'deathlessness' if you wish, or 'that in the *martya* [mortality] which is *amrita* [immortal]', is the crux of Ramu as I read him.

Ramu explains the mutuality, the far from obvious mutuality of faith and inquiry as the heart of his *sadhana* (contemplative path), in his essay, 'Philosophical Scepticism and Theistic Faith' (Chapter 12 of the present volume). He speaks here of 'the luminosity of faith', namely of faith, or shraddha, as a source of light and lucidity, without which self-inquiry, an inquiry toward the self, is not possible. 'This contradicts', he tells the readers, us, 'the idea that faith is necessarily darkness, a mode of blind faith'. Not of blind faith he speaks, then, but of faith as opening one's eyes, or if you wish, one's inner-eye, or self-eye.

'Is ahimsa non-violence?'

'Advaita is Ahimsa' is the title of a short chapter of *I Am Thou* (2011 [1984]: 238). Here, Ramu suggests that the first instance of violence does not take place when one raises one's hand to hit the other, or to destroy his temple. It is rather the gaze that sees the other, you, as different from me, which gives birth to violence. This differentiation, before any action is taken, is for him the cradle of violence. If one can 'prioritise' the common ground between you and I over the obvious differences between us, or metaphorically, to see the clay substance 'before' seeing the different pots and vessels made of it

(I draw on Shankara's Brahmasutra-bhashya 2.1.14), then violence as the logical implication of a segregating gaze becomes redundant.

Still in 'Advaita is Ahimsa', an interesting statement by Ramu caught my eye. He writes here that 'Gandhiji was right, notwithstanding the limitedness of his translation of ahimsa as non-violence'. According to Ramu, ahimsa, as concept and ideal, does not signify 'the opposite' of violence or pertain to non-action (that is, refraining from a violent action) instead of action. It rather stands for an existential position derived from a deep contemplation on violence as integral human tendency; a position that goes beyond violence and non-violence; a position that is no longer the opposite of anything, but indicates that one has perceived that 'clayish' common denominator, preceding the I–You partition.

Ramu further elucidates his position in a chapter titled 'Is Ahimsa Non-violence?' (2011 [1984]: 159–62). Here, he suggests that that ahimsa cannot be non-violence, since non-violence has—always, necessarily—exceptions, such as in cases of self-defence, whereas for the Mahatma (or Gandhiji, as Ramu refers to him), ahimsa is an ultimate, exception-less value. Here I wish to add two interlocutors to my dialogue with Ramu, Patanjali of the Yogasutra and Martin Buber. For Patanjali, just like for the Mahatma, ahimsa is a *mahavrata*, or 'great vow' as he puts it (in Yogasutra 2.31). As such, it has to be observed and practised 'irrespective of birth, place, time, circumstances, or even a sense of duty (such as animal-sacrifice by a Brahmin, or fighting a war for a Kshatriya, Vyasa explains in his commentary)'. No exceptions, then, for Patanjali. Buber is relevant to our discussion, owing to a letter that he wrote to the Mahatma, dated 24 February 1939. Buber's letter is a reply to an article by Gandhi (published in *Harijan* on 26 November 1938; see Sharma 2002), in which he offered his views on the Jews in Europe under the Nazi regime and their dream for a 'national home' in Israel. In a nutshell, Gandhi recommends that the Jews adopt the ahimsaic *satyagraha* (truthfulness in non-violent action) approach that worked for him in South Africa. Buber, in response, challenges the universality of ahimsa as ideal and guideline. He agrees with Gandhi that ahimsa is a desirable approach, effective in 99 percent of the cases. But the Nazis, he proclaims, fall under the last percent. 'Do you know or do you not know Mahatma', he writes passionately, 'what a concentration camp is like, and what goes on there? Do you know of the torments in the concentration camp, of its methods of slow and quick slaughter? I do not presume that you know.' In this case, Buber implies, ahimsa will not work, and a measure of *adharma* (the articulation is mine) is needed to protect and restore a dharmic state of affairs. Gandhi never replied to Buber, or to another Israeli philosopher, Judah L. Magnes, who also wrote to him around the same time, challenging the universality of ahimsa with a different argument (which I cannot present here; see Magnes's letter in Sharma 2002). Shimon Lev, author of *Soulmates: The Story of Mahatma Gandhi and Hermann Kallenbach* (2012), tells me that the letters must have reached Sabarmati Ashram, but for some reason were not read by Gandhi, who when asked about them by Louis Fischer (Magnes's friend) could not remember these letters at all.

Nevertheless, Buber does receive a reply, a belated reply, from Ramu in place of his illustrious grandfather. It is not just the title of his book, *I Am Thou*, that corresponds with Buber's *I and Thou* (1937, first published as *Ich und Du* in 1923). In a nutshell again, if Buber speaks of transforming the position of the other from the third person to the second person, namely from 'it' (consisting of 'he' and 'she') to 'thou' or 'you', then Ramu suggests taking one more step toward the advaitic formulation 'I am thou'. Buber was not unaware of the Upanishadic notion of an all-encompassing *atman* (self), that echoes in Ramu. So immense was his interest in Indian philosophy that in Part 3 of *I and Thou*, Buber offers a short narration of the famous Chandogya-Upanishad story about Indra, Virochana and Prajapati. But he rejects the Upanishadic standpoint which advocates 'absorption', as he puts it, and instead declares that 'the reality of the everyday hour on Earth, with a streak of the sun on a maple twig and the glimpse of the eternal Thou, is greater for us' (1937: 87–88). Buber prefers the maple twig and you, a 'real you', or 'eternal you', not a 'tentative you', to be finally immersed and lost in me, just as 'I', tentative like 'you', am reciprocally absorbed and molten in and with you.

But I wish to return to what I see as Ramu's reply to Buber on the universality of ahimsa in 'Is Ahimsa Non-violence?'. We saw that according to Ramu, ahimsa cannot pertain to non-violence since, unlike the latter, it is an exception-less mahavrata. 'Ahimsa', Ramu writes here, 'is non-injury, not non-violence, etymologically as well as metaphysically and morally, and admits no exceptions' (2011 [1984]: 159). Yet, in what way is this alternative translation contributive to the understanding of the Sanskrit notion at hand? Making an interesting move, Ramu explains that the practitioner of ahimsa aims to become non-injurious primarily toward himself, or toward 'his soul', the very soul that he essentially is. This soul, he continues, strives for 'God, or Freedom'. The capital letters, as well as the equation of 'god' and 'freedom' (for the Mahatma it is 'god' and 'truth'), are Ramu's. Any conduct of 'unjustified violence or unjustified non-violence', he suggests, distances my soul from this yearned for freedom. His move sits well with Patanjali, who writes (in Yogasutra 2.33–34) that in order to stop 'contrary thoughts' (*vitarka*), namely thoughts that could motivate the practitioner of yoga to deviate from the *yamas*—the ethical precepts prescribed for him—and primarily ahimsa, one has to reflect on their consequences, which are 'endless suffering and ignorance' (*duhkha-ajnana-ananta-phalah*). Ramu implies here that unjustified violence and unjustified non-violence are equally self-injurious, or soul-injurious, thus contributing to unfreedom. He explains what 'unjustified non-violence' means through the Bhagavadgita. The Mahatma famously argued that the Gita is a manifesto of ahimsa, even though Krishna pleads Arjuna to fight in the great Mahabharata war. Ramu explains—interpreting the Mahatma and elucidating the meaning of ahimsa as he sees it—that 'the violent battle is also ahimsa, because to let the Kauravas – Nazis of antiquity – get away with their plans of Earth-domination would be to injure not only those who would be subjugated or killed by them, it would also amount to injury to the Kauravas themselves' (2011 [1984]: 160). This is an astonishing statement by Ramu. First, the phrase 'Nazis of antiquity' implies that Ramu has read Buber's letter to the Mahatma, and agrees with Buber that non-violence is not the right approach toward the Nazis, as it falls under the category of 'unjustified non-violence'. On the other hand, an action against the Nazis, involving a measure of violence, falls under the category of ahimsa. Not acting against them, he suggests clearly, would be harmful, or injurious, both to those who suffer under their brutal rule, and to them, since if they continue to pursue brutality, they (as 'souls', and for him, even the Nazis are not exempted from the all-inclusiveness of the atman) will move away, far away, from 'God, or Freedom'. Ramu, then, justifies a violent action against the violent Nazis, for the sake of victim and oppressor alike. Ahimsa, as presented by him, is a matter of a broad vista that takes into account every party involved in the situation. Ramu further explains that 'ahimsa is like the divine mother, with both a benign and a terrifying face, Lakshmi and Kali' (ibid.). It means that there is something protective about ahimsa as attitude and way of living, whatever 'justified action' it gives rise to, violent (Kali) or benevolent (Lakshmi).

But who will decide what is justified? In the Gita, Krishna is portrayed as the ultimate 'deciding authority'. In Bollywood, I am tempted to add (and it is Ramu who interweaves classical texts with Hindi cinema, I just follow his lead), Amitabh Bachchan is the voice of authority, for instance when he appears on the screen for a brief cameo as a *kajal*-eyed shepherd (The Lord is my Shepherd, Ramu would comment), to solve the burning riddle of self-identity in the film *Paheli* (2005, directed by Amol Palekar). But who can decide what is 'justified' in 'real life' (as against the cinematic 'reel life')? Who can decide what is 'good' and what is 'bad', and what needs to be done? Ramu, as I read him, assumes that deep down, one knows the answer, presuming that there is a capital-A Answer for these ethical questions. Take for instance Duryodhana, a second generation of blindness (not sight-wise like his father, but heart-wise), who confesses honestly: *janami dharmam na ca me pravrttih, janamy adharmam na ca me nivrttih* ('I know what dharma is, but I have no inclination for it; I know what adharma is, but I cannot resist it'). This popular verse from the *stotra* Pandava-gita, quoted in Madhava Vidyaranya's fourteenth-century work *Panchadashi*, suggests that the 'villain' knows what the 'good' is, even if he refuses to follow it. Ahimsa as refuge and shield, preceding and transcending both violence and non-violence, the Nazis of antiquity in correspondence and agreement with Buber—I find all these features creative and thought-provoking. But the religious bottom-line—assumption in the guise of conclusion—that 'the truth' is here, available (or even unescapable) for its ardent seeker, is an aspect of Ramu that I respect but can hardly accept. A student of Daya Krishna, Ramu's contemporary, I feel more comfortable with questions than with answers.

Sambodhana

Despite his self-confessed craving for the great silence embedded in the not-two-ness of the advaitic experience, Ramu—like other *moksha* thinkers—speaks his way to this beatific goal. He uses language, and plays with language, and makes an attempt to carefully listen to language.

In his acclaimed essay, 'The Task of the Translator' (in fact, in the Translator's Note appended to his 1923 German translation of Charles Baudelaire's *Tableaux Parisiens*), Walter Benjamin suggests that 'the task of the translator' is to de-conceal the 'Language of Eden' (a phrase that he coined in his earlier 1916 essay, 'On Language as Such and on the Language of Man'). Benjamin envisions a primordial universal language, which had been 'broken' into countless languages owing to the human hubris symbolised by the Tower of Babel, which brought about God's curse (in Genesis, Chapter 11). Benjamin's hunch is that this 'first language', resonating in each and every other language, can only be reached through translation as inter-linguistic dialogue. It is implied that only the translator is sensitive enough to cut through 'the surface' of language and reach 'the source'. Benjamin's formulation sits well with my reading of Ramu's advaita project, aiming to retrieve a 'pre-partition' mode of humanity. I use the word 'partition' not (just) in its contemporary political sense, but thinking of the 'primordial partition', depicted in the Vedic-Upanishadic corpus, of the 'one' (*ekam-eva-advitiyam*, as in Chandogya-Upanishad 6.2.1) becoming 'many'. Like the 1947 political partition, this primeval, or mythological partition is portrayed in the scriptures as involving violence. It is depicted as an act of dissection or cutting apart, with a sacrificial overtone (for instance in the Purusha Sukta of the Rigveda). The idea is that under the manyness on the surface, the long-lost primordial oneness is waiting to be disclosed. And the pre-partition language, a language of identity, can only be carved out, or 'remembered' (in the Platonic, idealistic sense) if one listens, closely, carefully to language.

'Sambodhana' is the title of another chapter of *I Am Thou* (2011 [1984]: 239–41). A quick search in the dictionary reveals that *sambodhana* means 'addressing', 'recognising', 'causing to know', 'reminding' and 'insight'. Ramu suggests here that every attempt to communicate with the other, you, is, in fact, an attempt to overcome the illusion of dissimilarity between us. Ramu further suggests that if one is addressed by another, this common situation is nothing short of an occasion, or 'invocation' as he puts it, for self-inquiry. When addressed as 'you', one is obliged to look into this 'you', into the '*tvam*' of '*tat tvam asi*' ('you are that', namely the 'atman' or 'self', the famous utterance from Chapter 6 of the Chandogya-Upanishad, used traditionally as a wake-up call from the phenomenal-daily existence into a deeper sense of selfhood). Elsewhere, Ramu explains that 'in being addressed, as opposed to being referred to, we are stirred to limitless self-awareness' (2002: 160–61). In the segment 'Is Our Heart On the Right Side?' (Chapter 7 of the present volume), he beautifully writes that, 'therefore, we may regard everyone who addresses us as a guru, drawing our attention to our *nirguna* absolutist mode of self-consciousness, restoring us to our atmic status'. But whoever is addressed, and fails to see the invitation involved in this very act, remains oblivious to non-other than oneself. The call of the other, then, echoes an inner-call, the call of the self, and can work (now I return to the lexical meaning of sambodhana) as a reminder, igniting an insight into the nature of the self, oneself, or even better, 'one self'. Ramu calls attention to addressing words, that we use all the time without paying attention to their power and meaning. For him, they are ethically the most significant part of every utterance, since they convey my recognition (sambodhana as recognition) of the other, of you. And moreover, they allow you, through me, and me through you (when I am the addressee), to discover yourself which is no other than myself.

I spoke of a 'pre-partition language', which is a language of identity. But what does it mean? What does a 'language of identity' look like? My safest way out of this question would be to suggest that someday if I ever reach 'the archaic roots of language', I will let you know. But instead, I wish to draw, like Ramu often does, on Ramana Maharshi. In a recent visit to Sri Ramanasramam, at Tiruvannamalai, I heard this chant:

> *Arunachala Shiva, Arunachala Shiva, Arunachala Shiva, Shiva Arunachala* |
> *Arunachala Shiva, Arunachala Shiva, Arunachala Shiva, Shiva Arunachala* ||

This couplet, an instance of the 'pre-partition language', is made of two identical stanzas, two that are actually one. Each stanza consists of two words, Arunachala and Shiva, two words with a single reference, God Shiva, or mount Arunachala as his physical manifestation, or even Ramana Maharshi himself as an avatar of the 'beyond' that the words Arunachala and Shiva point at. The couplet is dualistic, but at the same time brimming with non-dualism.

Man and Hanuman

Another chapter of *I Am Thou* is titled 'Man and Hanuman' (2011 [1984]: 295–96). The joke works only when you see the two words written in English, the word Hanuman 'hosting' the word Man. The interconnection between the philological and the philosophical is a salient feature of classical Indian philosophy. Ramu creates here a pseudo-philological language-game. Who is Hanuman, he asks (and as a Ram, he is qualified to answer), and offers the following meditation: As a body, at the corporeal level, on the surface, Hanuman is a monkey. In the same way, on the surface, each of us too belongs to the family of monkeys or great apes. At a deeper level, the *jiva-atma* level as Ramu puts it, Hanuman is an insider-outsider, participating in and transcending the world and the worldly at the same time. There is a 'divine spark', a spark of the atman in this monkeyish envelope. At the deepest level, he is the atman, free from dualism. There is a future to mankind, Ramu drives his point home, only if it discovers itself anew as Hanumankind. This is to say that there is a future to the human being only if he manages to become more than the monkey that he is. And if I may play with words (like Ramu, with him), then the word 'kind' means both 'species' and 'generous', hence a sense of generosity, a much-needed generosity, awaits to be discovered and applied in our life, in the world.

I read 'Man and Hanuman' as a philosophical joke, joke as performance which is intended to enable us, readers, to go beyond our 'monkeyness'. There is something in jokes that cuts through the surface, and in their 'outcome', namely laughter, that takes us away from our 'ordinary' self and allows a sense of rare freedom. On Ramu's jokes, here and elsewhere, Arindam Chakrabarti writes (in a review article on *I Am Thou*, 2011): 'If you are a Ramu type of thinker-about-thinking, you must make the ridiculous sublime, and the sublime ridiculous.'

I agree with Chakrabarti twice, first when he portrays Ramu as 'thinker about thinking' (Ramu himself defines philosophy as 'thinking about thinking'), and second, when he underscores the interconnection of the ridiculous and the sublime in Ramu. For an exponent of advaita, of not-two-ness, this interconnection is indeed a must.

One final insight about 'Man and Hanuman': It is my feeling that the notions of evolution and involution are hiding here between the lines. First, the evolution from monkey to 'more', not in the Darwinian sense of 'natural selection', but in Sri Aurobindo's sense of 'evolution which would raise man to a higher and larger consciousness', as he puts it in his famous '15th of August 1947 Message', broadcast on *All India Radio* on the eve of India's Independence. Aurobindo suggests that 'Man is a transitional being, he is not final', and envisions 'volitional evolution' at the level of consciousness towards a 'super-consciousness'. But the metamorphosis from monkey, or body, or external costume, to the atman can be also seen as a process of 'involution', or 'return to the original state' (pratiprasava, as in Yogasutra 2.10). In this respect, Ramu often speaks of the need for *adivasa*, which he renders as 'source-inhabiting'. But the source, again, is hardly Darwin's monkey-hood; it is rather a sense of atman-hood, blending together classical Upanishadic ingredients with Ramana Maharshi's contemporary (Ramu would prefer, eternal) silence.

Hospitality

Hospitality is a significant feature of Ramu's project. It is the heart of *Sita's Kitchen*, the crest-jewel of his 'philosophy of now and here'. In the prologue of this original treatise, he confesses that Babri Masjid (not yet demolished as he visited Ayodhya) is for him a paragon of otherness. 'It is the very embodiment of otherness, sheer, indissoluble otherness', he writes, 'and at a commanding height in one of the holiest of Hindu shrines, the capital-city of God-incarnate Rama's kingdom on earth' (1992: 11–12). But here comes the twist: What could be (or could have been) a better occasion to practise hospitality? What could be a better occasion to practise ahimsa, in Ramu's sense of excavating the subterranean common human denominator, that his motto 'I am thou' aims to convey? For Ramu, the Ayodhya saga can be approached not merely, or necessarily, as a discourse of hegemony, but also—and this is what he attempts to demonstrate here—through a spiritual prism (he sees *mandir* and *masjid*—Hindu temple and Muslim mosque—alike, together, as a powerhouse of spirituality). According to Ramu, the mosque ('sheer otherness at a commanding height') is (was) an opportunity (alas, a missed opportunity) to disclose the transparent thread that connects 'you' and 'I', Muslim and Hindu. Thinking of a political-religious dispute, involving two rounds of violence (in the sixteenth century when the Ram ka Janmasthan temple was demolished, and in 1992, when the mosque was destroyed), in terms of hospitality is not just intriguing but moreover, fruitful, and hopefully even effective. The advantage of this unique prism is that unlike other concepts—for instance, 'tolerance', which is often used in the political discourse in India today—which may 'feel' too abstract, or theoretical, or academic, or even vague—we all know, in practice, what hospitality is all about. In our day-to-day life, we often find ourselves in the position of a guest or a host. We are all acquainted with the labour of hosting, with the (un)gratefulness of the guest, with intimacy and goodwill, but also with the tensions that often arise between guest and host. This 'knowing by living through' we can use in our attempt to unravel complex controversies at the broader collective arena.

The focal point of *Sita's Kitchen* is naturally Sita's kitchen, 'a largely ignored structure', Vinay Lal (1993: 83) explains, 'which, standing apart from the now-demolished Babri Masjid, nonetheless constitutes a part of the entire complex'. In his visit to Ayodhya, Ramu was in search for another angle to the entangled dispute, when his eyes fell on a new sign telling an old story, hardly told, unnoticed: 'Sita ki Rasoi'. Besides the obviosity of defusing the patriarchal narrative, the kitchen plays a significant role in the interplay of hospitality. The crux of the matter in Ramu is not the food, important as it is in every instance of hospitality. Instead, he implies that in the light and warmth of the kitchen fire, a dialogue—direct, informal, without masks—can take place. This *rasoi*-type of dialogue, Ramu suggests, is exactly what the political arena needs. This dialogue, for him, is the heart and soul of hospitality.

In his talk 'Translation and Displacement' (2016), theorist Homi Bhabha touches on the notion of hospitality apropos India's partition, an attempt which coincides with Ramu. The conjunction of translation and hospitality is interesting. Bhabha depicts the translator as simultaneously a guest and a host, a guest in the text she works on, and a host of this very text at the 'target language'. I would like to suggest that in Ramu—a sensitive reader, not a translator in the technical 'from-to' sense of the word—the gentleness and curiosity with which he approaches a text, especially a classical text, are guest-like, whereas the way he 'makes it his own' (I think of Rajashekhara's notion of *svikarana*), or plants it in his own garden, is that of a host. Bhabha further looks into the concept of hospitality through the works of artist Zarina Hashmi, whom he introduces as artist of 'partition and displacement'. His pertinent dialogue with her through her work reminds me of Ramu's dialogue with artist Tyeb Mehta in his book *Svaraj: A Journey with Tyeb Mehta's 'Shantiniketan Triptych'*. The title, as always, is intriguing (*svaraj*, journey). Moreover, there is something singular, even advaitic, in Ramu's choice to dedicate a whole book to one painting, the *Shantiniketan Triptych*. He meditates on the painting, allows it to 'colour' his consciousness (I think of the term *uparaga*, as used in Yogasutra 4.17). Like in Bhaba, the dialogue is primarily with the text, with the artwork as a text. 'I have a strong feeling that the painting has sometimes spoken to me', Ramu writes (2002: *xxii*). Hashmi's 'dislocation', as portrayed by Bhabha, is not just a matter of her personal biography, but of her eclectic technique. She works with a variety of materials that she 'extracts' from different 'contexts' and assembles together, thus creating a new context.

Like Ramu, Hashmi is both a guest and a host. Like him, she is a 'witness', a specialist in violence and partition, offering remedy and solace through her intertextual work. Like Hashmi, Ramu—the conceptual artist—is not just a collector, but a weaver. In his 'Nirmal Smriti Vyakhyan', presented in this volume in Tridip Suhrud's translation (Chapter 4), he creatively interweaves the Upanishadic story of Nachiketa not merely with the biographical account of Ramana Maharshi, but moreover, with his friend Nirmal Verma's story 'Kavve aur Kala Pani' ('Crows and the Exile', 1983). Or for another instance of weaving, take Chapter 33 of *I Am Thou*, 'Isaac, Nachiketa, Christ, Ramana' (2011 [1984]: 133). In Ramu's eyes, these four iconic figures comprise a single whole and convey mutual interreligious teaching of self-sacrifice.

The two main influences on Ramu, as he himself affirms, and as each of his later works illustrates, are Ramana Maharshi and Mahatma Gandhi. At first sight, they are altogether different from one another. Ramana is the personification of the Upanishadic utterance '*upashanto 'yam atmeti*' (silent is the atman), an immovable rock, apolitical, 'Master of Ko'ham (Who am I?) Sadhana', as Ramu puts it (in 'The Peacock and the Sage', Chapter 5 of this volume). The Mahatma, on the other hand, is an activist, world-changer, perpetual traveller, a rare combination of politician and *karma-yogi*. 'It is amazing that Maharshi and Mahatma never met', Ramu writes in 'Is Our Heart On the Right Side?' (Chapter 7), and makes sure that they do meet in his writings. He sees the two as a single whole, again a single whole, always a single whole, Ramana and (the Mahatma who surrenders to) Ramanama (or Rama-nama). The former, you see, Ramu shows, is included in the latter. They are inseparable.

Before closing, I wish to return to intertextuality and dialogue in Ramu's work. Still in 'Is Our Heart On the Right Side?', he writes: 'What a pity Wittgenstein never met Ramana!' And a few lines down the road, he says: 'What a pity Simone Weil and Albert Camus did not visit Tiruvannamalai!' There is a lot of talk today about comparative philosophy transforming (or of the need of such metamorphosis) into dialogic philosophy, a conversation between equals, no longer a one-sided affair based on Western standards willingly adopted even by non-Western scholars. Ramu's philosophical jigsaw-puzzles in his later writings achieve exactly this. In Ramu, the thinkers mentioned earlier, and not just they, but also Søren Kierkegaard, J. L. Austin, A. N. Whitehead and P. F. Strawson, all 'visit India', and 'meet' Ramana Maharshi and others. Their materials and ideas, 'hosted' on Ramu's canvas, are interwoven with Indian ideas and materials, as to create an amalgamated, advaitic whole.

I will close with a few stanzas by Ben Okri, the Nigerian poet and novelist, from his poetic essay 'Hospitality', that he read at the Jaipur Literature Festival in 2012. I dedicate these lines by Okri to Ramu.

> 1. Hospitality begins in the soul.
> 2. Hospitality is more than a rational, deliberate act. It is a way of being.
> [...]
> 6. Hospitality takes us back to the root of humanity, to the source of rivers.
> [...]
> 8. Hospitality is a secret affirmation of the oneness of humanity.
> [...]
> 20. There is also intellectual hospitality, the hospitality to ideas, to dreams, to ways of seeing, to perceptions, to cultures. We will call this invisible hospitality. This is the most important hospitality of all and it includes all other hospitalities.
> 21. Beyond that, we are talking about the hospitality of the infinite, which should be pursued in silence and through initiation, following a secret path towards the eternal.

Daniel Raveh

References

Benjamin, Walter. 1970 [1923]. 'The Task of the Translator'. In *Illuminations*, trans. Harry Zohn, 69–82. London: Fontana/Collins.

______. 1979 [1916]. 'On Language as Such and on the Language of Man'. In *One-way Street, and Other Writings*, trans. Edmund Jephcott and Kingsley Shorter, 107–23. London: NLB.

Bhabha, Homi. 2016. 'Translation and Displacement'. Lecture delivered at Graduate Centre, City University of New York, May. Available at https://www.youtube.com/watch?v=TVQcdbSV6OI&t=183s (accessed 11 March 2020).

Buber, Martin. 1937. *I and Thou*, trans. Ronald Gregor Smith. Edinburgh: T&T Clark.

Chakrabarti, Arindam. 2011. 'I Am Thou: Meditations on the Truth of India by Ramchandra Gandhi', review article. *Seminar* 636. Available at http://www.india-seminar.com/2012/636/636_books.htm (accessed 11 March 2020).

Gandhi, Ramchandra. 1992. *Sita's Kitchen: A Testimony of Faith and Inquiry*. Albany: State University of New York Press.

———. 2002. *Svaraj: A Journey with Tyeb Mehta's 'Shantiniketan Triptych'*. Delhi: Vadehra Art Gallery.

———. 2003. 'Moksha and Martyrdom'. Lecture delivered at National Institute of Advanced Studies, Bangalore, 14 November. Transcribed in *The Seven Sages: Selected Essays by Ramchandra Gandhi* (2015), ed. A. Raghuramaraju, 121–141, Pengiun, India. Available at https://www.youtube.com/watch?v=NPYb3BsoCI0 (accessed 11 March 2020).

———. 2011 [1984]. *I Am Thou: Meditations on the Truth of India*. Delhi: Academy of Fine Arts and Literature.

Lal, Vinay. 1993. 'Advaita's Waterloo', review of *Sita's Kitchen*. *Social Scientist* 21 (5–6): 82–89.

Lev, Shimon. 2012. *Soulmates: The Story of Mahatma Gandhi and Hermann Kallenbach*. New Delhi: Orient BlackSwan.

Okri, Ben. 2011. *A Time for New Dreams*. London: Rider.

Radhakrishnan, S. 2005. *The Principal Upanisads*. Delhi: HarperCollins India.

Sharma, Arvind. 2002. *Modern Hindu Thought: The Essential Texts*. Delhi: Oxford University Press.

Verma, Nirmal. 1983. *Kavve aur Kala Pani*. Delhi: Bharatiya Jnanpith.

Publishers' Acknowledgements

For granting permission to reproduce copyrighted material in this volume, the publishers wish to make the following acknowledgements.

India International Centre, for 'Nirmal Smriti Vyakhyan'. Talk delivered in Hindi at India International Centre, New Delhi, 3 April 2007. Translated into the English by Tridip Suhrud.

India International Centre Quarterly, for 'The Peacock and the Sage: Reflections on the Advaita of Architecture'. Originally published under the same title in *India International Centre Quarterly* 15 (2), Summer 1988: pp. 27–30.

Postcolonial Studies, for 'Is Our Heart On the Right Side?'. Published under the same title in *Postcolonial Studies* 6 (1), April 2003: pp. 57–64. Reproduced with permission of Taylor & Francis Ltd.

International Philosophical Quarterly, for 'Whitehead on the Distrust of Speculative Philosophy'. Originally published under the same title in *International Philosophical Quarterly* 12 (3), September 1972: pp. 389–414.

Indian Philosophical Quarterly, for 'Self-consciousness' and 'What We Do and Say in Saying and Doing Something: An Exploratory and Experimental Move from Austin to Advaita'. Originally published under the same titles, respectively, in *Indian Philosophical Quarterly*

1 (3), April 1974: pp. 167–81; and *Indian Philosophical Quarterly* 11 (2), April 1984: pp. 145–60.

Leela Gandhi, for 'Philosophical Scepticism and Theistic Faith: Theistic Inquiry Cannot Be a Denial of Advaita, Only a Necessary Preparation for It', 'Testing Times' and 'Towards Nuclear Non-violence'. Unpublished essays.

Chandan Gowda, for 'Ethics, Ecology and Enlightenment'. Originally published under the same title in *Lankesh Patrike*, 21 September 2003.

Rajiv Mehrotra, for 'In Conversation with Ramchandra Gandhi'. Originally from *In Conversation with Rajiv Mehrotra*, for Doordarshan, New Delhi, date unknown.

Rajmohan Gandhi, Founding Editor, *Himmat*, for 'Private Knives, Hives' and 'A Sense of Rumour'. Originally published under the same titles, respectively, in *Himmat* 17 (23), 1 November 1981: p. 40; and *Himmat* 17 (14), 15 June 1981: p. 47.

St Stephen's College, for 'Stephen Lila'. Originally published under the same title in *The Stephanian*, St Stephen's College, date unknown.

Shankar Ramaswami, for the photograph of Ramchandra Gandhi.

Every effort has been made to trace copyright holders and to obtain their permission for the use of copyright material. The publishers apologise for any errors or omissions made, and would be grateful if notified of any corrections that should be incorporated in future reprints or editions of this book.

Acknowledgements

I am extremely thankful to several individuals: Gopal Krishna Gandhi, Leela Gandhi, Kamini Mahadevan, for their continuous encouragement and suggestions; Vidya Rao for asking me to edit this volume. Several friends and admirers of Ramchandra Gandhi encouraged me and reassured me with their support. I am thankful to Daniel Raveh for writing the Foreword to this volume. I am also thankful to Tridip Suhrud for translating from Hindi to English the talk titled, 'Nirmal Smriti Vyakhyan', delivered at India International Centre, New Delhi. I thank Nalini Bhushan and Tridip Suhrud for endorsing this book. Chanda Gowda sent me two unpublished works of Ramchandra Gandhi on peace and nuclear non-violence. Rajiv Mehrotra sent me the DVD of his conversation with Ramchandra Gandhi, recorded for *Doordarshan*. Gurveen K. Singh gave me some of his valuable unpublished works, one of which is included here. She also gave me cassette recordings of his talks on the Upanishads. Bhanu Kale and Sanjay Palshekar procured for me two short essays published in *Himmat*. Rajmohan Gandhi sent me two essays published in the journal *Swarajya*. K. P. Shankaran located for me a short piece published in the St Stephen's journal. This short piece was brought first to the notice of M. R. Venkatesh by Mani Shankar Iyer. I am thankful to both of them for this. I am extremely thankful to all of them for their help.

I am thankful to G. Vedaparayana for his generosity in reading some parts of the manuscript. N. Satyanarayana Raju, Kalidindi Girija Kumari, Laxmi Narayana Kadekar, M. Mohan Raju, M. Sudha Raju, C. Radhakrishnama Raju, C. Madhavi, Sundar Sarukkai, Aparna Devare, Ananda Sagar, all extended their support at various stages of this project. It was very kind of Mishka Sinha to have transcribed Ramchandra Gandhi's last talk, which was delivered at the California Institute of Integral Studies. I am really thankful to her for this kind gesture. I also thank my students, D. Viswanath for transcribing some talks, Anuradha Raghuram, Shobha Rani and Purushotam Kumar for transcribing the other talks, and Suyasha Singh and Deepalee Rout for proof-reading during difficult times. I thank Prabha Shankar Dwivedi for helping me in translating Sanskrit words. R. V. Harnoor has really undertaken the difficult task of copy-editing and punctuating the talks, and for this, I am thankful to him. I also thank D. Balaganapathy, Nivedita Jena, Narmada Pujari, Vanlal Vempuria and Pankaj Varma.

At the Indian Institute of Technology Tirupati, my director, Kalidindi N. Satyanarayana, and deans, P. C. Deshmukh, K. Krishnaiah, V. Raghavendra and N. N. Kishore have been instrumental in providing a congenial academic atmosphere that made my work not only easy but also enjoyable. I also thank my colleague C. Bharath Kumar for his generous help. At Orient BlackSwan, I want to thank for their professional help Nilanjana Majumdar, Insiya Poonawala and Veenu Luthria.

A. Raghuramaraju

Introduction

Ramchandra Gandhi makes an important intervention in contemporary Indian thinking, clearly discernible in the volume of his work, the range of subjects he dealt with, as well as the variety of themes and genres he traversed. He authored seven full-length books and edited two volumes on a variety of topics—one of them a special issue on K. C. Bhattacharyya's famous essay, 'Svaraj In Ideas' (1984), for which he was one of the guest editors. His books include *Two Essays on Whitehead's Philosophic Approach* (1973), *Presuppositions of Human Communication* (1974), *The Availability of Religious Ideas* (1976), *Language, Tradition and Modern Civilisation* (ed., 1983), *Svaraj In Ideas* (ed., 1984), *I Am Thou: Meditations on the Truth of India* (1984), *Sita's Kitchen: A Testimony of Faith and Inquiry* (1992), *Svaraj: A Journey with Tyeb Mehta's 'Shantiniketan Triptych'* (2002) and *Muniya's Light: A Narrative of Truth and Myth* (2005). There are, in addition, several published papers and talks, lectures, interviews and newspaper articles. Some of these are published earlier in a volume titled *Seven Sages: Selected Essays by Ramchandra Gandhi* (2015). The remaining works—except one essay titled 'A False Lead in the Philosophy of Language' (1973), originally from *Philosophical Studies*, is not included in this volume due to permissions-related issues—are included in the present volume. His topics range across speculative philosophy, philosophy of language, analytical philosophy, Indian philosophy, religion, spirituality, politics, art, aesthetics, modern Indian sages, secularism, nuclear proliferation, ecology and several other overlapping areas.[1]

Ramchandra Gandhi is perhaps one of the very few academic philosophers who seriously, that too very early, engaged with the modern Indian thinkers of the nineteenth and twentieth centuries, including Ramakrishna Paramahansa, Sarada Devi, Swami Vivekananda, Ramana Maharshi, Sri Aurobindo, Mahatma Gandhi and J. Krishnamurti. In philosophically rejuvenating the modern philosophers in India, he not only reactivated both classical Indian and Western philosophies, but also broke open the exclusivism prevalent around him, of doing either Western philosophy or classical Indian, or comparing the two. He succeeded in bringing together and assembling Western philosophy, classical Indian philosophy and modern Indian philosophy in a novel way. His works have a dialogical tone and are largely in a debating mode in the *purvapaksha* tradition. They are also often anchored in contemporary issues, which makes them all the more interesting and lively. For such similar attempts see Akeel Bilgrami (2002) on M. K. Gandhi; J. L. Mehta (1974, 2004) on Bhattacharya and Aurobindo, respectively; and Alam Khundmiri (2001) on Iqbal.

Ramchandra Gandhi experimented with several styles and genres including a rigorous analytical style of writing. He also collaborated with the classical dancer Shovana Narayan. He wrote scripts for her dramatic performances, *The Clown of Assisi* (1993), *The Sadhu and the Sage* (1993), *Mohan and Rambha* (1994), *The Temptation of Vivekananda* (1995) and *The Unmasking of Death* (1995).

In addition, he inhabits the Upanishadic mode of inquiry and exploration, though in pioneering new areas and intellectual pathways. His notion of permanence, though an advaitic version, has within it enough scope for change and growth.

Ramchandra Gandhi is an interesting case to examine, whether we see the various stages of his explorations as discontinuous or recognise an underlying cumulative continuity, which may not be immediately apparent. Such an examination has not yet been carried out. One of the reasons is the apathy of Indian academics. However, it is also partly because Gandhi's works, though available in many scattered places, are not all accessible in one place. This is even truer for his essays, talks, lectures, interviews and newspaper articles than of his longer writings. The present volume assembles some selected works, and some of his talks appear here for the first time in text form. Interestingly, philosophy as an assemblage was one of the themes that preoccupied Ramchandra Gandhi in his very first book on Whitehead.

While most of Ramchandra Gandhi's books are available, and at least some of them are in libraries, this volume, in addition to the earlier volume *Seven Sages* (2015), seeks to add one more book to the existing corpus. The essays presented here run parallel to the full-length books; at times they repeat an interesting selection, incident, idea or an argument in a stimulating and concentrated manner. In this sense, this volume can serve as a window through which to look into the books and also into the essays and talks not included here. However, it must be noted that often there are significant and substantial overlaps between the contents of a book and those in this volume. This series of eight talks on 'Modern Indian Spirituality' that Ramchandra Gandhi delivered at the California Institute of Integral Studies is one of the best series that one can think of to compile into a full-length book. According to Gandhi, his 'attempt in these lectures is to present a coherent account of a group of sages ... to set up a theory which will explain all of them in the light of a coherent set of ideas so that is what it is'. Three out of the eight talks are included in this volume. In fact, the book starts with these talks, which are being made available for the first time.

The purpose of this volume is to bring together in one place a selection of his essays, talks and unpublished papers, present a parallel picture to that created by his books. This volume contains Ramchandra Gandhi's philosophical papers as well as those that presented larger issues at a serious level in a more accessible style. Some of these short pieces published in magazines present large and complex concepts in a brief flash of illumination.

This volume, in its first section, includes three out of the eight talks mentioned earlier, that he delivered in 1988 as part of a larger series on 'Modern Indian Spirituality'. They are 'Modern Indian Spiritualism' (Chapter 1), 'Sri J. Krishnamurti' (Chapter 2) and

'Indian Spirituality and the World' (Chapter 3). The talk on Nirmal Verma (Chapter 4) is also included in this section. While 'The Peacock and the Sage: Reflections on the Advaita of Architecture' (Chapter 5) shows how a peacock was a close disciple of the sage Ramana Maharshi, the other short piece, 'The Firefly's Prayer: A Parable of Sri Ramakrishna Paramahansa' (Chapter 6), discusses a parable of the well-known sage. In 'Is Our Heart On the Right Side?' (Chapter 7), Gandhi shows how, according to Ramana Maharshi, the 'miracle of transformation is not possible if we remain attached to the idea of ourselves as being exclusively our bodies, driven by the biological heart on the left side of our chest'. He says, that our 'true heart', Sri Ramana teaches, 'is on the right side where there is nothing, only a depth and vastness which holds everything in its embrace of compassion, including our bodies!' This claim of 'anatomical identification of atman' on the right side, Ramana Maharshi cautions, 'is only for the benefit of those who are unable to be rid of the false identification of themselves with their body and mind, body for short'. The last paper in this section is his Foreword to the biography of Harilal Gandhi, M. K. Gandhi's eldest son. In this Foreword (Chapter 8), he brings out some novel observations on the father–son relationship.

Part II has essays that are more philosophical. The essay, 'Whitehead on the Distrust of Speculative Philosophy' (Chapter 9) emphasises how 'speculation as controlled by reason is the very foundation of all progress in life and thought'. In his essay 'Self-consciousness' (Chapter 10), while denying the notion of self-consciousness as it makes no sense to talk about non-referential identification of oneself, he, however, admits that it '*is* possible to speak of oneself *imagining* that one was being non-referentially identified by another person', and 'the notion of self-consciousness should be regarded as being, at least, the notion of oneself *imagining* that one was being non-referentially identified by another person'. Ramchandra Gandhi reminds us that 'self-consciousness also has a moral and political dimension'. This is in addition to ontological and epistemological dimensions. In this context, he introduces a novel distinction between eliciting and soliciting, and concludes that the 'possibility of altruism is rooted in the nature of self-consciousness'.

In his essay, 'What We Do and Say in Saying and Doing Something: An Exploratory and Experimental Move from Austin to Advaita' (Chapter 11), he develops the notion of what we say in doing something, the exact opposite of the Austinian notion of what we do in saying something. Using Ramana Maharshi's declaration that '*mauna* [silence] is the most incessant eloquent speech', he concludes that 'communication is the many-centredness of self-consciousness', and 'self-consciousness is not the internalisation of communication'. The essay, 'Philosophical Scepticism and Theistic Faith' (Chapter 12), argues how the 'theory of karma' and 'theory of reincarnation' would be the '*generalised* theories of the human condition, and not theories restricted to the private careers of individuals', and this, according to Ramchandra Gandhi, would be 'profoundly illuminating'.

The last section has his interviews and short pieces. His interviews by Chandan Gowda (Chapter 13), published in *Lankesh Patrike*, and by Rajiv Mehrotra (Chapter 14) for *Doordarshan* traverse a large number of issues and problems of contemporary times. These issues include the urgent and imperative need to overcome all sectarian views and to become more integral and non-dualistic. He continues to maintain that dualism is the root cause of all conflicts, misunderstanding and suffering. In the interview to Gowda, he claims that more than Eurocentrism, the problem lies with the 'implicit anthropocentrism of the secularist imagination'. His political concern continues in his unpublished, later short essays. His earlier piece 'Confusion and Communication' (Chapter 15) shows his stint in active electoral politics of India. And 'Testing Times' (Chapter 16) and 'Towards Nuclear Non-violence' (Chapter 17) reveal his concern for contemporary problems. In addition to being a serious and sensitive philosopher, Ramchandra Gandhi has sharp wit and humour, and this comes out clearly in his short pieces 'Private Knives, Hives' (Chapter 18), 'A Sense of Rumour' (Chapter 19) and 'Stephen Lila' (Chapter 20). I have not been able to access the scripts Ramchandra Gandhi wrote for Shovana Narayan's dance performances, and the archive prepared by Suresh Sharma and Tridip Suhrud.

Making his works available may facilitate a serious, critical and evaluative work on these important modern Indian thinkers in the future. The long-overdue work in this field, if undertaken, will contribute to philosophical scholarship cumulatively. Such an undertaking can avoid the present tendency of merely, solipsistically, producing works bereft of relations and interconnections that merely and mechanically accumulate without having any progressive cumulative effect.

A. Raghuramaraju
Indian Institute of Technology Tirupati

Note

[1] For discussion on Ramchandra Gandhi, see my interview to Richard Marshall, for *3:AM Magazine*, 'Ramchandra Gandhi and Contemporary Indian Philosophy', 24 February 2018.

References

Bhattacharyya, K. C. 1984. 'Svaraj In Ideas'. *Indian Philosophical Quarterly* 11 (4), October–December: 383–93.

Bilgrami, Akeel. 2002. 'Gandhi's Integrity: The Philosophy behind the Politics'. *Postcolonial Studies* 5 (1): 79–93.

Khundmiri, Alam. 2001. 'Iqbal on Time and Self'. In *Secularism, Islam and Modernity: Selected Essays of Alam Khundmiri*, ed. M. T. Ansari, 177–89. New Delhi: Sage Publications.

Mehta, J. L. 1974. 'The Problem of Philosophical Reconception in the Thought of K. C. Bhattacharyya'. *Philosophy East and West* 24 (1): 59–70.

______. 2004. 'Sri Aurobindo: Life, Language and Yoga'. In *Philosophy and Religion: Essays in Interpretation*, 121–84. New Delhi: Indian Council of Philosophical Research.

Raghuramaraju, A. (ed.). 2015. *Seven Sages: Selected Essays by Ramchandra Gandhi*. New Delhi: Penguin.

— one —

Modern Indian Spiritualism*

How does one connect ... with Mirra [Alfassa], with the Mother, with this incredible person? An adventurer—I don't like adventuress, the expression, as though the woman can't be an adventurer. Expressions like manageress, totally unnecessary I think, manager, controller, a ruler, a woman or a man. She is a spiritual adventurer, a realised sage, no doubt, and a wonderful human person, I never encountered her in [the] flesh. In fact, I have only encountered Mahatma Gandhi and J. Krishnamurti in this crowd, and not Sri Aurobindo, not Ramana Maharshi or any of the others. I never encountered her like that. I encountered her through her books, through Sri Aurobindo's writings and through reflection on what she means, what she symbolises. But today I am going to try and talk about Mirra and Krishnamurti in a joint sort of way. Because there must be continuity and transition, because these group of sages I have not selected arbitrarily—there is a very important connection between them all. It is very interesting that

*This is an edited version of the lecture on Modern Indian Spirituality, delivered at California Institute of Integral Studies, July 1988.

Linda herself has made a transition from the Mother to the Buddha, in her own spiritual search, in her own special way. And I do think that the spirit of Krishnamurti is very, very similar to the spirit of the Buddha in our own times. And the spirit of the Mother to the more elemental, more atavistic, more mystical traditions of the Earth. And to move from the concentration of the one to the expansiveness of the other is a beautiful, powerful, liberating experience.

And this is exactly what happened to me. A sense of this, when I was in Varanasi, Banaras, many years ago. As a Hindu, I visited the Vishwanath temple, the ancient temple of the lord of the Universe there. You really have to go to something like a cave, concentrated in a space, it's almost like the interior of an atom when you get there. And it is intense and magical, and small and powerful, it's like the power-house of the Universe, all concentrated in one place.

And a few miles from there is Sarnath, where the Buddha preached his first sermon, so from Vishwanath, I wandered all the way to Sarnath, where it's the open sky. The Buddha taught his first sermon, not in a temple, but under the open sky. This tremendous, extramural university of the Universe, under the open sky. And the spot where he actually stood, there is nothing there. You were told this is where he probably stood, or sat, so the contrast, and I am holding forth to both items of contrast, the catacomb intensity of Vishwanath and the complete open sky of Sarnath. If you like, Hinduism with its concentrated tantric intensity and Buddhism with its total unfurling of everything, all energy, all interconnection, all possessiveness. It is a wonderful, beautiful contrast and the Mother, Mirra Richard, does represent some of that energy of Vishwanath—why? Because she and Sri Aurobindo decided in their spiritual search, determined in their spiritual search to visit the tiniest, the most concentrated form of divinity, of reality, the atom and the cell, and to do some of their work there, it's unusual, it's a fantastic story, it ought to be taught to nuclear physicists everywhere in the world, this story. But here, where two spiritual scientists, who visited the atom in another way, at the time when others, less spiritually gifted, oriented, who visited the atom for other purposes. So here is the story of two sages, who descended in the yoga, in their spiritual exercise to the tiniest unit of existence.

As I told you ... I have difficulties with many of the positions that they adopted. As a philosopher, I think it's my duty to voice these difficulties too. Now if you read all their works, you do get the impression that they felt something wrong with the matter. The atom was deeply deluded, was obscure and this may or may not be the case. I haven't visited the atom, and I haven't been on intimate terms with the atom. But I have a feeling, in this, they were really influenced by the philosophical and the spiritual ideology of our times, and of several centuries, which makes a very sharp contrast, between spirit and matter. And they thought that matter, of course, was an area of the darkness of the inconscient—terrible words Sri Aurobindo coined. He coined some terrible phrases and made some marvellous use of these terrible phrases [laughter]. Anyway, they visited this in the hope that they might undo some of the damage that ... the matter was doing to the Universe. I had a feeling that they were pleasantly surprised that the residents of this small space probably said, 'Welcome, we are so happy to receive you, no one has bothered to come and see us, but we are all right, we are doing your work, and we have been doing it all along. But thank you for awakening us to the sense of our own importance. We are very glad to receive visitors from out there, and we are doing our job quite well, do not worry, the Earth is all right, the atom is all right.' This may well have been the final revelation to them. But they didn't write about it, I am only speculating, and I tend to prefer this outcome of their tremendously exciting journey. And the fact that it was undertaken, under the impression that there was something wrong there which had to be put right, darkness there that had to be removed and replaced by light, is okay. I don't hold this against them at all.

The important thing was that they chose to make this journey nobody else had. Often people have talked about Heaven. Often people have talked about illumination, but no one really has talked about the matter. I don't think if Ramana Maharshi did not talk about it. It does not mean that he wasn't interested in it. It is the uniqueness, the distinctiveness of this pair of sages to have talked about it in the idiom that they were familiar with and to have actually in their spiritual mind to have visited it, to have encountered it and tried to do some of the scavengings that they wanted to do. But I have a feeling that they encountered there, sages and saints in the way in which when Mahatma Gandhi visited the huts and the homes of the scavengers, he found saints there. I think it is the same surprise that they experienced. I do think that while I feel uncomfortable about the language that they use sometimes, Aurobindo and Mirra, about the necessity of undoing the contradiction of the heart of the nature of matter which I think is a very dualistic way of looking at things, and something in which matter has hardly been consulted, I think [mild laughter].

While I am uncomfortable about this, I felt for this journey, for this tantric dangerous journey, in yoga inspired by the highest motive for the good of the Earth. You might almost say that the atom represents the ultimate proletariat of the Universe, they are the hardest workers and they probably almost wanted to organise them in a kind of revolutionary bid for power, I think [laughter]. I think in this they were probably misled by the images of revolution because all such bids fail, the working class is not something to be manipulated. They have a very rich tradition too. I am sure this cosmic working class of atoms also asserted quite a lot of independence when they were solicited by Mirra and Aurobindo, I think. And who knows what their partnership might eventually amount to; it might amount to, perhaps, a kind of cosmic socialism with a human face, who knows. Whatever it is, I am so glad they visited this region and, who knows, I have often worried about this, mind you!

The fact that they didn't explicitly condemn the bomb has worried me all these years. As far as I know—if I am wrong I will be delighted—bothered me, it cannot be they favoured destruction, of course not, but they were devotees of Shakti, they were not willing to be scared of any evidence of power, *shakti*, they want Divine power. So they were not going to say, 'Oh! This is terrible in some way.' But I think their desire to discover the heart of shakti in the atom may one day, who knows, if there is power and truth in yoga, I believe there is, and in their yoga certainly, but who knows some contacting of matter by sagehood has occurred, and if in the future some really non-violent source of energy from the atom is to be discovered, not the current kind, who knows it may be because of this spiritual journey that was undertaken. And this conclusion I have reached through a lot of turmoil. I had to come to terms with the fact that there was no ... I am grown up in the Gandhian tradition, in the peace tradition, and I thought anyone who did not shout down the bomb was somehow inadequate, but I don't think so anymore at all.

All energy is Divine. What we have encountered in the way of nuclear energy is, I think, a caricature of something else which lies coiled up there, like the *kundalini* [yogic-meditative technique] shakti, and who knows even if under a mistaken philosophical impression, which was the result of the conditioning of their times, they have met with this energy, who knows what this combination may produce for the good of the Earth, in the future, I don't think it's going to lead to or even that it ought to lead to what they sometimes wrote about, namely a bodily immortality, I don't think very highly of bodily immortality frankly, not to be able to die for this body to remain ... apart from the fact that it might be difficult, it would be very boring. I don't want indefinitely to be landed with one body even if it is an ageing body, how boring! I would like a vision where I am many bodies including this dying body, and all verities if you like an immortal body also to be in my wardrobe to be worn sometimes. But no, I am surprised that philosophers of their imaginative power did not see this. I am a little surprised, but who knows I am just a philosopher, I am not a sage. They may have found something there. This may have been a neglected theme ... I think there is a way of saying, don't think this is impossible to you, and that I accept, an unageing body is not impossible to us, I don't think that it is the ultimate price, a sense of being all bodies and nobody at all. All forms and no form, even this humble dying ageing form is very beautiful, there is nothing to compare the beauty of that dying face. That picture is taken in [1926] or somewhere there, that woman must be old now, but there is a beauty to her youthful face and whose mask is next to her, and even if that face is aged, that aged face is probably like that mask now. Must be very beautiful, if that is an unageing face, how boring it would be to meet with and say, 'Oh you are the beautiful woman photographed in 1926 or 1936, wherever, you have not aged, how disappointing.' So I do think that the sense of the beauty of the flesh not only of the immortality of the flesh, the sacredness of the Earth, of the atom, of the self, of the face, of the body, as these things are also very important, and I do sometimes miss these things in the writings and yet, this is no final judgement, I could be wrong. They are yogis, sometimes I feel the philosophers can also be right and yogis can be over-enthusiastic, who knows [laughter]!

Let me tell another story, but of course, my favourite image is not the catacomb power of Vishwanath, the nuclear reactor of the Universe, nor even the open sky of the Buddha, but of the humble holdall which I saw in a cave in Varanasi. I was visiting Varanasi with a friend, and you know those lanes, Linda has been to Banaras and you can be killed by a bull in those lanes easily, even if you are a Hemmingway, you can easily be gored and killed. And all sorts of other dangers more moral than physical are also to be encountered there. So we encountered some of these things and overcame these things, and then we found ourselves standing in front of a cave. And inside this cave wall was a *pandit* [scholar] writing in a little book, and he was not disturbed by us at all, he went on writing. I stood there transfixed, and I wish I had some of the concentration of this pandit in relation to my work, which was not doing very well then. Then I wondered, looked around what his *ishtadevata*s were, favourite deities, there was nothing. They were hanging on a wall from a big nail, a holdall, a bed-roll, very popular in India, holdall, it is an old English term, it is a Victorian term, I do not think you use that term in America to describe these bed-rolls, it is an enormous thing, it can carry everything including goats, and beds, and all sorts of things in India, and it occurred to me that that is what I would like ultimate reality to be, a holdall, something which held all, everything. And that's my favourite image of ultimate reality, of the Divine, I wish I could get hold of a holdall for you next time, to hang from the wall. Something which is both the sky under which the Buddha taught, and the little cave where the energy of the Universe resides, and everything else also in between the city of Banaras, all its filth, all its sacredness, the visitors, the natives, the hope, the despair, everything holdall but that's my personal preference, and if you like, prejudice.

It is a very Hindu preference for everything. We can never make up our mind because we don't believe we are the mind, it is to be made up.

Well, there is the fear of nothingness, which haunts us, which haunts all life, and I think the Buddha, 2,500 years and more ago, faced this nothingness and decided to visit it, that is one way of regarding. He did not put any name to it, God, self, nothing, but, of course, he couldn't, he wanted to encounter it and said that all things go, whatever they are, big things, small things, they die, let me reject everything, we seek that which is not a thing and this really is nothingness, something that we fear. He faced it, entered it, and found that it was unconditioned without which he would be wasting his time, as he himself said. He didn't call it eternal, he did not call it God, he called it nothing because nothing, it is very discourteous to give a name to nothing. So he did not, but he faced the fear of nothingness and entered into it.

I think J. Krishnamurti in our own times, does that too. He doesn't give this nothingness a name, and he does not call itself, God or anything. There is another fear, the fear of nothingness and there is a fear of matter, there is the fear of lifeless, inert, purposeless, mindless or something, everyone has feared that. Aurobindo and Mirra entered that, they did not fear it. They said, 'Let us find out what it is to be there, to be dead like that, to be small, to be concentrated, dark there, let's go there.' I think it is a comparable story of courage. I am not saying there have not been other sages who have not done tremendous things, but in the Buddha and in Aurobindo and Mirra and in Krishnamurti, you will find that I cannot think of only one form as representing anything. Buddha, I also think of the Upanishadic sages who probably did the same thing. I think of sages in ancient Greece whose names have not come down to us, the most gifted group of human beings, race, if you like, and they have disappeared from the Earth, such was their humility, the Greeks. So there are many ancient Egyptians all over the place in space and time. So my list of sages is infinitely long. See, if I mention the Buddha, it is only to dramatise, to highlight something. If I mention Aurobindo and Mirra, it is again to do the same thing, Krishnamurti [and Aurobindo and Mirra] but they were in our own time. So Krishnamurti and Mirra, let's forget Sri Aurobindo tonight. Mirra and Krishnamurti represent two kinds of courage, fundamental kinds of courage which have been exhibited, down the ages, the courage to face nothingness, the courage to enter into the very small dark, the tiny, the dangerous. And I think this is tremendous. This is why there is continuity to Mirra and Krishnamurti, but more of Krishnamurti later.

Some of my friends know I worry a lot about everything, about positions and propositions. I do, of course, think the infinite sky is the self, is the self's own image of its limitlessness, and the very tiny is the self's own destruction of the idolatry of bigness. I do think it is the self that assumes both forms. But I am not going to talk about the self tonight. I am going to talk about the sky and about the atom.

I don't know about transformation. This word is a sexy word. I don't like it very much [mild laughter]. I don't know about transformation. Not because I think I am okay as I am, but any radically new picture of who I can become will not interest me very much. I don't want the atoms to dance in a new silly way, and they dance pretty well as they do now. And men and women too, and I don't know what a supramentalised woman is going to be if she is going to be necessarily an improvement on the ordinary variety. I really don't know about this language, I think it is the language of our times, and as I have pointed out on earlier other occasions, Mahatma Gandhi fell for the word non-violence, it was lying around. Sri Aurobindo and Mirra, I am a little more surprised with Mirra because the French are more sensitive about these matters, but she was a learner and a seeker, and they picked out the word 'transformation'. I think atoms are going to violently resist any such transformation, and not because of inertia or anything but out of sheer good taste, I think [laughter], so I don't know about that. I think we need to be awakened to the truth of the very small, and the truth of the very big and leave it there. Try transforming your daughter for instance by saying, 'You got to become this, and you got to become that', you will have difficulties [laughter]. But try loving her, acknowledging her truly and you will be transformed. And I think that is what really happens. And I am convinced that Mirra and Aurobindo and Krishnamurti, in their willingness to confront this guy and the very small, became transformed, the atom was the sage who probably gave Aurobindo and Mirra liberation. It is not they who are going to give the atom transformation, probably not at all. I think we are in for a lot of surprises in this *leela*, play of the spirit.

And well, there is an ancient story of Vishwamitra and Vasishta. There is somebody here who had acquired a new name Vasishta, and I would like to tell the story for him which teaches me ancient wisdom on this whole subject of transformation. Vishwamitra, one possible etymological reading of that, although people question this, *vishwa amitra*, the foe of the world. That can be a complement because the world in its ordinary way is no good, you can regard Sri Aurobindo and Mirra as foes of the world, of the ordinary world, of the dull, inert, tamasic, all right, inconscient world, they don't like this, they want a better world, they are entirely in the progressive revolutionary transformative tradition of our age. How amazing that the secular spiritual in any given age are structurally so similar, it is very, very interesting.

Anyway, Vishwamitra in sacred antiquity, that means at all times there is a Vishwamitra in us who wants to transform everything. He is a Kshatriya in the ancient story of Ramayana. He is also the one to whom the Gayatri Mantra, the most sacred *mantra* [a recitation] of the Vedas, was revealed finally. Vishwamitra was a Kshatriya, a warrior, and he wanted to be a Brahma *rishi*, the ultimate in sagehood. So he went to Vasishta, who was the sage in the court of Raja Dasaratha, whose son was Sri Rama. He said to Vasishta, 'I want to be a *Bramharshi*.' Vasishta said, 'You will have to try pretty hard.' So he tried very hard and millions of years of austerities. But something or the other always tripped him some temptation whether it was for woman, kingdom or whatever, he tried again and again and again. While he was still in the process of trying, let me inform you he did eventually become a Bramharshi [sage among the Brahmans].

In the process, he had one weakness. There are many pitfalls in this spiritual path. One is, if you are susceptible to the flattering of any kind, you are not quite there, and Vishwamitra, as he was advancing, was approached by a king who had leprosy. These ancient Indian stories are very gruesome. I don't think there is a filmmaker who can truly make these films without driving away audience. You have this powerful image of this king with leprosy. The king or crown with a face distorted by leprosy approaching the sage and saying that 'you are a very great sage'. And the sage is immediately flattered, but probably took longer than that. You have to have this scene, this very contemporary motion picture scene of this sage who is trying very hard to attain the highest realisation being approached by this king whose body is decaying and this king says but who is unaware of this, unembarrassed by this. He says, 'Master, I want to go to Heaven in this body and who but you can help me.' And this rather pleases Vishwamitra, who wants to transform everything of course. He wants physical immortality. Everything, and this is laudable, the tradition permits these experiments, it does not promise success, that's another matter.

So he organises a great *yagna*, a great sacrifice, and he invites all the great rishis of the time to the sacrifice, and Trishanku is the name of this king who wants to go to Heaven in this body. That simply means who wants physical immortality and leprosy is only an image, it means it's an image of mortality but this king wants to go to Heaven. So he organises the sacrifice and he invokes all the Gods and the Gods don't come and the assembly titters and it is terrible for ... and the sage is furious and then he almost lays a curse upon the God and says, 'I don't care, if you don't come, I pour all my *siddhi* [attainment] into this yagna and Trishanku will now rise in his body heavenwards.' And the cosmos is scared and the Gods are scared, of course, Trishanku rises the body rises heavenwards. That means the cells begin to change, that means there is something like physical immortality beginning to take place. He rises, rises, rises, and of course, he reaches Heaven and there the doorman at Heaven says, 'Who is this? Get out, you filthy fellow' [laughter], and gives him a kick at the back, and he begins to fall, and he shouts and says 'help, Vishwamitra, I am falling'. Vishwamitra by this time is very pleased. And he hears the shouts and he says, 'I will create another world for you.' He started creating an alternative Universe in the sky, through his yagna: new sun, new moons, new Earth then the God's thought, they come to Vishwamitra. Enough, enough, we knew you can do it, but don't do it and that is his first advance towards

Bramharshi when he says, 'All right Trishanku, stay where you are.' He stays back.

Many of the clusters of the stars are supposed to be the relics of this stage in evolution, where something extraordinary contrary to the spirit things of things was tried permitted and stopped, as proof of our capability, but as proof also of this being not being strictly necessary. The sun, the Earth, the atoms are miraculously enough. Anyway, there is the Vishwamitra story. Who knows that may be necessary from time to time to revitalise the existing energy, who knows. A little bit of experiment, a little bit of daring is always useful in life. It does energise everyone. If there were no circus, there wouldn't be even ordinary acrobatics in life; because I have seen the circus even in my middle age, I can do a few dangerous things. So thank God for circuses, thank God for the Vishwamitras and the Aurobindos and the Mirras of the Universe. I do think they keep the spirit of adventure alive in the cosmos, but strictly and miraculous alchemical transformation, of everything, is not necessary. And it is not a nice thing to want I think, because things are okay, in their internal deep structure, I am not saying that they are okay in their manifestation. But in their internal deep structure, they are also okay. Manifestations are meant to change, but they don't change, if you find fault with the deep structure. If you acknowledge your daughter then the deep structure looks after the manifestation, not otherwise. If you say, 'Well, daughter, there is something wrong with your deep structure, I want that to change' [laughter], you will get what you deserve there I think. So, that's the Vishwamitra story.

After this Vishwamitra saw two things, both the power of consciousness to produce an alternative Universe [and] to change the very structure of things, to achieve bodily immortality and so on. But that it was strictly not necessarily ... when he saw the true glory of the deep eternal structure of things—the sky, cell, everything—then he quickly became a Bramharshi after that. And he is the one to whom the Gayatri Mantra, the sacred mantra of the Goddess, and of the sun, of the shakti, was revealed. And he was the one who took Rama and Lakshmana away to the forest on their first visit to slay demon, to slay all the obstacles. The Ramayana is a deeply symbolic story, the Divine on Earth was first initiated into heroic activity by

Vishwamitra. This is rather good, I think the Divine on Earth with probably, if there is to be transformation, and I rather think that it would be of the heart not of an atom, will still be encouraged by the shakti generated by Aurobindo and Mirra, and those like them throughout history.

That is my considered verdict on the sages. You see, I like this about them, their ability to say, no, we want to do something different, and they use some choice phrases, oh, Sri Aurobindo says I don't want this old fiasco, and unfortunately, they include people like the Buddha and others in this fiasco, and I think that is not fair at all. But I like this, the Buddha and Shankaracharya are going to grudge them, this language, not at all. Try anything. And if you have the spirit and the sincerity of a Mirra, then you certainly should, because whatever your impressions, you will certainly help things. And Mirra, like Krishnamurti who came later, has helped Hinduism enormously, this woman from France, she has enabled Hindu thought in a variety of ways. I am not a subscriber to their vision, but I do feel their influence, Aurobindo's, Mirra's, I'm enabled in the modern world to think daringly as a Hindu, to think courageously and to think globally, helpfully, for this we are all eternally grateful to her. She became an Indian citizen, as has Mother Teresa and so on, we love her, I do think this is a tremendous story of love, Aurobindo's and Mirra's. Don't be shocked, those who are absolutely pious in these matters. Here is a yogi, here is a philosopher, here is a revolutionary, who indeed loves this woman, long after political and social equality between humans is achieved, spiritual equality will stay much longer, men are always going to resist, we are politically equal but spiritually still unequal. I am delighted to find not only that Sri Aurobindo attributes equality to her but superiority. Here is a woman, encouraged by him to exceed him in yoga. She is the Mother and the symbol of motherhood, of womanhood, of the feminine, it is so important in our life today. I am very, very grateful to time and eternity, that it was an Indian sage who took this bold and fantastic step of love and in truth and it is a tremendous love story.

If Sri Aurobindo stayed in one tiny room for, well, how many years, say 22 years, Mirra stayed much longer for nearly, not in a tiny room, but in the same ashram, for almost 50 years. Her dates are 1878–1973, 95 years. She did what is that song, 'Anything you can do I can do better', I think she proved that in relation to Sri Aurobindo. I think he wanted it like that. He was a good loser and but in his losing he won [mild laughter]. He brought the intellect of France and of Europe deeply to come to terms with Indian spirituality, to produce a unique and interesting, fantastic, if in the end, slightly uncomfortable for me, mix of things and that is a tremendous contribution to philosophy. You should read not only the prayers and meditations that Linda had talked about but the several volumes called *Mother's Agenda* by a man called Satprem, a Frenchman, a disciple of hers. There you see a creative, powerful, daring, tantric, French, ancient Egyptian, Jewish mind at work. Incredible! I do think that to say that she is a great woman philosopher is an insult! She is a great philosopher of tremendous power in our times. Why worry about whether she was a woman or a man in relation to her achievement? So I would teach her in any course of philosophy, not in a course merely of feminine philosophy, that would be to damn her with faint praise. She is available to all of us, for the real philosophical and spiritual excitement. Of course, I worry about the language of manipulation involved there.

Satprem, her French disciple, is always quarrelling with the matter, and darkness, ignorance, and he is poking fun at everyone else in the delightful French and the completely misguided way I think [laughter]. But it's very enjoyable reading and I have never been more instructed by anything in recent years than by that kind of writing and I know that all of it comes from the spiritual illumination which must have been Vishwamitra's illumination. It is good to dare. It is almost like this. They have consulted with one another's spirit, they have done all the other yoga and said, 'Well, could it be that all the yogis have neglected matter. Let's go there, you and I, and put things right there.' It is a heroic journey. And I think myself that they were surprised to find I think, everything okay there. But they were not unchanged, they became transformed and that is the great story.

Well, I must say a few words about the great work *Savitri*, which Aurobindo wrote. It is really a love poem to Mirra. *Savitri* is a poem which makes use of a short story recorded in the Mahabharata, which I will tell you. It's a very simple story of a king, Ashwapathi, lord of the horse, who didn't have a child. So he prayed and he practised *tapas* [penance] and austerities, and he was gifted with a girl child. And in those days they didn't kill female children, as they do now in China and in India. So he was honoured. All this is fantastic to discover, in antiquity people had so much better sense than we do. She is so beautiful and wonderful ... it was very hard for him to find a husband for her. So he said, 'Why don't you find one for yourself?' And so she decides to wander all over the world. And in Sri Aurobindo's poem, it is in a chariot, a motor car of antiquity that she wanders all over the world looking for a husband, and finally she finds a woodcutter in a forest called Satyavan. And he is also of course ... you know the class distinctions are modern [...] we want today [...] the story writer would say, and of course, she met a member of the proletariat. No, everyone is a king or a queen or a prince or a princess in ancient literature. Satyavan and his parents are, of course, royal, but they are going through some difficulties. They have been thrown out of their kingdom, that's all that there is to it. And this is what is so delightful about the literature of antiquity when, when the time comes for the Buddha to die, 'Ananda,' he says, 'This is where I want to die'. And Ananda says, 'What is so great about this small place?' But the Buddha does not say why don't [we] have a great place like this, no ... once upon a time this was a great kingdom. Every place is a kingdom. Everyone is a king and a queen. There has to be levelling up and not levelling down.

Where was I? Yes, Satyavan and Savitri are in love, and Savitri returns to her father and says, 'I want to marry this man', and he says, 'Of course.' Good sense again. But Narada, the spiritual minister, suddenly arrives, [and says] but this man is going to die a year after they get married. Ashwapathi says to Savitri, 'You still want to marry him?' She says, 'Yes, of course.' They get married. But she is not going to accept his mortality. She is with him and in tapas, in austerity, and when death comes, he follows death, she goes with the spirit of Satyavan to the death chambers, matter, and says, 'I want my husband back', but he says, 'Why? You can choose, you are so beautiful. There are hundreds and thousands of husbands you can choose.' 'No, I want him back.' 'Why, why', in the way in Kathopanishad, I will have time to talk about it later today or next time. The young Nachiketa is likewise sought to be discouraged by death, when he wants his immortality at the age of 16, in the way in which Ramana Maharshi did. Persistence is a very great yogic virtue, in India, if you want a cup of tea, coffee, or a ticket or anything like that, persist, like Savitri, like Nachiketa, and you will be rewarded. And so death says, okay. There it is, and she returns with her husband, that's the story.

But in the epic poem *Savitri*, which is a fat work in thousands of verses, this becomes a story of the Universe as a whole, where Savitri, the shakti of the Universe—of course, the structure of the story is retained—endeavours to alter the structure of the nature of things, of atoms and battles with the forces of death in those recesses, a complete mistake I think, to battle, to go and love I think, an alternative version of the Savitri, also I think, is meant to be written where she really discovers love, where she expected hostility, she discovers cooperation where she anticipated resistance, but that would be another version, I don't have Sri Aurobindo's gifts to write a Savitri. But I do report this to you that a magnificent poem in the English language exists, which is a story told in the framework of the vision, of the victory of shakti over death. Now, I don't think death is meant to be overcome in that way at all; death is meant to be understood, to be acknowledged, and overcome in that way, there is nothing wrong with the deep structure of death. Its manifestation ought to be different, it ought not to be premature, it ought not to be humiliating, but it ought not to be banished.

You recall a story that I told you in the very first of these lectures of Rama, again of the kingdom of God having arrived and the only person unhappy was Death, and Death had an audience with Rama and clearly, Rama tries to talk to Death into giving up this sordid business of killing. But it's not so easy, Death said, 'I never destroyed' ... Rama says, 'Okay, maybe, you need to retire', something like that. And just then suddenly enters, without appointment, an angry sage and Death looks over his shoulder and finds in an angry sage, no doubt, says in his heart, so long as there is anger even in sages, it is going to be business as usual for me [laughter], people are going to die, and I do think this is important if we all had the immortal bodies, I am not sure that we would be less covetous than we are, I would not want this one immortal body, I would want ten immortal bodies. So I don't think the problem of covetousness, of greed, of hate, of fear, of anger, this problem is overcome by an immortal body, I am not saying it is overcome if our bodies are underfed, or without joy, or without sufficient longevity, no, but without the blessings of death, and of ageing, there is no charity, there is no making way for other bodies, other forms and I think all this has to be taken into account before any reconstruction and reinterpretation of the Vishwamitrian, or Sri Aurobindoian or Mirra Richardian vision, and may others more competent than I do it.

It may be time to move to Krishnamurti a bit. Very briefly, I only want to introduce him, very briefly, because there is a connection between the two. Of course, they are very similar, they were in some respects non-Indian, Aurobindo, Mirra and Krishnamurti. Aurobindo knew some Indian language, but he had taught himself these languages ... he spent between the age of 7 and 21 his years in England, totally and his adopted parents there were given strict instructions by Aurobindo's father not to bring Aurobindo into contact with anything Indian at all and they faithfully followed these instructions. The English are very good at obeying such instructions. No, they didn't expose Aurobindo, but of course his innate patriotism, but he had to teach himself, I think he, till the end I am sure, his dreams, if yogis have dreams, were in French and English, or maybe Latin and Greek if you like. But I don't think they were in Bengali or whatever.

Likewise, Krishnamurti, at a young age, he was picked up by theosophists, by occultists, a guy called [Charles Webster] Leadbeater, found this boy on the beach and said he is going to be the next Maitreya, the bearer of the new spirit is going to come. Now in Buddhist terminology, a new bearer of Lord Maitreya is picked up and he is put through a new form of training, he is not, he is not encouraged to speak in Telugu any more. Krishnamurti is made to forget Telugu, beautiful language. And he is put through training in English and horse-riding and all sorts of other kinds of silly things, I think [laughter]. But anyway, he emerges I think and he survives.

He is sent to Oxford, and England and Paris, and I was delighted to find that he failed the matriculation examination three times in London [laughter]. You can't expect to put a sage through this kind of routine and still expect him to pass the London matriculation examination. That is when he protests. This is where I have put my foot down. I am going to become something else if you like, but I am not going to pass your matriculation examination, so he failed three times. That should be a great consolation to slow learners everywhere, I think [laughter]. Anyway, totally transformed, French- and English-speaking, and really he lived all these!

And in America he lived many years in California in Ojai, that's where for many years later his brother Nityananda, who was also with him in this training, in this sadistic training period. Oh! The extent to which the agents of the Divine will go to produce a sage out of ordinary human beings! Anyway, when his brother died, Nitya, that's when his heart broke and was filled with light. He loved his brother very much. That's a beautiful story. We have talked about Ramakrishna and his wife and their disciple, Vivekananda; we have talked about Ramana Maharshi and his mother; we have talked about Aurobindo and Mirra. Here is Krishnamurti and Nitya, two brothers, one of them dies and fills the heart of the other with the compassion which the Buddha knew. Compassion for life, for death, the loss of his own brother, broke him, he was already a sage. He had had [a] mystical experience, he broke down. And all this was predicted by occultists, that he will not be allowed to die, while you are on your way to attend the major theosophical conferences of the world. And all of this happened and he stopped believing in believing, because how could a brother die? What are these predictions worth, if a brother's life can't be safe? He broke down and his heart filled and expanded with love and then became the sky and that is Krishnamurti.

And I don't want to do anything than tell you two stories of Krishnamurti, then I am going to ask Kusum Behan, if tea is ready, after two short stories, which will give you a sense of Krishnamurti and next time I will talk about Krishnamurti at great length, but again somewhat not without irreverence, and this is something which he would entirely approve of, I don't know about his disciples.

I actually encountered him in Madras in 1980, and I was very privileged to be invited to a smallish group of people for a dialogue with Krishnamurti, Rupert Sheldrake was there and George Sudarshan, I felt very greatly honoured and very nervous to be in the presence of such notabilities. There we were, Krishnamurti sat and he had lectured then. He spoke to us and he suddenly played the following game. Without warning, he is a great actor, 'I am dying, I am sick, I am troubled, I have been through it all, through marriage, through a divorce, through health and sickness, I am dying.' And of course, we knew by the power and the beauty of that acting, he was acting. Then he said, 'But you give me no help.' It is a powerful image of even a guru who might be in trouble and we give them no help. 'Help me, tell me what I should do and I have seen it all, it is terrible.' Rupert Sheldrake, who is a Christian, he said, 'Well, try praying.' He said, 'That's a priestly trick' [laughter]. And it was my turn and I am an *advaitin*, I said, 'Well, try finding the self.' 'I have touched the blasted thing' [laughter]. And there was a physicist, George Sudarshan, who went on, and said, 'Be simple'; and there were disciples, Pupul Jayakar, who said, 'But Krishnaji, what would you say if somebody came to you.' 'Ah! And now you are talking.' Then he said, 'I would say nothing at all to such a person, I would simply hold their hand', and he got up, did namaste and went away. That was Krishnamurti. Then when somebody is in real need, simple compassion and love is what you [are] meant to give, not a prayer, not meditation, not physics, not anything of the kind.

My last story—and I really must have the chai, it is very good of Kusum, and her mother, they have come and prepared this for us. So many people help this event. Well, this story was told to me by Pupul Jayakar, after the death of Krishnamurti. She said Krishnamurti—this should interest Buddhists—was very close to Buddhism and Buddhists. They sought him out, so at a meeting between the Buddhist and Krishnamurti, Krishnamurti said, 'Tell me what does Buddhism say about death?' So they gave him the *pratiddhasamupada* view of dependent origination, death simply occurs when certain conditions, in order to take something called death occurs and, of course, there is reincarnation, in the specialist Buddhist way, they told him this, he said, 'Don't tell me this, my friend is dying, I don't want philosophy', so they gave him even more complicated and sophisticated philosophy. He said, 'Don't do that, I am dying', so they are trying to give some more, then he said, 'No, no, no, if a friend of mine were dying, and they were in distress and wanted to be told about death, I would, of course, say nothing, I would simply hold their hand.' But this time he added something before I could say, 'I have heard that before' [laughter], he added and I might say to them, 'Let me die with you.' It was so beautiful when this was told and my understanding of that is, the sage has already died, he has allowed his ego to die, we are all afraid of our ego dying when we fear death. A sage is able to say, look, that what you fear I have already gone through and I am okay. Let me die with you again, let me show again to die to the self, the ego. That's a beautiful story which moved me so much and I am very happy to share with you the story and other things and we will come back after tea for some discussion. Thank you [applause].

I forgot to explain the meaning of the word *'aravinda'* in Sanskrit, and *'aurobindo'* in Bengali, in relation to the teaching. It is the Sanskrit word for lotus, and another word for the lotus is *pankaja*, which means born of mud or muck even, I think, and lotus is the flower of consciousness that is born out of the mud of ignorance, *avidya*, and it blossoms. Indeed the lotus grows in especially dirty ponds in India. I don't think you have to have a dirty pond to grow lotuses, but it tends to do that, and to symbolise out of impure improbability, can arise this beautiful flower. And it's an open flower and in traditional Hindu iconography, there is always an open flower like that, whether it is an open flower which is a flower or the open flower of the *sahasraya* [harmony], it's an invitation for the Devi, for the Shakti, to descend into it, and some of the more popular calendar design, my favourite pictures of Goddesses you find Lakshmi, most beautiful Goddess, standing on a lotus without upsetting even a tiny petal there.

So I do think of Aurobindo as that lotus which opened like that awaiting the descent of Mirra, that flower which opened out of the improbability of his life. Look at the odds against him, seven-year-old England, out of that this flower of yoga opening, into that coming, this magnificent companion, friend and philosopher, sage. You are only to remember the word 'aurobindo', 'aravinda' in Sanskrit, and its meaning, and almost all of the philosophy can be got out of it. There is the yogic readiness which is the opening of the flower and an invitation to the shakti, to the coming. That is what there is, okay let's have a discussion. Yes, Linda.

Question: You kept saying that you were convinced that at the end of their careers Aurobindo and Mirra discovered that the atom was okay, but they did not say so. What do you base this on, your kind of confidence that they made this discovery? Or is it a kind of view of yours?

Ramchandra Gandhi: It could be the latter and if I am wrong, I am sorry, but I teach more than I wish because I have met with people who have had *darshan* [the occasion of meeting a deity face-to-face in a temple] of Mirra towards the end of her life. And they saw in her a very, very, much more gentle, non-strident philosophically person, and who may have, mind you, may have continued because there is a kind of rigour to this yoga. But there was a quietness and an acceptance of the body, of the death. There was no resistance to the old body, it is very, very frail and old, I am convinced the old body in its own gentleness and softness had nourished her. Even Sri Aurobindo, when I look at the dead body, pictures of it, and read many of his letters, I do find that there is an acceptance of it as it was, a tribute paid to the dead body by the Mother herself. As, oh! We thank you for being the receptacle of Ma ... It is a tribute to a non-supramentalised, non-immortal body, and so on. My own confidence is that then if they had failed, I think they had the honesty to admit it. They did not find it necessary and it may have been quite entirely not clear to them even, but it is only a conjecture that in the total, the entire range of their discoveries would have included many surprises. Look, I am not saying that no cells are ever going to be transformed. I think the Earth is a wonderful place, where the Gods, Goddesses, the humans and the others, the mortals and the [im]mortals are all together. That has been the picture in all ancient literature, of every kind of being, being here, and look at even evolution, all of the big bang or whatever, is precipitation out of nothingness, of something, but not all of nothing has become something, much of it mercifully remains. And out of this something, precipitates organised matter, not all matter is organised mercifully, out of this organised matter something precipitates as life, not all matter and out of that and so on and so on. And I think this is the basic style and pattern of evolution, and so they must have encountered both. If they only looked at the faces in the mirror, here is the sage in this body, which is dying, that's okay, somebody who was totally ... Look, unlike many a guru, who is not able to face his own fall in some sense and would wish to hide this, they did not hide their dying bodies. In fact, some of the conversations with some of their attendants I am told by devotees are of a kind of helplessness of the body, which is beautiful. I am not interested in proving this in some historical way—that does not interest me. But I would be surprised if something like this did not occur. Because they are truth-seekers, and if their dream had been shattered ... and in a sense, the dying of their bodies does on one level shatter this dream. There are some statements when Sri Aurobindo dies, oh! This has occurred because of the disciples this or that, Mirra says herself. This is corrected later on, 'no', this is not necessary because their victory is assured. There is room in the Universe for the dead body of Aurobindo as well as to some possibly, alchemically transformed body of somebody else, both. If you say this is my wish ... okay. But, this is not a wish not based on considerations of a serious kind and when I talked to people who knew, had darshan of the Mother towards the end and read many letters of Aurobindo, later on, one letter of Aurobindo specially where some over-enthusiastic disciple is trying to say, 'Oh you are greater than Buddha', [he says], 'What are you trying to say? Their realisation comes to nothing?'—like that. But as I said I am not a devotee of [Sri Aurobindo], this hypothesis doesn't shatter my love for them, no. If I were a devotee of the literal kind, I would, but I am not. I am an admirer of theirs and I do think that even if my hypothesis is correct, there is a way of interpreting the teaching in a way which is entirely restorative of confidence in them. That is of really having shaken things out of a bit. That is what evolution does and if life has evolved out of matter, this is done a lot for the matter to restore its confidence in its power.

But one family in a village produces an educated person in India. All the other families are greatly honoured and comforted by this, for this is possible and they needed [it] too, if everyone became a graduate student in a village in India that would be terrible I think. That's just an analogy ... okay, let me be very clear, the explicit statements do not satisfy me, but I would wish to reconstruct the teaching in a way which would restore in my heart honour and faith and love for them which I always felt, and also enable me to see the value of the teaching. Although in its explicit form, I don't think it can be sustained but it is like that, and I would also, of course, wish to look for evidence, which would of a literary, historical kind, which will support or tend to support my hypothesis. But all this is still work in progress. I only expressed some of the results of my thinking. And I would wish to if I were interested, but I am not, in establishing any historical thesis, if I was really, I would talk to many more people, look at all letters, look at the records, look at Satprem's works [themselves] and find out much more about what happened. I am not interested in that because I don't think anything stands or falls on being able to prove this.

Q: You mentioned that Aurobindo encouraged the Mother to surpass him. In what way do you think that she did?

RG: Well, I think there must have been a pace of a yogic development and he did not say 'hey, don't go fast', and he didn't guide her after a certain point. He acknowledged her as the Mother, as the energy, as the shakti, and I am sure that guided him. If he wanted her not to progress, he would not have done that at all, when she was a disciple, a devotee, when she became something else, what does this mean, unless it is flattery. It is not. It means you have gone beyond certain stages which I have attained, where I must stay for certain other purposes, but you are free to go beyond. I think it does mean that. Think of how many people have done this in relation to their companion. Sri Ramakrishna, yes, when he offered all his siddhis to his wife, but there was there I think an absolute equality and absolute identity if you like. Sri Aurobindo is tantric and there is going to be an excess in creativity and continuing realisation. And that is as well because even after all the siddhis there is still the yoga which continues.

The notion of something which exceeds all given realisation is a good notion and in one of her letters Mirra says to a disciple, never mind what the experiences that you have gained in yoga, never mind how brilliant and wonderful it is, there is something greater even than that, don't ever forget that. So I think that Sri Aurobindo must have realised this in his own yoga and this must be one reason why ... But of course, I think that this is still at the quantitative level greater than, greater than. There must be that which is smaller than the smallest too, that which includes everything and nothing, which is itself a nothingness, and that is the self, that is the *sunyata*—but that is another idiom. I don't think the two cancel each other under the sky, infinite sky of realisation, every kind of experiment is in order, if it aims at furtherance, at a deepening of yoga, that's okay. I think a sky which knows only no storm is no sky. I think storms and thunders and lightning are all permitted I think, not just dry Californian weather all the time. That's good too. I like that.

The question that has just been attempted to be answered is, it is difficult to really portray but. In what way did Aurobindo let the Mother Mirra exceed him? I said that she did, I tried to answer in a certain way, but the question is a profound and an important one, and I think the answer is correct. I noticed a hand behind you.

Q: [The voice of the person asking the question is not clear on tape.]

RG: What a beautiful utterance! I hope the mike has picked you up, I cannot repeat it, but it is a reflection on the possible connection between Linda's recollection of her darshan with the Mother when she held her hands, and Krishnamurti's story I told about Krishnamurti wanting simply to hold the hands of the person who was dying and of saying 'let me die with you', and the statement is, is this what I want of course, not consciously at all, dear friend, if this has happened it happened by the grace of my guru, and that's all ...

Q: [The voice of the person asking the question is not clear on tape.]

RG: Question is about the transformational experiences of Mirra, the mother; after the death of Sri Aurobindo, she did say things like 'he is still here with me', and he had often said before he died and he had written that whatever she says is the truth and we are meant to follow her, beautiful little work called *The Mother* that he wrote. What a tremendous prose, love-work that. I do think so. But there is another idiom of saying the same things even a strict advaitin who doesn't use the idiom of transformation would say, of course—the sage is in everyone. So there is nothing here which cannot be stated in another idiom, but theirs is this idiom. So they choose this way of putting things. The omnipresence of Sri Aurobindo is described in the more tantric, more occult language [that] has been present in a body. Likewise, the eternal *chit* [consciousness] part of *satchidananda* which is the energising shakti, which is, of course, the leader, the *neta*, the language of the Upanishads is described by Sri Aurobindo in this very powerful idiom of the Mother, the source.

I always give long answers to questions. Let me take advantage of this question and talk about something which is in my notes but I forgot. I want to blame the light for it, but it is not, for it is not my own forgetfulness. Mother, the word mother, the word father, you really, it is a pity Lisa left her anthropology, a teacher here, but kinship terms, my prediction is that the next real insight into spirituality will come when we examine the meaning of kinship with mother, father, brother, sister deeply.

Mother means what? When you call your mother, mother, or mom or *ma* or *amma*, you are not thinking of the grandmother whose daughter she is, no, you bring the series to an end. When you call somebody, mother, that's a powerful metaphor from the very heart of our life for the notion of the source of all being. The mother of all, father likewise, mummy, daddy are profound, are the words for Brahman. And the child knows that the being in question is not omnipotent, but being able to call upon the being is a profound experience of entering the source of everything. I would say that our first spiritual experience is when we called somebody *ma*, dad. Because we do through metaphor and through the power of the metaphor enter into the source of all things. So, when somebody set up as the mother for us to call mother, we are I think reminded of this and this is dramatised in one body, which is the body of a sage and in one personality, and I would say that we are, whether or not this is exactly what he meant to relevant. I would take it like that.

This is an invitation for us to do at least three things. To be mindful of the source of all things, Brahman. It is the notion that he uses very consistently. Source of all things, the vast thing, the cause of itself God, the notion of God understood metaphysically and mystically, not theistically alone. Why mother? Why not father? I think the reason for that is that symbolically and in other ways, the gifts of life are brought out almost like magic from the body of a woman. The self-images of the father as it were are produced by the mother. The father here is the formless Brahman that which has no form, the creativity of consciousness produces the forms of the formless exactly analogous to the way a woman brings forth the forms of life, feminine. So it is a very powerful image of the creative process of the Universe which is a way of giving form to the formless continuously, ceaselessly; I would prefer this idiom Sri Aurobindo does not. This is more a language of creating something out of something else, but these are the translations. I would say the magic work of creation is done by the source conceived as a mother. Because our understanding of the mother is [...] ask a child whose mother is expecting another child. 'When is my baby brother going to come?'—expectant, complete, all this I think, this is overdone, the desire to determine the sex, and everything of the baby in the womb, I think that ruins the surprise element totally I think. I would just wait for this expectancy, this waiting on the Universe, all these things are powerfully ... you don't have to be biologically a mother to understand this, but the form of a woman is the form of that energy which is ceaselessly producing images of that which has no image. So there are all kinds of powerful reasons, and in our age, when we need this when the formless Brahman is not properly understood and the Buddha's *nirvana* [ultimate freedom] is not properly understood, and we need a sense of creativity and also we need to honour women sages.

For all this to be done, by this sage Aurobindo in relation to this other sage who is a woman, a philosopher is nothing short of miraculous, and I think this is the reason, and what I don't myself favour, an occult interpretation of these things, because so what, if it is only in Mirra's body, not in another body, that is nothing much. I would like to believe that a sage is in everybody. Maybe some bodies are more open to that, I would not like to believe that miraculously in some occult way that this body of Sri Aurobindo is in that other body, no, it is okay, it is not a big deal, so what? It is okay.

Q: [The voice of the person asking the question is not clear on tape.]

RG: J. Krishnamurti was a profoundly humble man, always very intimidating, a strange combination of intimidatoriness and humility, he would say nothing at all. He is not self-centred at all in that way. If you tried to touch his feet, he would try and touch your feet, so this went on quite humorously often [laughter]. I always thought that the Earth goes round the sun because the sun is trying to touch the Earth's feet but the Earth [is] beating [the] sun going round and round, it is a bit like that. The humility of that sage would ... I don't think, no, no, and I wasn't so sure about these things till I read a lot of him, and met with him, still was not sure, but I do think that there is a quality of great humility to him. It looks almost good manners sometimes that used to worry me. But when I read some of his more angry exchanges with people, then I said, 'Well that is okay, there is an angry sage also.' So, I don't know Karan, what he would have said. I don't know if he had said nothing at all, I wouldn't be surprised. This is what I am saying but I don't have a sense of his presence in the way in which I have a sense of Ramana Maharshi's presence, but that's my fault, not his.

Let me explain a small point. My attempt in these lectures is to present a coherent account of a group of sages, if you like, to set up a theory which will explain all of them in the light of a coherent set of ideas so that is what it is. I am not offering documentary evidence for everything but I am setting up a theory which is claimed to be true.

Q: [The voice of the person asking the question is not clear on tape.]

RG: Certainly. I had said at an earlier lecture. Was reminded of something that the philosopher [A. N.] Whitehead had said about the great philosopher. He said that—I am almost quoting—the philosophy will never revert to its former position after the shock of a great philosopher. We can be a post-Ramakrishnite, we cannot be pre-Ramakrishna. In some areas, in the areas especially of the connection between religious relations, we simply cannot think in the exclusivist ways easily after Ramakrishna. We cannot. We may wish to be more sophisticated in our description of the unity of religion. That's okay. But we can't talk in the kind of exclusivist way of those who spoke before Ramakrishna and nobody does now. Why are the people talking about interface dialogue and song, because of a hundred different kinds of reasons and Ramakrishna? Okay.

Likewise, Ramana Maharshi, that there can be a central experience of non-duality, which in every way matches the experience that has only been reported in books. He is something that we know, to have happened in our own, maybe there are other instances too, we know of this one instance. So the possibility, see for a long time all of this realisation, all attainment of the divinity of something that happened, probably in antiquity, is gone now. It can happen all the time. So I would say Ramana is again like that. And the complex things about Sarada [wife of Ramakrishna Paramahansa] and Alagamma [mother of Ramana Maharshi] I am not going into.

I would say Aurobindo and Mirra that it is possible to make profound and new discoveries in yoga which at least seek to connect with all that has gone before, and not merely eccentric, or indulgent, but that all of this can be sought to be connected with the whole process of transformation, which is understood only in a historical and ideological way by, say, Marx and others. But, this can be understood in a yogic way, even if we find fault with all this as I have done. The possibility that there can be a contacting of the historical and temporal process by the consciousness of yoga, and this might lead to startling discoveries, some think that can't really be doubted, no one can doubt the authenticity of the Mirra and Aurobindo experience; one may quarrel with their interpretations of it, but no one can quarrel with the authenticity of that, with the attempt to connect spiritual consciousness with historical process.

So, I would say, J. Krishnamurti is a healthy reminder that all of us remain rebellious and irreverent, and it is possible to be all of this and still be a sage and that's a wonderful discovery, I think, for our rebellious age. We do not really have to bow our head in premature to submission to anything or ever. But you have to be as empty as Krishnamurti was. I think, furthermore, the possibility that the essence, say of Buddhism, can be independently rediscovered or essence of *advaita vedanta* can be independently rediscovered by Ramana Maharshi, who knew nothing of scriptures. This is great hope, we don't really have to go the traditional way. But we have to go a much difficult way, a very deep way and we can find we have almost rediscovered what the Buddha said or reattained what he did and so on. So I do think that there are a variety of ways of showing what you want. This age is a very special age, and in spiritual attainment, we cannot be prior, in our spiritual thought, in our religious thought, in our thought about history and time and, of course, I still have to talk about Gandhi. That is important too. There are many things that come through with him which don't through the others. Real coming to terms with the difficulty of our times, with the perils of industrialisation and with the meaning of poverty, with all that humility, all that non-violence, so it should become clearer after I talk about Gandhi. But I do think this is an age which is such that we cannot revert to an earlier picture of things. We may have to go beyond this age. Do not think we can slip to an earlier age. And in this way, it is reminiscent of other great ages.

That is an excellent and a very deep question, Vashista, the question was, what exactly do you mean by saying in relation to Sri Aurobindo and Mirra and Krishnamurti and others what you said about Sri Ramakrishna, that we can't go to a stage of understanding prior to Ramakrishna and I have only attempted to answer that question.

Q: [The voice of the person asking the question is not clear on tape.]

RG: That's a wonderful way of putting it. The question is, or the thought is, I have said something about how the acknowledging of matter, the anointing of it if you like, the honouring of it, transforms the sage. All this may not [be] how they put it, but this is at least what they accomplished or what happened to them, how this affects. Is this why we cannot go to an earlier time, because they have their awakened things, this I would say 'yes', the catholicity of our hearts has been touched by Ramakrishna, the self-confidence of the soul has been stirred by Ramana, and the tremendous possibilities of experimentation and of change in the very nature of things have been awakened by Aurobindo and Mirra, and I think the truant and the rebellious spirit in us has been honoured by Krishnamurti, in a way which doesn't result in the chaos of loyalty and disloyalty of being with one guru or another. But in a deeper, deeper beautiful way. And all this has touched us in a way and it is very hard to forget this. I do not think that we can go back to the time when this was not the case. Thank you for that.

Q: [The voice of the person asking the question is not clear on tape.]

RG: Excellent, but I must repeat, I think that certain things are still missing, as I have often pointed out in these lectures. A sage is awaited who will—he or she, maybe together, I don't know—will teach us more explicitly the way of a spiritual sexuality [mild laughter], a way of sexual love, which is real, not only metaphorical, but also it will teach us the meaning of it, the meaning of restraint and responsibility in ways that are not merely alarmist, the ways that go to the heart in explicit terms. I don't know what they could have written explicitly on the subject of sexuality. Ramakrishna says it probably would be very boring, I don't know [mild laughter], but who knows, but I am still waiting for a sage like that—so many things which are there in the womb of the future. There is only one thing and there are many other things to hear, a reawakening, a true rediscovery of aboriginal spirituality by contemporary sage. And a true internalisation of it, not merely in political and cultural terms of honouring, but in real internal terms all that is needed too. So there is much that is to be ... By no means has this extraordinary team exhausted the subject matter of realisation, I don't think so.

— *two* —

Sri J. Krishnamurti*

In a way, this lecture is going to be for me the most difficult so far, and not only because I, like you, I am a bit tired but also because of the subject of Krishnamurti. I talked a bit about him last time, is a very difficult one. He died only a couple of years ago, a master like him or anyone is not really fully understood or even begun to be talked about really exploratively until many, many years after their death. And not that it matters very much, the death of that body, the ending of that body, and yet there was a radiance of power of presence, and many questions which he raised are still being debated. The corpus is not yet determined. What he said, what he did not say, in a way, this is exactly as you would have wished, because and then we are thrown back upon ourselves.

There isn't a neat shelf in every library, which says *The Collected Works of J. Krishnamurti*, and that is just as well. I have been reading biographies of Krishnamurti, the most recent one is by Pupul Jayakar which I recommend. It is simply called *Krishnamurti*. I think it arrived in the market a year ago and not much longer than that, and the earlier one by Mary Lutyens. They are full of a very charming incompleteness. Lutyens says in the chapter, 'Who and

*This is an edited version of the lecture on Modern Indian Spirituality, delivered at California Institute of Integral Studies, July 1988.

What is Krishnamurti', in the end, she says, 'I don't know.' There is an illusiveness to Krishnamurti, which is also the illusiveness of Krishna, whose name he bears. Like Sri Krishna, he was the eighth child, and he barely survived. And something about him which is very hard to understand. Please do read Lutyens' biography called *Years of Awakening* and *Years of Fulfilment*, I like that book. When Mary Lutyens first saw him, she writes, there is a 'silliness, a vacancy, a very unimpressive gentleness, pliability', he was like that. So something like 70 years after she first knew him like that, she asks him, 'How is it Krishnaji that you are able to think these complex thoughts?' And by the way, Krishnamurti's thought is very complex: 'How have these things come from that vacant head that I knew, vacant boy that I knew, how is it that vacant boy becomes Krishnaji?' That's a tribute to Krishnaji, only a guru like Krishnaji could have a pupil who could ask a courageous question like that, I think. It is rather nice. But his reply is very interesting. He says, the vacancy, I am not quoting, the vacancy remains. It's only out of a completely emptied mind, that thinking, true thinking, speaking can come, so it is quite possible that the early vacancy which Mary saw and was horrified by, that something of a very big promise to it, maybe it was already a realisation. We never know about these types. They are very strange. Who could have predicted that Sri Ramana Maharshi, when he was the boy Venkataraman, could be that? He was not very interested in his studies, he was sports-oriented and so on, but a deeper look at that would show that's just a quality of playfulness which remained with him always. And a certain illusiveness and vacancy remained with J. Krishnamurti—those big eyes, and when he wrote of something very poignant, he said, 'I saw a picture of seals with big eyes being battered.' I thought that he was thinking of himself, perhaps. So there was to Krishnamurti a great mystery.

And although mind you, he broke away totally from the occult dimensions of the theosophy movement, which in fact discovered him, I think, and I think rightly that we do owe a debt of gratitude to the strange reverend Leadbeater, interesting name, Leadbeater, and the whole occult movement, which I find quite silly after a certain point, but I do think we owe a debt of gratitude to them for having spotted this child on the seashore. They said of course that the Lord

Maitreya, the Bodhisatva, was going to use this child's body as the vehicle for his crowning *avatara* [godliness, or embodiment of the Divine], and this vacant child, probably when he first heard this, remained vacant, until the end he remained vacant.

But who knows? There might have been something to it, there might have been triggering off of a process which is greater than occultism, but maybe it took occultism to start something greater than occultism, I think [we] must not be ungrateful to [Helena] Blavatsky, to Annie Besant. Annie Besant loved Krishna. Krishna called her 'amma', which is the dearest word that a south Indian child can use for mother. Throughout his life, of course, he grew beyond all attachment, but he retained a very special love for Amma, and when you read the accounts they are probably slightly biased in favour of Krishnamurti. I don't yet know any work written from the theosophist point of view on Krishnamurti. But when you read all the accounts, [you] get the impression that here are midwives who are struggling to bring a very difficult birth into the world, Annie Besant, Leadbeater, and I think, that even when they are clumsy, I think they are doing an important job. So I want to begin with a thought of gratitude to a group of thinkers who I don't myself admire all that much. But I do think in relation to Krishnamurti, they performed a task of midwifery which is remarkable and for which we must remain very, very grateful.

So here is this vacant boy. What does he do? Is he at all permanently touched by the occultism, by the magic, by the mythology which surrounded his identification? In a very quaint way, yes. When he was 80, he said to Mary Lutyens in a room, 'Do you feel it?' She said, 'What?' 'Oh, the presence. I have always felt protected,' he said, 'There's something which protects me always.' You could read it at various levels that he was a channel—he was not. Krishnamurti, a channel and he hated all kinds of dependence. He would have told whoever wanted him to be a channel to go away. But he said but there is a presence, something is protecting, and Mary felt that force too. So [like] Krishna himself, Krishnamurti had a keen sense of the occult. As a child, he could see Krishna. It is remarkable that somebody who had an occult capacity was able to disown it. Somebody who was hailed as the new Messiah, the Maitreya avatara, was able to disband the order of the stars. These are acts of very great and beautiful renunciation, I think. If you have occult powers, you tend not to give them up very easily. They are impressive, and I have a feeling, I have a hypothesis, I am such a hypothesis-maker I know that this is one reason why I probably had the touch of the flu the other day, I went out and I saw all kinds of occult forces [that had] invaded me said that you are creating many theories and hypotheses [laughter], you should speak with a little more reverence. So I am trying to propitiate the occult forces a bit. Because I don't want to remain with my flu very long. But there remained with Krishna a sense of the occult although he had no use for it. That never became a part of his teachings but it's there, there are all kinds of mysterious forces, I have a feeling that the occult force is no more mysterious than my neighbour next door who plays her music too loud, that's also an influence. That's my only grouse about these things. That they may be wonderful, but things closer to us are even more wonderful. I think the influence of somebody actually sitting in front of you, and looking at you, and smiling at you, is infinitely greater than some occult influence which makes your arm go stiff, I find it a bit silly, I think Groucho Marx would have had a good line on it, but I can't think of a good line straightaway.

Well, so what does Krishnamurti achieve finally? Everyone knows that he attacked the idea of gurus, and I am so glad Bobs reminded us that the guru nevertheless remains. But it was necessary for a certain idea of the guru to be attacked, and attack with the brilliance, and the authority of a Krishnamurti. Because our age is an age of great insecurity and, despite Krishnamurti's attacks, everybody is looking out for some kind of guru all the time. And Krishnamurti was once talking to a traditional Hindu, who said, 'Oh! But the guru is within me.' He said, 'Within you, oh my God! I hope not!' [laughter]. So without, or within, the notion of a guru is a dangerous one for Krishnamurti. Of course, as a vedantin, I am mildly irritated by that. But I think I am put in my place too. The guru is no one, you must do it yourself, that covert independence is so tremendous, that our age which prides itself on its independent spirit, when it comes to spirituality is so subservient to somebody else, or something else, is quite a paradox. I think Krishnamurti does draw our attention to this, and I think we are meant to be grateful to him, but this does not mean that we are meant to abandon our search for the meaning of what a guru is.

I think in strict conformity to Krishnamurti's own teaching, we must not depend on Krishnamurti either for what ultimately turns out to be the nature of the guru. We ought to be grateful to him for stimulating thoughts, for a kind of iconoclasm which was greatly needed. Remember I told you, I am afraid there will have to be some references to what has gone before, and those who had come for the first time will forgive me, but I did talk about Ramakrishna's story, which connects with the subject and the style of Krishnamurti in an intimate way.

Ramakrishna, one of his pupils began to learn English, quite unnecessary, and it was reported to Sri Ramakrishna. He said, 'Aha! Now he will start whistling and wear boots.' That has a very profound meaning I think because in India we have tended on the whole to make very poor use of English, which is analogous to the status of whistling, which I like, I don't know why whistling is disliked, but it has this sense of triviality let's say. And boots because if you know a little bit of English, you become a very powerful person in India and you trample upon native cultural soil. So Ramakrishna knew the dangers of that, but Krishnamurti is an exception to that. He certainly internalised English, very, very profoundly and deeply, and he was no whistler, and he wore no tyrannical boots, so that is an exception to that warning, that danger that Ramakrishna alerted us to. Krishnamurti's use of the English language alone would be a remarkable subject for a long lecture, but my own limitations prevent me from venturing into that field. Some scholars of English ... his English is quite interesting. There are Victorian things there, mind you, like, sir and madam and so on, quite intimidatingly he would say, 'Sir, I don't know what you are talking about.' I worry about that. But then he was a product of his time, but he is remarkably fluid and simple in his choice of words but in the way they connect and construct they become heavy, and his writing has a strange illusive simplicity to it but it is not, his writing is very interesting. You should read him as a writer too. He has written several journals and things like that. At the end of these lectures, I will give a long list of readings to all of you. I don't want these lectures, the flow of these lectures, and of your attention to be interrupted by reading lists and things like that right now. But I do promise that at the end of the seventh or the eighth talk, I will give you hopefully in several copies the reading list.

Now Krishnamurti is [of] our times. He is the media sage if there was ever one, he is talking, lecturing, he is a jet-set sage if there ever was. Not one of those who travelled to make money and to bring a kind of spiritual slavery, not one of those, but he flies in jet planes, all the same, he is wandering around all over the place. He is in Bombay today, he is in Sydney tomorrow, he is in New York all over the place, Krishnamurti. Tirelessly how he managed to be, I imagine you have to be a sage to handle jet lag on that scale I think, he managed to do that. Well, that's a good incentive to being a sage, I think the only way of beating jet lag. So that's Krishnamurti, he is very much with us all the time. And yet, when I look at this group so far—Ramakrishna, Sarada, Ramana, Ramana's mother, Vivekananda even, and Krishnamurti, Aurobindo, Mirra—I think of them all as sages who shrank from direct political activity. For one reason or another. It is very interesting going to their reasons for this. Even the great Vivekananda who was a charismatic figure, he would have been the dictator of India if he wanted to, he chose not to, Sri Aurobindo, who was a very powerful thinker and writer and a very passionate arouser of emotions, chose after a brief skirmish with politics, not to have anything to do with it.

Krishnamurti hated politics. The word politician is invariably an abusive word in his writings. Gandhi did not share this ... So there is a kind of line here. Up to Krishnamurti, you have in this period we are talking about sages who, mind you, are not escapists by any means. There is a deeper politics that Krishnamurti is doing, and there is another occult politics of the cosmos that Aurobindo and Mirra are doing, and of course, Ramana in my heart remains the arch politician of our age, who explodes this bomb of self-realisation. But I don't mean in those occult and metaphorical senses and perhaps metaphysical senses, but in the honest, goodness, straightforward sense, they don't. But I don't judge them for this. But with Gandhi you have a very different, we will come to that, but Krishnamurti was quite irritated by Gandhi often. We must talk about these things too, because I do love him and this gives me a right, therefore, to disagree with him sometimes. But he thought that Gandhi's non-violence was a form of violence. And I don't think he had a very high opinion of the political aspect of Gandhi's life, mainly because not for any personal reasons I don't think because he felt that politics of the conventional kind had better be left severely alone, but I am afraid he had rather a touching, romantic belief in the persuasiveness of his words, especially when it came to world leaders and others, they are not so easily persuaded, although we must keep trying. I am not saying, therefore, there should be violence, but there has to be other modes of communication too which is politics in the wider sense of the word, which involves saying 'no' to evil, politically in the field, not with hatred, and not only in your home, and office and factory and farm, but out there, where the battle lines are drawn. We will come to that, but with Krishnamurti, increasingly I find sagehood, which is totally divorced from the politics of the survival of the Earth, a bit irritating. Of course, politics that's divorced from spirituality I find even more irritating [mild laughter], but I do think that Gandhi's example is going to lead us to try and evolve a mode of spiritual life which would honour the exclusiveness of a spiritual truth of course, but also seek actively, not violently but actively, even militantly, but not militarily, but militantly relate spiritual truth to the ongoing struggles of our life. There would be the struggles of nationalism, I don't think so, or of ideology, but of survival of nature, of peoples, of sexes, of children, of old people, of oneself, of the body, the mind, spaces, but we will explore that more next time.

But back to Krishnamurti and to my notes. I said it's hard for me to talk about Krishnamurti not only because he only recently died, but also I am an advaitin, I am a vedantin, I believe in the self. Krishnamurti hated the self. It's taken me many years and the struggle continues, taken many years of struggle not to want to put down the book which when I encounter some kind of negative thought on the self. But I will try to communicate to you some of my results in this struggle. Oh! By the way, talking about the occult and the protection that, this is a great source of support to lecturers and non-stop talkers like myself, Krishnamurti said that this body has to be protected because it was meant to speak, he said. Here you have a sage who values speaking and this is rather nice, that there are sages who value silence, and that's very good, but that has often been taken to mean indifference, running down of the gift of speech. But Krishnamurti honoured and valued this, not a ceaseless chattering, but the use of speech for illumination, for exploration. And he was tremendous, he I think did manifest the old art of speaking. Speaking as an art form, to perfection, I think. And I do think that all show business stars, would-be stars, ought to get tapes of Krishnamurti, I think they would learn many things from that. But also lovers of sound, he had a very beautiful voice. I remember closing my eyes, only half in meditation when he was speaking, but more for the acoustic enjoyment of his voice and words. And then certain things that used to irritate me, a certain sharpness of the language still began to look more and more like a kind of poetry. So there is that aspect too, I think to Krishnamurti. So what a gift to the English language I think Krishnamurti and Aurobindo and others, and he loved this country, Krishnamurti, he stayed in Ojai, for many years. That's when he had this first significant spiritual experience, he writes about it in the language partly of theism. He says, 'I am God-intoxicated and I have reached the source of it all.' So he did acquire immigrant status to be here, so, that's interesting, he was no nationalist, it did not matter to him, he loved this part of the world too and his brother died in Ojai, Nitya. And as I tried to point out last time, the death of his brother, various things triggered off, didn't they?

In the case of Ramakrishna, it was the storming of the citadel of Goddess, as blackmailing of God to show herself to him, and she did. In the case of Ramana, it was this straight encounter with death, and this pure enquiry, crystal-clear enquiry, 'Who am I?' In the case of Krishnamurti, many things, but I think it was the death of his beloved brother Nitya that broke his heart and illumined his mind. What he writes about, it is so wonderful. He prayed, he said, 'I prayed to everything, everyone, save my brother's life, no, why have you done this? Why have you permitted this, the occultist! Why did they lie to me?' Why was ... a brother dies and I think the root of Buddhism, of the compassion of Krishnamurti lies there, the root Buddhist experience of Krishnamurti, the root illumination of compassion, my brother has died, that happens in Ojai the sacred place, I must visit it really, that is it.

As a vedantin, as an advaitin, for me the biggest challenge of Krishnamurti, the biggest attraction is his Buddhism. I am not saying he is a follower of, in the conventional sense, but more than two millennia ago, Gautama of the Sakya clan charted another path to liberation, to enlightenment, not the conventional path of the Upanishads, of self-realisation, nor the conventional path of traditional theism of God out there, worlds out there, but another path which had to do with the perception of the transitoriness of everything, the changefulness of every[thing]. Just what breaks our heart turns out to be our salvation, when we go deep into it, without fear, without desire, with a total identification with the stream of life as it comes into being and as it goes away, as you embrace the total flow and stream of life, just what you fear you want to stand outside from it and say I am a soul, not this body, I will survive, all these will die, I will go in this occult aeroplane to Heaven. Or cynically, of course, everyone dies and there is no need to make any further enquiry, neither cynicism, nor nihilism, nor complacency, but something in between, I can see Gautama saying, 'No, why is everyone afraid of death, let me face it, let me enter into it, not by suicide but by a process of identification with that which dies, namely the flesh, the mind, the living creature, but that must mean all creatures. If I really wish to find liberation through this other means, not through a standing apart and finding that which does not die.' That is also legitimate enquiry, unnecessarily pooh-poohed by Krishnamurti. But there is also another enquiry, the reason why I salute Krishnamurti although I find his anti-vedantic sentiment irritating. The reason I salute him is I think, like the Buddha, he has found that other path too, the path of saying, no, this is very problematic anyway, this soul, the spirit, the self and God and of course, one is not meant to be cynical either. Let me identify myself with this flow, with this body that dies, this mind that dies, or let me die, and then when you die like that, you are born again. Remember I told you the story last time, maybe there is a repetition.

Some Buddhists were talking with Krishnamurti, and Krishnamurti asked them to explain the Buddhist position on death, and they gave very beautiful accounts of *pratitsamutpada*, of causality, of the obtaining of certain conditions and the obtaining of life, of the non-obtaining of certain conditions and the non-obtaining of life, very beautifully in its own way. But Krishnamurti kept saying, 'Oh, do not give me words, my brother is dying, my friend is dying, I am dying so they gave me some more', and he said, 'Wait a minute, if somebody is dying and they wanted to know about death and so on, I would say nothing at all. I would hold their hands maybe, or maybe I would go on to add "let me die with you".' So I suggest that Krishnamurti's method and the Buddha's method is the method of 'let me die with you'. It doesn't mean if somebody is about to jump off the Golden Gate, you would say 'let me jump with you'. No, it does not mean that at all, it means if you are lucky sitting down with them and saying look what you are afraid of in life that you have this separate something, being which will come to an end because of the misery and the pain, and so you want to die before. No, but this can come to an end without life going by a total identification with all lives, you and I are not other than one another, we are one, all being is one, everything is changing like that, let's be with all of this in compassion and love and then something will die in us, but something will be timelessly born, something, the timeless will be born, let me die with you, it means that. Let us, you and I die to the self, to use the Christian expression, or ego die, and then Krishnamurti wouldn't say that the real self is born, he is too wary of that, as I think was the Buddha, because the moment you say self, we will begin to think only of their own ego and personality. They are not even to hold fast the idea of pure self-consciousness, and more is the pity I think because we are that, I am, you are. So I do think that this is something panicky in that strategy of Gautama and of Krishnamurti, but who knows it may have been greatly needed, it is permanently needed, because we have both deeds, and constantly thinking of myself only as this man, of you as only that person, and of the world only this region. And then Krishnamurti and Gautama suggest, let us think of this collectively, let us immerse ourselves in this temporality, in this flow, and then something will die and something will be born in that play. He doesn't use the wordplay, but as I see it, that experience, he doesn't talk about it, would be something like taking the plunge and finding that you haven't sunk, haven't drowned. That you are swimming, but you are under the sky, the infinite sky which sustains the oceans, ocean *samsara* of all life and in that what was originally a destructive-looking thing, the dying, the losing the battle becomes I think to play, because without that separateness of ego, but with this all-embracing compassion and love, everyone's victory is my victory, everyone's sorrow is my sorrow.

Krishnamurti says something so beautiful about sorrow. He says the only way out of sorrow is to be in sorrow, to be it. So somebody asked, 'I am bored', and he said, 'Be bored', not in the way of shocking you, but I think in the way of identifying. He said something which used to irritate me in my more analytical moments. He says that I am anger. But I have grown up in the tradition which says I am not any of these things, but there is a sense in which I am angry too. If I am thinking of myself as this person, not as pure self-consciousness, most people do think of themselves as the persons, that they are the bodies and minds that they are. If that is so, there is still a way and they worry about their separateness, they say, 'Oh but I am just this, I will die, she is just this, she will die.' Krishnamurti and Buddha are saying, 'Why do you worry about that? Immerse yourself in this process, accept that as the truth of the nature of things, this dying, this changing and you will find something happening. If you really do that with that universality, it can't be a limited sympathy. Then you are born again. He says something very beautiful. He says, 'You want to continue that which is continuous cannot be creative, how can that which merely remains this man with all his greed, his fear, remains, remains, remains, for eternity, there is no creativity, nothing radically new is going to come out of that even if I change my form into several different kinds of life forms. It is still the 'I am', but this thing, even if I became the immortal body I would say after one million years, I am but this immortal body. Boredom is the ultimate obstacle to illumination. The boredom of Heaven alone I think makes the search for illumination possible. This is why sages who are probably Divine beings and celestial beings come to Earth to experience the changefulness, this mortality, this compassion and that's what Krishnamurti does. He says often, but I first heard him say, 'I and the world are one.' I thought he was making a vedantin statement. That the world is no other than the self and the self is all that there is, and it creates for itself, he was not saying any of those things I thought for a moment wishfully that he was, it became apparent fairly quickly that he wasn't. What he meant was, 'I and you are different in very many interesting ways. We are also so similar and so profoundly similar in fundamental ways, we all grieve, we all hunger, we die, we suffer this torment of existence, this weight, this burden of it, we shared its sweetness also, we are one.' That is another mode of non-duality. I have a professorial phrase for it, non-duality of the ego. There is the non-duality of the self, which is advaita vedanta, that the self, ultimate pure self-consciousness, is one, you and I are not other from one another.

This is what Ramana Maharshi would say. He would say, I see no other, you are not other than I. Somebody came to Ramana Maharshi, and said, 'Oh! You teach a different doctrine.' Ramana taught no doctrine at all. The questioner who was probably a dualist said, 'We believe in the separate reality of God, the world, and the self, you only believe in the reality of the self.' Ramana looked at him with great compassion, said, 'No, no, my dear friend, you got it all wrong, I believe in the full reality of the world and of God and of the self, because they are all self, you only believe in one-third reality of the world, one-third reality of God. You divide it into three,' but that is not what Krishnamurti is saying. He is saying that at this level of non-realisation of the self, if there is such a realisation, there is still a way out. He and the Buddha offer a direct path, even to those who despair of *mukti* [ultimate freedom] and self-realisation. We can still feel the real one, what is the profound difference between a child and an old man. There is no profound difference. Mortality comes to both, and what is the 100 years of time in cosmic time, nothing, they are one and all life is one. And not only that, all things die, change, so thing-hood of any kind is necessarily mortal, necessarily involved in flux and that should inspire us to be very compassionate straightaway. And if we are able to do that, throw ourselves into this fire, this yagna of self. He also used the word self-knowledge,

Krishnamurti. Again I used to wishfully think that 'Aha! This is where the vedanta, when he likes it or not, is entering into through the backdoor.' No, of course, I am disappointed that it is not entering, but what he means is, and I think that the compassion of a Buddha is something that Krishnamurti has taught me. The compassion of the Buddha, this is my own vedantic view of the Buddha, so don't be shocked. Self-realisation as a path, the authentic path of advaita, of non-duality, is hard and authentic teachers are hard to find, but suffering remains, ignorance remains, what are we to do, and as I see the Buddha, he is thinking about, then it probably occurs to him that is not necessary at all. The embracing of change, as a total condition of all that is, could lead to that compassion and he tries it and he attains nirvana, because the result is the same, only they don't use the word self. Although I think they do sometimes. The reason is that they feel that is a non-starter for many people, the moment you say, 'Oh! Realise yourself', the man will say, Oh! But where am I? What do you want me to realise?', but if you say, 'Love your brother, your sister, love everyone, be compassionate to others', it is the beginning, and if you say not only as a duty but as a way to supreme enlightenment, they say, 'That's an incentive?' So I do think that it is the compassion of the Buddha that you find again in Krishnamurti.

These are hard things for a vedantin to say, mind you, but I say very gladly as a tribute to this unique master in our age, who I think in contemporary English, has found words to express what the Buddha must have done, of course, the entire discourses of Buddha have not come down to us, but I do sometimes think, I have meditated for a long time today tried to see Buddha as Krishnamurti, Sakyamuni. He may have had similar discourses too, but I think he would probably have been less irritable sometimes, I think, than Krishnamurti tended to be. But who knows, he may have been quite impatient with so-called gurus also. He may have wanted again, out of the compassion of his heart, to teach everyone *sharana* [to surrender to the divinity] to immerse themselves into the flow and liberate themselves at the same time. Amazing! It is a bit like the truth of 'jump into the river and you know how to swim'. It's only an analogy. You are afraid of the flow of life, but jumping into it, not as a separate diver, but have a sense of everyone being in these waters, and you will know that no one is, that everyone is free, do that. Everything is on fire, enter that fire, and you are free, it is a unique path, almost a tantric path. I don't mean in the sense of the Buddhist *tantra* that emerged historically later, at the very root of it, there is tantra in the Buddha's way. Tantra is what, to convert supreme adversity into a supreme advantage. Death, mortality to enter that and to convert that into a supreme experience, that is tantra if anything is. Krishnamurti might choose to do that.

And then, one of the doctrines of which rather epistemological matters have been written, dully academic and philosophical things, and I say this as a professional philosopher, it is very difficult for me to say that, but he says the observer and the observed are one. Now, this echoes the theory of relativity, the principle of uncertainty, you have professors of physics writing ... and engaging Krishnamurti in very expensive international seminars all the time, that's okay and I don't grudge them any of these. I wish I was invited to some of them, that's another matter. But I think ... Krishnamurti had read no books at all, Mary Lutyens says that the few books he had read he had forgotten, that vacant boy, and she says that his memory is appalling, he does not remember anything about his boyhood and gets his dates wrong. Lovely, for a sage to risk such fallibility, it's quite a good thing, most people would think him a fool, indeed he failed his matriculation examination three times. I bet he knew everything, and then he forgot everything. Because he attached no importance to learning, to the past, to the conditioning, his attitude to the past was carried over to his attitude to his own past. Remember how much he loved his brother! He used to say, 'Oh is it not true that I had a brother whom I loved much? Tell me about him', meaning, of course, there is no specific brother that I loved. I loved all as my brothers! So this was his way of saying I have forgotten this specificity now, remind me, so that is Krishnamurti's tantra if you like. That is Krishnamurti's way with adversity.

He says the observer and the observed are one. The meaning is I am the observer and you are observed. One way, direct way into the heart of the illumination that Krishnamurti is exhibiting is, I am there. You and I are one. In that new non-advaitin way, mind you, non-vedantic way. Not only in the profound sense that pure self-consciousness is one and it manifests as all these people. I prefer that image frankly. But not only in that way, but in this way of the flesh we are one ... observer and observed are one. So this is a very great way of direct love and compassion, and it must be distinguished from a merely ethical attitude, although of course, it is an ethical attitude. Merely ethical attitude would say we ought to love our brother, love our fellow human beings. But you expect the plunging into it, into the process of why should we love. Not because they are immortal souls, that would be selfish kind of love, wouldn't [it]? You say to somebody, 'I love because of your eyes, because of your head, because of your immortal soul.' I think they would be talking nonsense [mild laughter], I love you because you will die, because you were born, and you suffered the torments of living. The few joys that there appeared to pleasure become pain again, because they go, I am one with you, the moment you say that those that sorrow becomes compassion and that compassion becomes joy, peace, so that is a very great mystery. I wish he could have said it all, a little more straightforwardly, Krishnamurti you know. He doesn't! He chooses a kind of convoluted style which is probably something like Zen teaching, but no, I don't think so, I think here is a vacant boy, to whom the English language comes in torrents and he makes use of it, I think he loves it, he is a talker, he is naughty, like Krishna. He will defeat your expectations, suspend you, think you are about to understand and he will change his tune, tone, you should read a dialogue with David Bohm and Krishnamurti. David Bohm must have been exasperated, good for him because he is always quoting etymology at Krishnamurti. And he is slipping out of the nets of etymology all the time. But they loved each other. But that was Krishnamurti. He was always keeping us alert and awake! And reminding us that our duty really is to throw ourselves into this stream to become one with it, not separately, but totally and then he did believe that if any one person is able to do this, transform their consciousness, the consciousness of the world itself is affected. And quite literally, he meant that! And I think what that means roughly is this, a bit like Sheldrake's theory about rats learning something in this corner of the world, everyone learning. But this is more than learning, this is unlearning, unlearning the bad habits of the past, which tell me that I am only this, I am only that, and separate from you and not you, that is the past.

Krishnamurti loved to poke fun at the past, I think again he overdid it. I think the past too has its elegance, has its simplicity and remembrance has its value. Not all remembrance is remembering, not every sage does everything, we can't expect Krishnamurti to have talked about the past in a loving way, if I love everything, I must love the past too, must [have] compassion for the dead, that which is gone. Anyway, he was rather present-oriented, in a way which I admire but also find slightly disappointing, because I love my friends and relatives who have died. There is something there too. And they had become one with everything. They are continually separating, perhaps the dead are the greatest yogis, they are continually becoming multiple. All the atoms continuously shattering themselves. Who knows? I think we must love the past too, it probably energises the present in a mysterious way. Anyway, Krishnamurti is talking about the world and I being one, in that way of shared mortality, shared changefulness. Why? Because his profound insight is that only that which comes to an end can be creative! When I read this I was really moved and really thrilled!

You know often the doctrine of the self or of the soul is presented as the doctrine of that which continues forever. This is a silly way of looking at the matter. But Krishnamurti is surely right, if there is something which remains forever exactly, as it is that is very dull, that is not creative. But of course, if something compulsively changes all the time, you know the kind of guy who was trying to say something different all the time, and then he manages to be exactly himself. Ah! There comes a guy who is trying to be different all the time, so everyone knows him. He defeats its own purpose. But there is something to, you know the kind of person I mean, we are all a bit like that sometimes, when we are trying to impress.

So ... Krishnamurti's is a way of dying, I have realised. Let me die with you. Is also, of course, saying let me live with you! The only way of learning to live with you is to die with you! When you fear the death of your ego, let me die with you there and then prove to you and to myself that something else has come into being, the timeless, that which is not in time at all, that which cannot die.

Not because it is non-living. The Gods are not non-living, they are timeless because otherwise the question to ask God would be, 'How many million years old are you?' That's terrible! To admit that you are a billion years old. That's not a compliment I think, to say ... Oh! Meet my friend! God so and so, he is a billion years old! Good, the Gods and the Goddesses are timeless. They are therefore timely, they can at all times be with us or not with us, so dying of the false, it is false that I am only this! Now I am not quoting Krishnamurti, I am trying to interpret him. It is simply false, it is an illusion that you are only that! This illusion must be shattered ... a friend of mine who came here a couple of a few weeks ago asked me, 'why do you talk about the shattering of the ego, is it not a bit coercive, violent, implied these things. Well, I don't think so, because shattering that really takes place is often, is illusion, and illusion shattered, that's the music of their going, shatter. And this is dying. True dying is the shattering, the noisy. Shattering of illusion, the illusion that I am only this! Krishnamurti doesn't use this language, but I would suggest that it could be used in a way in which we would retain his teaching. This must go. The reason we are probably annihilatory in the world, so, nearly bringing about the end of all life on Earth is that there is another kind of ending of the world in ourself, which we are not doing.

I have always maintained as a general principle that there is no evil, which is not a caricature of some very great good. The evil, the profound, unique evil of our time, the unconscious desire, and sometimes less than unconscious, more conscious desire to put an end to everything, is probably a caricature of the other shattering of the illusion, that the world and I are different. You are different, that is also a kind of false world. There is a false world of illusion, which we haven't smashed, shattered, exploded, brutally, because we haven't done that, we want to do this. Because we haven't, ego died, we want to kill the person, ourselves. The person is not just the ego. The person can be an ego. But the person is also him or her who overcomes that and therefore becomes, I think, an image of the Divine. The Man Ray picture is in repose there, the person who wears the masks of all like that girl does. But in Krishnamurti, there is not much use for the word 'self' in a commendatory sense, so I have put on the easel bird picture of Margaret that's called more of the sky, more of the non-self. Even the bird has transparent wings, you will notice, that is more appropriate to Krishnamurti and the three eggs there might be our three kinds of ego, three kinds of false self if you like. They are meant to be offered to this bird, so something may come out of it, something may be hatched. Krishnamurti is a bit like a bird himself, you watch he looks like a bird. You can look at that picture, that's of the old Krishnamurti. More like a bird again. But there ought to be surely as a sculpture in the museum of the modern art, showing Krishnamurti is birdlike I think ... so I find Krishnamurti's thought when I managed to understand when I read his words, I am thrilled and irritated by turns. I will read some words which thrilled me. And I will try not to read those that irritate me.

The order of the star is disbanded by Krishnamurti in the following words: I maintained the truth is a pathless land and you cannot approach it by any path whatsoever, by any religion, by any sect. I do not want to belong to any organisation of a spiritual kind, if an organisation be created for this purpose it becomes a crutch, a weakness, a bondage, and must cripple the individual and prevent him from growing from establishing his uniqueness which lies in his, forgive the sexism of that, he means, his or her. His discovery for himself of their absolute unconditioned truth, because I am free and conditioned whole. I desire, though there is something vedantin here because I am free, unconditioned whole. You would never say this is in 1929. In later years, he chose to be, explicitly more Buddhist in his language, but you know, you can't get rid of the self so easily [laughter].

You are all depending for your spirituality on someone else. No man from outside can make you free. You have been accustomed to being told how far you have advanced. The theosophists always needed somebody to tell them: How far have you progressed? Give us A, B, C, grades in our paths. For two years I have been thinking about this slowly, carefully and patiently, and now I have decided to disband the order as I happened to be its head [laughter]. Disbanding it from the top, not undermining it from within, but explicitly ... You can form other organisations and expect someone else, with that I am not concerned. Nor with creating new cages, new decorations for those cages. My only concern is to set men absolutely, unconditionally, free. Wonderful words, I think, and he does do that. But sometimes in a way which is hurtfully iconoclastic. But then no man, no sage, no one can do everything. And their hurts are not intended to be hurts, they are meant to awaken us! I thought little hurt, when I suggested to him in that other game he played, I said, oh, try overlooking for the self, he said, I have touched the blasted thing [laughter]. But I was glad I was put in my place. It's a game that he deserved to win. He has been playing it much longer than I have. That's okay.

And another thing to go back to that Man Ray, he was sitting on a kind of futon. We all sat in chairs and he said, oh, you can come and sit next to me, there is plenty of room here and like that. What he meant was there can be a lot of people speaking too, lots of gurus if you like, lots of teachers, I am not going to be the only one and like that. So those are the kinds of words that have thrilled me when I read Krishnamurti. Then I again, what is it that continues, idea, thought, is it not, the idea of yourself as a name, this could be Sakyamuni, this could be the Buddha speaking in Pali. The idea of yourself as a name, as a particular identified individual, which is still an idea, which is memory, which means the word, surely most of us are clinging to that, aren't we? You are not afraid of leaving your family, your children, that is just an excuse. Actually, you are afraid to come to an end. Now that which continues, that which has continuity can that be creative? Is there a renewal in that which continues? Surely there is renewal only in that which comes to an end! Paradox, dangerous, if you are potentially suicidal, don't read this [laughter]! Where there is an ending, there is a rebirth! Play on the doctrine of reincarnation! If you don't want this ego to end, you will never be reborn, you will be much the same. What is the profound difference, it might be Ramu Gandhi here and somebody else in the next birth, only want simply to be, and to be under the illusion that I will not die? That is no rebirth. If I continue as I am, as I have been in this life, with all my ignorance, prejudices, stupidities, illusions, memories, attachments, whatever, and yet it is that we cling to tenaciously. So these are profound words. But don't get lost. I don't think this in any way has the slightest tendency to prove that the self is not! That you are not that! This is a way of saying that is hard perhaps, people get it wrong, don't worry. Accept the fact that you think of yourself, go beyond it, see that everyone is like that and that you are everyone. And you will die and be born again because this must come to an end and now I am interpreting because the false must come to an end. There is only one thing which necessarily comes to an end and that is an illusion. The notion of an endless illusion is an impossibility. So, only if my thought [is] that I am, only this is, an illusion, can I come to an end?

Now, I am arguing as a vedantin, of course, and I would love to debate Krishnamurti on this. I would say yes, Krishnaji, I accept your teachings and it is beautiful, and it is wonderful and I am not trying to flatter you, in fact, I could do the opposite. But notice that the only thing of which we can be absolutely certain that will come to an end is an illusion, something which is not an illusion may go on and on, on, forever. Why is nature changing? This appearance is there because the thought that tree is only there is false and so the tree changes. My thought that I am only this is false, so I change. Anything which is false necessarily changes, and since everything is changing at the level of appearance everything is false. This is why there is change, but these are arguments which I offer from the side of vedanta. But they are not intended to dismiss Krishnamurti at all. But of course, I will feel obliged to produce arguments because when you read brilliant, beautiful, passages like that, don't think that anything on the side of the self has been demolished ruthlessly. Many a follower of the Buddha thinks unfortunately that, oh, with the Buddha the whole of the pursuit and search for self-realisation comes to an end, forgetting that Buddha himself was one of the chiefs amongst the self-realised ones.

And that beautiful story of the woman slave, who, no, I told the story so many times especially some friends of mine who heard it ten times would say, oh, no, there goes Ramu again with that story [laughter]. But I am afraid I am like that. You have to blame that story, it is so beautiful that I can go on telling it, it's about these beautiful people who are having a great time in this forest, where precisely at that point in time in another part is Buddha after nirvana walking up and down like a lion, savouring it, and these other beautiful people are also doing their thing, and they are very happy too. But one of them is a woman, who has no partner and she is a slave woman, whose task is to look after the valuables of these beautiful people while they are having this great time. And while they are having this great time, she runs away with those valuables. I think she does the right thing. Good for them, I think, you can't do that, you cannot hire a slave to do that, especially if you don't even try to provide her a partner. So, when they are wakened and they are furious, they mount their elephants, their horses and their trumpets, and they virtually destroy the forest. The peace of the forest, the peace of the *sadhus* [renouncers, wanderers] there, the animals there, the birds there. They are looking for this slave woman. And who do they run into eventually, the Buddha? And as I see, they see this sage, so they get off ... and say, 'Have you seen that woman go this way?', in that way of the aristocracy. The Buddha says, 'Why do you seek her? Seek the self.' In a little section called 'Bhagdavadiyavathu', which occurs in the Mahavagga of the Pali canon. Now, you can't change that, it doesn't mean something else, like, oh, Seek yourself, not the self, no, because these guys have found their selves, they are the aristocracy of their time, you know. What he is saying is, look, your own ancient teachings you have forgotten. That is the true extra, the true other, instead of seeking that other, let's call that other, the mother, you are seeking the slave. Let her go! Let her be free, and if she has run away with some of your valuables, you jolly well owed her ten times more than that anyway. That's tremendous teaching, which combines compassion with pure advaita, but that is another story. I will have to be invited as I have often said for another series of lectures to do justice to that.

But that doesn't take away from the negative, I don't mean in the pejorative sense, but in the logical sense, an idiom of the Buddha. It's very important to remind everyone that, has this side of illumination we are, we think of ourselves only as this, or as that and this changes continuously, and this is the cause of our sorrow, what do we do? Plunge into this stream, become aware of the rich interdependence of everything indeed the identity of everything, in the flash. Become compassionate, doesn't mean become a collective, you can have this feeling without being in a crowd, you can be in a crowd and lose this feeling, a crowd has an ego, a crowd can say we, one and me and only 27 people. You can be alone and say, let us all creatures be totally compassionate. You don't have to be a politician of the collective in order to be all compassionate. But that is the way of the Buddha, and of Krishnamurti in our own age, and I salute Krishnamurti as I would salute the Buddha too.

Well, time flies and I must bring this to a close in some way, although a few words more. And I know Kusum is probably quite irritated that I have exceeded the time, and the tea is probably getting cold ... [loud laughter]. So, thank you, Kusum, I don't mean for the cold tea, but for the warning.

But Krishnamurti said something and I will only talk about that. Okay. It was something so poetical and so complete that I forgot everything else and I really loved him from that point onwards. He said, you see he was sitting on the floor and he had that beautiful, slightly high pitched voice ... tremulous old-fashioned English voice, and he said something which would have made T. S. Eliot jealous, I think. He said, 'Thought is fear.' Three words. Thought is fear. Lovely sentence. Desire is fear. Time is fear. And I have spent years that were in the eighties, trying to understand this. And let me offer you my brief understanding of that and then I will close. Thought is fear because if we think anything at all, we are afraid that it might be false. Desire is fear because we desire anything we might think that we would not be fulfilled or that it would not be worth having after that. Time, because time will soon be time past, we live in the world of thought, desire and time and fear is based on that, so only if we go beyond thought that to that which immediate, love, compassion, awareness, intelligence is a word, not IQ intelligence, but attentiveness, that which is beyond thought, observation of the other as oneself, if we go beyond desire to love.

Krishnamurti said, look at a beautiful person and stop right there. Look at a tree and stop right there. Go beyond desire we find love and fulfilment. Go beyond time by dying to the ego. What is the time? We are afraid of time because we are afraid that we are coming to an end. Well, before we come to an end, we can come to an end in our thought. Go beyond time. Then there will be no fear. So the way of fearlessness by the tantric way of dying to the false self is probably one way of describing what Krishnamurti's way is. Of course, if he was present he would say, 'What nonsense!' And his followers too would be irritated by any interpretation of his thoughts, but let me add, his last advice to one of his followers was, 'Don't say you are quoting me or you are my mouthpieces, interpret me, but do your own thinking.' Important thing is to do our own thinking about the notion of the self and the not-self and death and the timeless. If only because he has energised our age in this way and stimulated us to think daring and beautiful and dangerous thoughts about the nature of things, we must salute this incredible vacant genius. Thank you [applause].

In my quiet time, I saw his face very clearly, very clearly, and the face as it appeared in a movie made of him before he died, his hair was blowing in the wind, looked like a comet's tail, white and black, he was standing on a beach and the wind was blowing and his hair was windswept, it sort of looked like a tail, the caption said: 'Krishnamurti's hair looks like a comet's tail, star.' And then apparently he did 'namaste' to the four directions, north, south. That was his last time in India. And the same beach where he was discovered as a ten-year-old boy, perhaps less, as the 91-year-old, he died in 1986, he was born in 1895, of course, I would like to think that he must be one-year-old when Ramana Maharshi attained illumination, so that must have had its influence. But he stood on the same beach, at the age of 90, 91, and offered his salutations to the four directions, which [is] rather interesting, because he is not going to prefer any one direction, so, that was my meditation. Now let's have yours. Yes, Vasishta.

Question: [The voice of the person asking the question is not clear on tape].

Ramchandra Gandhi: Subject of choiceless awareness is profound and he does use this word, and I think it is a very happy word. And it connects with the kind of understanding that I am going into of Krishnamurti. Because there has to be a catholicity, a shifting away from specific attention if we are to love in this compassionate way. If awareness is with choice, if I say, ah, I am looking at this audience and not that. There is already flow in my awareness, but if it is lighter so that I see all audiences in this audience, and this audience in all audiences, that is choiceless without being objectless but every object is seen in every other object, and awareness, in meditation is one-pointed, you prefer this to that. This spiritual man wants to be totally impartial and loving at the same time. If you like that is the fundamental problem of spiritual life. How to be supremely loving and absolutely impartial at the same time? Choiceless awareness is a phrase which captures something of that mystery. There can be no love without awareness. If you love somebody you are intensely aware of them, but not in that way of choosing them as supposed to be somebody else. They know this immediately, and then they are worried, they say, maybe he loves me because of my eyes, or because I have still got hair on my head, and when I don't, or when my eyes are tired, she won't love me. So, no, but if you love somebody, then you are aware of them, but of them as everyone, and also of everyone as them. This is harder to take. So I do think that choiceless of awareness is not something which is merely a meditation or mystery, although there it has its clear significance.

And in Krishnamurti, of course, he is attacking the idea of worshipping one form, one guru, one tradition, one object, and the phrase 'choiceless awareness' is rather a brilliant phrase to describe the possibility of full awareness, with absolute impartiality, because choice means partiality, I choose this, freedom has nothing to do with choosing, he says. There he is right. The great Spinoza pointed out that this kind of freedom is only ignorance of the laws of nature. Because I happened to choose this, because I have been conditioned to choose in this way. Advertising is like that. I think I am choosing that toothpaste that is because I have been conditioned by what I have been watching on television, but choiceless awareness would be a way of likely playing with the world of appearance, of loving it without succumbing to it, to any segment of it, or loving all of it, perhaps. And it is a mystery which I think we experience, when we truly love, without a possession, anyone at all, or anything, if you truly love your friends, you will set them free too, but you would not be anxious to be set free from them. That is another matter, but true love and real contemplation of beauty, when you see the sun setting, you also notice the sky, and you also notice the clouds, and you also have a sense of what is behind you. A great painting is a bit like that. This is why I like very much the practice of hanging paintings on walls, you see the wall, I did not look at the radiators in Museums, they are very beautiful too, the kinds of objects. And I think a great painting permits all that, a great piece of sculpture permits loving attention to its surroundings too. I do think our experience of love and our experience of contemplating beauty, and also of creativity. When you are really thinking creatively, that doesn't happen very often, you will find that you are not really obsessed with any one thought, the concentration of that kind of obsessive, results-oriented kind, gives way to a more playful exploration and that's when the subject you are investigating begins to speak to you. So the theme is vast and the phrase is brilliant, and there is so much more to say, thank you, for asking that question which was about Krishnamurti's phrase 'choiceless awareness', I repeat for the record.

Q: [The voice of the person asking the question is not clear on tape].

RG: Thank you. The question is what kind of relationship is there between Krishnamurti and India. What kind of reception has he had amongst Indian people and crowds and others? He looks quite different to other sages and saints of our time. That's a good question. But I do think that there was, and I recall my own meeting with him. But of course, I don't think he knew any other language, English and French, I think some Italian, are the only languages that he spoke. But, he would probably have forgotten the Telugu that he knew as a child because he chose to forget everything. That was not really needed. And he had no narrow loyalties, linguistic or national. So, he would probably have been at a loss to say anything to a peasant, say, who ran into him. But there is a very beautiful last shot in this film called *Krishnamurti*, where he is walking alone in the twilight. It is a beautiful shot, down, what looks like a beach, then he comes to a narrow wooden bridge, and just before he starts, there is another person following him, who is clearly one of the outcaste Indians, the lower caste, so he puts his arm around him and they walk, they cross this bridge together. His lips move, but I am not sure what he, he probably forgot that this other boy knew no English and continued to speak in English perhaps, and maybe some divine mechanism translated that English into the most beautiful Telugu for the other boy, who knows. But this shot is of this culturally uprooted sage with his arms around and culturally absolutely rooted, but unprivileged, underprivileged Indian walking happily, crossing this bridge of samsara to the other side together.

So I do think that sages are able to overcome this handicap very easily, professors are not. The fact that I can speak Hindi and two or three Indian languages is no guarantee that the people of India would love me, no [laughter]. Remember the joke about the man who knew 14 languages and had nothing to say in any of them [loud laughter]. I think he also dropped his mask when he met outside his lecture. He was very much more vulnerable, loving, and in a very enduring way, confused sort of person. These are qualities which Indians admire. They like people to be vulnerable, not to be absolutely sure of everything ... He never addressed the masses of India, I am glad he did not try because he would not have succeeded in the conventional kind of way. Why is it necessary? I think he addressed millions of people all over the world, he is an Indian who is doing something different, and I do think he touches India to a very deep point. For instance, although he had read very little works on philosophy, sometimes he comes up with amazing insights which would be beyond scholarship, for instance, he says, vedanta means the end of knowledge, which is quite literally correct. Veda means knowledge, *anta* means 'the end'. So, no vedantic scholar would have quite described it as the end of knowledge. But he translates it as the end of knowledge to make his own point, we must move beyond what is known. So, there is here a kind of insight which is more Indian than India, if you like. And likewise, I have watched him attend an Indian music concert. He probably knew nothing about it but lost in ecstasy.

And this was when he was old and when he had something like Parkinson's disease and he got up and held the hands of the singer for five minutes, he tried to [laughter]. And it would have been embarrassing for the woman, that he really loved her with his Parkinsonian hands. Very beautiful. Whether he knew much about Carnatic music or not is irrelevant. Those who knew a lot about that but wouldn't have loved the singer in the way he did. And that is the important thing, really. He was a loving human being, not only an illumined one. But that is a good question because we must ask that.

Many others, take Ramakrishna, there are many people who were annoyed by him, many Indians, although he was very Indian in many ways. You know sometimes it is better to be a little different from your own culture, in order to be loved better by your own culture, because then you are not in competition. He was not one of a kind; there were hundreds of Krishnamurti's around. So he was heard even by Indians, he did not wear the *sanyasin* [renouncer] robe and all this is interesting. There was a time when he wanted to become a sanyasin, he wanted to wear the yellow robe. But he chose not to, just as well, because ... he would have lost in the crowd of yellow-robed teachers. He did not. He dressed very immaculately. When he was in the West, he wore very sharp suits, and when he was in India, he wore Indian clothes, I am convinced by the explanation offered by his biographers, this is because he cared for the body, it had to be well clothed, fed, not fussed over, so things like that made him. Of course, some of this is mildly eccentric, 1920s English style, but all that is good, I think. We are meant to reflect our own culture also I think. We are not meant to be so utterly transcendent of our own times, we are meant to look like where we grew up, and he did look sometimes in the pictures, he looks like you know a sharp-witted Londoner. He does very-smartly-turned-out London wit, but much more than that. I love him. He went through what was called the process by his biographers. He had acute pain in his body and became unconsciousness for hours on end. He knew a lot of physical pain. So all kinds of occult things are happening in that body too.

So I am not dismissing the adventure of Mirra or Aurobindo. But I think that adventure occurs, wherever there is enlightenment. When there is enlightenment in a given body that all the cells I think both revolt and celebrate. Because they are used to receiving just one kind of ego message, do this, do that, don't do this, don't do that. But when that pressure is off, I think many of them are happy some are mad and so they become cancerous. This is my theory of cancer. That the cells receive a totally different kind of message and they go mad and start eating each other. That is what cancer is, insane multiplication and murder, at the cellular level. That's what happens to a population when a sage or an avatar arises, they get confused and start killing each other.

It is interesting that Krishnamurti dies of cancer, of the intestinal tract like the Buddha. And I think that is rather interesting because anyone who is emphasising change and flow is inviting cancer of the intestinal tract I think because that is where food goes and that is what keeps us going. So if he lets go of that, he is saying I don't necessarily want this to persist then that is where I think cancer will get you. Ramakrishna Paramahansa dies of cancer of the throat because he had a beautiful voice and he could speak and sing beautifully. To destroy the ego of that, cancer of the throat. My own supposition is that the Buddha too died of cancer but some Buddhist friends have objected to that. They said what is your proof, which book, I said well I am talking of a time when books were not written [laughter], and the fact that what is described looks like dysentery is no proof that it was not duodenal cancer, which produces dysentery at a late advanced stage. And I do think that the compassion of a Buddha would have invited the kind of madness which cancer represents, you know, which everyone hates and fears that. So my theory is that the human being because of this special role of the central nervous system is especially vulnerable to cancer because every one of us is a potential sage. So those of our friends who have cancer are in good company.

Q: [The voice of the person asking the question is not clear on tape].

RG: Okay, yes, question is, I probably did say something like he undoes or does not increase and this is entirely his style of not burdening humanity with more knowledge, more words, more institutions, more gurus, nothing, we are burdened enough. In fact, lightened some of our load, and he sometimes, therefore, adopts the strategy of demolition. Any word at all is capable of a second-rate meaning and often it is at that level that it operates. Take the word, knowledge, it really means a lot of received learning, opinion, although that is not the only meaning. But he fastens on to a less than the best meaning and attacks it. Discipline means regimentation, but not all discipline need mean that, but the fact remains that is how it manifests itself most of the time. Religion means fanaticism but doesn't have to mean that. But he fastens on to the unideal meanings and legitimately I think because this is how these things are manifested, but again he is not very consistent, thank God, he would sometimes suddenly use the word religion in an absolutely different way ... and self-knowledge and all the things that he attacks, he would again bring up but the general thrust is of that kind, of that destructive kind. He used the word negation in an entirely spiritual commendatory way, we must negate. The illusion that things are permanent, that we are other than one and other. The world is other than ourselves, negate. Somebody says, don't you believe in the unity of mankind? He says which means, why should I believe what is not a fact. There goes the idea of the unity of, and yet he would use the unity in some other beautiful sense later on. He is God as a spoilsport, I think [laughter]. Too many angels with too many clichés about God, so God walks off in a huff, I think.

You cause me to become visually very mindful of Krishnamurti. He was a short guy, but he walked with a kind of uprightness which made him look like a bird of some kind but also you did not notice his short height then but he had a very sensitive face, very plastic face with big pouches under his eyes, which made those eyes beautiful you know, amazing! All this nonsense which the cosmetic industry spreads about beauty, big baggy eyes look very beautiful if they are illumined. And really white hair, spotless simple clothes, but clean, and he could sit without backrest for hours like that but he meditated for many hours every day, although he hated the word meditation and so on, did *pranayama* [breathing exercises] for many hours, breathing exercises.

And he was quite accurate. When he was 80, he said, 'Oh! I have got to live for ten more years because I have got work to do.' And he died ten years later. There is no doubt in my mind that we had here an unusual sage, I had no doubt. If I had doubts, but it has taken a long effort of study and reflection for me to see that, also the need for it. But I do believe that there has to be a more combined strategy which would combine the more direct advaitin path of the self. And the more exciting iconoclastic Buddhist path of Krishnamurti. In our age, we need a kind of pincer movement, both things are needed I think because if you go and tell, say, a deprived, for instance, many Hindus, socially handicapped Hindus are becoming Buddhists. Wonderful! But if you are to go and preach emptiness to them, they would not understand. They want to be empowered too. You have to combine a way of teaching them both the self and the emptiness of the ego at the same time. So I do think that of future, the double strategy of vedanta and Buddhism of, say, Ramana Maharshi and Krishnamurti, would have to be adopted by more and more people. And between these two extremes you can, I think to accommodate all the other paths. These are the two austere extreme paths, one holding on to the timeless eternal self, the other holding on to the temporal flowing person and the world only. And between them, you have all the Gods and the Goddesses and everything, God, everything. What they generate between them, Ramana Maharshi and Krishnamurti, is a whole rainbow of possibilities, it is rather nice. But their orthodox followers will hear nothing of it, this is the pity of it. You know people have that strange smile on their face when you talk to them about their guru being the same as some other, very compassionate smile saying, oh, you are really misguided, but we have, you know that ear-to-ear smile, which means that we forgive you, but it's okay [loud laughter]. I dread that smile. I prefer an honest frown, any day.

Q: [The voice of the person asking the question is not clear on tape].

RG: Yes, at the level of formulation, yes. That's such a good question. Thank you Vasishta! Vasishta reminded me of an Upanishadic saying that the wife is beloved because of the self. The son is beloved because of the self. Yes, the wife is beloved not because she is the wife, because she is the self. The son is beloved not because he is the son, but because he is the self. Now, he wants to know how this could be formulated in Krishnamurti's way, if at all. Now I think he would not be able to say this because he has decided to have nothing to do with, but he might, well find himself saying, 'I am not other than my wife, I am not other than my son. We are together in this flow. So the wife is beloved because we are together, and because are in sorrow. And we are that sorrow. And at the heart of being that sorrow, we discover passion.' Krishnamurti's is a very imaginative translation of all that.

— three —

Indian Spirituality and the World*

You will recall, those of you who were here on the first day, and those of you who have looked at the announcement of these lectures, that these are dedicated to the memory of Dr Haridas Chaudhuri, about whom Jim has spoken. And we are all indeed very grateful to him at this Institute, and I know in this city also there are many friends who knew him, and I can see some of them here this evening, so welcome, again, to this [lecture]. I remember an old Beatles song called 'Sergeant Pepper's Lonely Hearts [Club Band]'—we are getting towards the end I think, when the donkeys start braying for some reason. It's a bit like that, I think. I need to be booed, I think, first, for being with you for so long, for all the trouble that you have had to put up [with], and all the parking, and the absence of sound, and the absence of other things. Thank you very much for being so patient. As the song goes on to say you are such a lovely audience, I think, and so on. Well, let me now retrieve my notes under this weight of paper, which has a list of some useful books. You might collect these during the tea break, I pass these on to Jim.

*This is an edited version of the lecture on Modern Indian Spirituality, delivered at California Institute of Integral Studies, July 1988.

1988—and Indian spirituality has been around for a long time. It's not quite like the ad for the cigarette, 70 and still smoking, or still going, or something like that. But it is still going strong in the West, and I really don't have to apologise for it at all, it is part of your cultural heritage now, and you are at liberty to assess it in any way you like. So it is part of the cultural scene of the world that Indian spirituality is in the West. And it is a very surrealist scene if you ask me. It is a mixture of odd things. At airports, you meet swinging *swamis* [Hindu saints] and all sorts of people. In India, you meet some blonde beasts in saffron. And then ... all kinds of wonderful phenomena are taking place. Certainly, swamis in Rolls-Royces and the white man and white woman barefoot in India, that is a wonderful sight. I don't know about the swamis in Rolls-Royces, but I do think that the other thing is pretty wonderful. I don't think it does any harm at all to ruin the shoe industry a bit in India, I think you can all quite happily do that, in India. But truly it is a surreal experience. And surreal is not a term of abuse in my vocabulary at all. It literally is, I think, a very good translation of the word, *maya*. It is a way of saying neither real nor unreal, which is exactly how *maya* is defined, *satasadvilaksana*, our professor of Sanskrit will I hope not, have to correct me.

Neither real nor unreal could also mean more than real and more than unreal. And the world is becoming like that. Partly because of this wonderful, chaotic, fateful exchange of spiritualities. And I do think that modern Western thought at its best is also spiritual. So when free thinkers, and deep-going thinkers and artists and others visit India, we welcome them as spiritual people. Nobody need have a halo around their head or be offering a lecture course on modern Western spirituality in India, or anything like that, but we can recognise the spirit in many forms in India, at our best. When people go to India and serve the poor there, or preach to the rich there, these are spiritual people, I think. And when you draw our attention to the terrible damage we are doing to our environment—that is spiritual advice.

So, Western spirituality also thrives all over the world. And I am thinking, of course, of good things, and not the bad things. As I hope you are thinking of the good things and not the bad things when I talk of Indian spirituality thriving in the West. And of course, I am not thinking of people being beaten by any sadhus, so-called, or whatever. So that is a shameful [thing] and I think there is a law against that, and I think you should put the man behind bars straightaway, for doing that. Well, let me talk a bit about this in a personal way, about how I encountered the West first, as a child. Then I will be able to understand, in the course of lecturing, how you are probably encountering India, Indian spirituality—Eastern spirituality. Of course, without in any sense of patronising Buddhism, we do like to think of Buddhism also as a dimension of Indian spirituality. So, when I talk of Indian spirituality in the West, I, of course, include Buddhism. But not only Buddhism, but many other things. So how you encounter ... I imagine it is quite funny for you to think of ... to see so many things going on all the time. Gods and Goddesses, and sadhus and sanyasis, and mantras and tantras, and sex and celibacy, and everything, all going on together. It is quite, quite mad, I imagine, for some people. Some conservative people—I have looked at their faces when they look at saffron-clad boys and girls in this country. They look puzzled and slightly disapproving, I think. They don't know what has happened to these good children of theirs—for they are doing all these very dangerous things. I daresay it's a bit like that when I encountered the West.

Of course, we had heard of the Englishman. And we had sometimes been able to see the Englishwoman, but much more rarely, I think, than the Englishman, when we grew up because she was well hidden and protected by her man. But he was often seen wearing a silly hat called the solar hat and sometimes he was seen beating people with his stick also. But, apart from that, we have a sense of the Englishman especially, being a bearer of some wonderful things too, like the English language, which, although it paralysed us in many ways, it caused us to repress our sense of our own language—by the way, I am very happy to be in this country but I feel terribly language-deprived—although this is something that happens to India all the time, when India is using the English language, [yet] it has also united us. People like Uday, who is sitting in the front row, and I—he speaks Bengali and I understand Bengali but I don't speak it so well, I bet he understands Hindi but doesn't speak it so well—we can talk to each other in our own Indian English and feel both amused and grateful [by this].

So this is a great gift [which] we knew that the Englishman had brought us. But we also had a sense of the Empire, and all these things were there, but it is only, believe me, when the Americans started coming to India during the war years, that another kind of white figure began to appear. Who—these were soldiers—who looked not at all intimidating, who looked more friendly, if slightly chaotic and irresponsible enough and drunk [laughter] ... but they looked distinctly friendly. And I was only about eight or nine, and I remember walking around Connaught Place and running into some of these guys, wondering who they were. And they looked distinctly friendly, they would often smile or, you know, try to make [a pass?] at children, and that was lovely. And much later I was told, and I discovered, and I read about them, that the Japanese war was likely to go on and on, and so they were there to be flown to Japan, and so on. But it is really with the movies that America became real to us. That was really my first Pauranic exposure to America, the mythology of the West if you like. The cowboys were always victorious, and the strongmen ... one thought that of course, it is only American actors who were he-men, who did all these incredible things on the screen. And of course, these gorgeous actresses, beginning ... with Greta Garbo and Marlene Dietrich, and going on to even more spectacular versions of that species [laughter]. It is when we said 'ah and they kiss on the screen', that's when the mythology, that something only the Gods did, became very powerful and real for us. And then, of course, came chewing gum, and bubble gum and things like that and all sorts of other—Coca-Cola and wonderful things; and then the Korean War, and then the atom bomb. This whole mix of terror and delight, this mix was Western civilisation for a growing boy. And of course, also from time to time, one read in books of great sages of the West, of the great philosophers. It is amazing for us [that] the artists of the West have always been more sage-like than the so-called or the more famous saints and religious leaders. When one looked at a Picasso print suddenly or even a Chagall, well that was something that opened our spiritual eyes to what was going on here. And this happens continuously to me. It is not in a church so much but in an art gallery that I encounter the spirit of the West, often. Although, of course, there are exceptions, I have been to great churches and pretty rotten art galleries too, that's another matter. Well, so things are beginning to reverse. When I read of Mike Tyson and saw his photo, I thought of him as Hanuman, flying in the sky, with his tail on fire, and carrying a burning New York City in his arms. Well, so constantly, the Pauranic, the mythological imagination of India interferes with my perception of the West and of America. But I have run into such a wonderful sensibility here, that I do think despite this chaos, or perhaps because of this chaos and richness, something really wonderful will occur—in both directions. And I hope Hollywood will never fail to produce the Garbos and Dietrichs and the Marilyn Monroes for us, and I hope we will never fail to bring our gifts here—and they are many; they come in many shapes and sizes. I was thinking of how Sri Ramakrishna Paramahansa would have reacted if he had been suddenly brought to Manhattan Island by a ship, say, and deposited there at the foot of the Statue of Liberty. He would have probably regarded the Statue of Liberty as the Divine Mother and gone into *samadhi* [a state of deep meditative contemplation]—that's perfect [laughter]. I think that is a rare occurrence these days when sadhus and sanyasis appear from India on these shores. But I hope there will be a sadhu who will look at that [the Statue of Liberty] and contemplate the Divine Mother, and will see this ancient land, with its ancient peoples and creatures, and the new ones, all as creatures of the Divine Mother, and that will be Ramakrishna Paramahansa again. I can't somehow think of Ramana Maharshi being brought here even by an aeroplane. He would have refused to sit in an aeroplane, I think, he would have been quite happy to remain in Tiruvannamalai. Although, he has less of the face of a comic, in the spiritual sense of the word than Sri Ramakrishna. I can think of Sri Ramakrishna doing a great talk show on television in Bengali, which no one would understand [mild laughter] you know. I think he would be absolutely fantastic in translation, you know. Somebody ought to do this, really, with subtitles, I think—the Sri Ramakrishna figure ... telling his stories to America—sort of a 'Good Morning America' show with Sri Ramakrishna Paramahansa would be very great. But, these masters like Ramakrishna and Ramana never visited [America]. But of course, Swami Vivekananda did.

Swami Vivekananda first came here in 1893 to Chicago and, of course, made a very big impact. I think that is when in a big way if you like in an American way, the West confronted Indian spirituality—of [the] nineteenth-century variety. The West had read, through its Indologists, about many things. But even Max Müller and others, the great Indologists of Germany, were writing rather snide things about Ramakrishna Paramahansa, also, you know, in a very funny kind of way. There is a book by him [Müller] on Ramakrishna Paramahansa, of course, it is a good book, but he is writing under the pressure of structural racism and imperialism, I am afraid, I am sorry to have to inform you. Read the Preface, and he says, 'But of course, he is not like those other terrible examples of ... etc., etc., etc. ... you know ... he is a good guy, in other words [...] read him', that sort of attitude. So even the great Max Müller is not without the kind of prejudice which creeps into cultures where there is structural prejudice, and there is such a thing in India. We can be terribly uncharitable about the West—that is because there is a reverse racism that operates in India, one has to be very careful. I find this in a lot of lesser sadhus, but I don't find this in a Gandhi, I don't find this in a Ramana, I don't find this in a Ramakrishna. But I'm afraid you'll find quite a lot of this in the caricatures who often arrive here, and, whom you often run into in India. So, when we talk of Indian spirituality in the West today, it isn't as though we are talking about the great saints and sages of recent times having this [...] with the exception of a few: Vivekananda. Krishnamurti, the consummate traveller: I have [...] run into him at airports and thought he was the president of the United Nations or something like that. A great pity he was never president of the United Nations but could have easily passed for that, or a philosopher of the West. He looked a lot like Bertrand Russell, I think, in his old years with that shock of white hair.

So, with the exception of J. Krishnamurti—and Mahatma Gandhi travelled a lot, of course, he looked reasonably ridiculous to many people in his loincloth and so on, especially to the King of England, I think—but you heard the story the other day, when he was asked—this is for those who didn't hear it the other day, and not for those who were here the other day—but when he was asked if he was properly clothed for the King's party, he said, 'Of course I am, the King's wearing enough for both of us' [laughter]. So, Mahatma Gandhi was, of course, a Westerner. He really was, in his very impressionable years, from 19 onwards, for several years, he grew up in London. And he can almost be seen, I think I pointed this out, as a member of the crank Society of Vegetarians of London [audience response unclear], and he would be perfectly at home there, and they would find him perfectly normal. And of course, all of them would be found deeply abnormal by everyone else [laughter/audience responds].

So Mahatma Gandhi is a familiar kind of eccentric. He almost passed for a kind of hippie, one of the early dropouts, who was very familiar with the West and travels a lot. He's like that. And J. Krishnamurti, he's a sort of a ... not a ... he's a sort of 'establishment revolutionary'. There are many like him one runs into. Very properly clothed, but absolutely revolutionary in what they say. No eccentricity in behaviour, in mannerism, in fact, a cultivated conservatism of speech, and of dress, and so on. But of course, they only had to open their mouths and you knew that it was a bomb that they were throwing [at you] [laughter/audience responds]. So that's another way to revolution, I think. It often works better than ... sort of ... manifest happiness and deep conservatism of doctrine. So, I think people were familiar with these two ... but, the traditional Indian sages, who were truly the bearers of Indian spiritual consciousness without being [traditionalist]—Ramana Maharshi, Ramakrishna Paramahansa—they never left India. So in a way, this is a hypothetical question—except in surrealist imagination: I can see in the sky over New York, Ramana Maharshi shaking hands with Groucho Marx or somebody like that, and blessing the city beneath, but only in surrealist imagination, and therefore [really] more deeply. So I would put my first request to you, [which] is to take the traditional sages of India, who were not traditionalist, absolutely as seriously as the ones who turn up here, easily, by a plane or ship, or repeatedly, whatever, and are perfectly at home with all the incredible pieces of technology that you have. Well, take them seriously enough, but not more seriously than the ones who never visited here, like Ramana, Ramakrishna, and Sarada and Alagamma. And—because there is a deeper Catholicity, there is a deeper one-worldness to Ramakrishna and Ramana—I'm not talking about Krishnamurti and Gandhi, they were exceptions. The fact that they have travelled is not something I hold against them at all. They are, they are new, there is something very new that they bring. They bring something which might be the idiom of our conversation in a 100 years, Gandhi, Krishnamurti. But Ramana and Ramakrishna are bearers of something more timeless, which is also greatly needed. The newer—and America is fascinated by the new, and so she should—but the timeless is also something that America would do well seriously to learn from Indian spirituality. And I don't mean by that a past orientation. There is a false contrast that is often drawn, between being slow and being fast. I meet wonderful people saying, 'Oh! I'm slowing down these days', and they think they are paying Indian spirituality a great compliment. Sometimes they are, by, well, not doing too many things, and by really cutting down on greed, and some wonderful things. But that is ... that is not the timeless. The timeless is a spirit, is a way of doing things, and nothing. Where past, present and future are all embraced and transcended simultaneously. Where one simply is. One is not here and now, or one was not then and there, and one is not going to be at a future time ... one simply is. And that is the timeless, which alone is timely I think. The timeless is always available, unlike the contemporary, the fashionable, which ceases to be fashionable every two days or so, something like that.

So 'cultivate the timeless', is something I wish to suggest to you, and not in the way of caricature, in the way in which the timeless has often been portrayed, as a throwback in time, as cultivation of antiquities, not that. The timeless, there is a timelessness to the contemporary production and lives, and speakings and doings, and also to anything in the past and anything in the present, and any ... can be timeless. Look for those things. A museum of the timeless would be a great new institution, I think, to be started perhaps in this city ... where ... it occurs to me that the Museum of Modern Art could organise a whole exhibition of Indian iconography, I think, as an example of wonderful, superior, surreal—art of the timeless. So,

I do really think that the cultural base of the process of assimilation of Indian spirituality in the West will have to come from art and not necessarily from traditional, religious pursuits. I'll tell you why, because many of these pursuits are imitating structures which are ecologically rooted in India, but not here. Separate ashrams I am not criticising—oh, by the way, if you think I am going to give a list of Indian ashrams in this country, I am sorry to have to disappoint you, I have no such lists in my pocket! No ... and I haven't even forgotten such lists at home. No, I didn't make these lists. Partly because, I don't like to talk about those who are living and functional in this ... this list, as you have noticed, includes only those who have died. But anyway, the creation of separatist ashram communities of any kind is less well understood here than it might be in India. I often said this to my Western friends, that for all our ignorance of worldly matters and so on, when it comes to spirituality, we are a pretty shrewd lot in India. No one, no guru, or so-called guru, is ever in doubt about this. They know that we are going to be seen through them if they are fake, very, very quickly. And no one is going to write a newspaper article even about them. They are just going to say namaste and go away.

Whereas I think this quality of perception is less well-cultivated here. But it is not only that, but there is a kind of sectarianism which is almost the fate of that kind of spiritual institution. So beware of it. I am going to give a large number of pieces of advice, unsolicited advice [laughter]. You can truly be ... hoot and boo ... and be glad this is over. But I have decided to speak with a sense of responsibility towards what India can give. And I have nothing against ... [there's] no law against any such thing. But I don't think that's the best.

The best will come from a deeper perception, from science, from art, from living, from lifestyles, of the entire corpus of Indian spirituality, to be integrated in a creative way, in your own lives, in Western life, in politics, in economics, in living, in marriage, in divorce, in whatever ... a new spirit. You don't really have to become a part of one sect, however attractive that sect might look like to you. Because it is not at all clear to me that the different sects of Hinduism, say, here [in America], or of Buddhism, are doing enough to clarify the position ... their position, in relation to other sects. And [they are not showing] how there is a rich unity of Shaivism, Vaishnavism, Mahayana, Hinayana, Vajrayana. So one keeps running into fundamentalist Vaishnavas here, fundamentalist Shaivas, fundamentalist Mahayanists, fundamentalist Hinayana ... enough to bring tears to my eyes. I say, is this what India has brought here? A sense of division? A sense of separateness? New sects within sects will crop up here: you have a genius for categorisation in the West. You will really, in the end, transform Indian spirituality into something like that if you are not careful. And of course, you can be careful. These are times of great freedom, and of an urge to be free of division and hatred. Bring the same energy, against division and categorisation, that you do [bring] to other things, to Indian spirituality. I am not going to be very popular with many Indian sects after having said that. But I do hope that you will demand of sects that you encounter here a statement of their Catholicity. How do they understand Hindu comprehensiveness? Buddhist Catholicity? And if they are not able to satisfy you on this point, if they, by implication even, suggest that, 'Oh, we are not quite like that other sect here, you know', well it's a bit like Christians in India: the Catholics will always tell their would-be converts, 'We're not quite like the Protestants, you know', and the Protestants, 'Oh, we're not quite like the Catholics, you know', and so on, and so on.

But I think this is far more embarrassing for Hinduism, because Hinduism has, I think, rightly claimed, I think, a more developed sense of the unity of things. And if this [is] betrayed, if this is lost, then that's like many shirts, Indian shirts that I buy here, poor quality export, I think they ought to be returned [laughter].

So ... excuse me [pause for water] ... oh, by the way, the shirt that Jim's wearing looks excellent to me, so don't return that! You really look splendid in that [pause].

Right, that's home-grown, and still valuable here, that's basically what I'm trying to say. Well ... sectarianism—of any kind—is foreign to the spirit of Indian spirituality, both Hindu and Buddhist, and, I hope, one day Jainism, the much-neglected tradition, will also be represented here, without *their* sectarianism. There's a big quarrel there, between those who ... saints who are *digambara*—who walk without any clothes, whose garment is the sky, but this they have forgotten, it is only the absence of clothes, not the presence of the sky, [that] becomes important—and the *svetambara*—who only wear white, so between the naked and the white-clad there is a big quarrel. Yes, this is absurd, and so I hope you will not learn any of these things at all. And anyone who ... be he a swami or a professor, who tries to teach you these things, you should get up and tell them to shut up [laughter].

Well, Peter Brooks made this great play, *The Mahabharata* [1985], which I haven't seen, maybe some of you have seen, maybe many of you have read about it, I have read about it. The casting of it, I don't know the details of it, an English friend wrote to me the other day and said, the only Indian actor there is Draupadi, the wife of the five Pandavas, she's the only Indian there. And the [only] Indian in the sense that this actress happens to be Indian. But, others are chosen for other reasons. Bhima, the [most] powerful of the five brothers is a black African—I think it's rather tremendous, this choice. There are five brothers in this epic, this sacred epic, and they are married to one woman. If you say, oh, we knew Hindus were polygamous, don't say that, this is a rich symbolism of the five senses being married to the one mind, which is rightly described as a woman. And these five brothers in Peter Brooks' play are represented, I believe, by actors from different races. There is a black African, there is an Italian, and a Japanese and so on, and wonderful that the five, five is a wonderful element: five elements, five continents, five races, five fingers, say, five races, five varieties, married to one Draupadi, one *India*! I wish India could be wed in that way to all the variety there is in the world. Without, and it was important for Draupadi not to take sides. Draupadi, these five brothers won her in a marriage game, and brought her and asked their mother before their mother could see their prize, 'We have brought something for you, Mother!' She said, 'Oh, then you must share it equally.' And also, part of the meaning of this was that she should not love one more than the other. So India should not love one continent more than another. We should really be married like Draupadi to all the peoples of this Earth, for them to love us and for us to love them. And so, this great play, oh, by the way, Peter Brooks is an Englishman, so Krishna, of course, is an Englishman in this play. And he's a very, very—I believe—this friend wrote to me that, 'Oh, he looks absolutely like an English politician or a bureaucrat.' It may well be that it is only English diplomacy that will save the world in some ways, some subtle negotiation with the devil I think, I hope so [laughter]. So, I am not offended at all by the fact that Krishna is portrayed by an Englishman. So, I do think that that casting is the best image of how India can serve the world, spiritually.

Marry us! And marry only one of us. Don't try and marry many of us. Be polygamous in relation to us. Marry the one, the one central Indian spiritual truth is that of oneness and of unity, of course, which comprehends variety ... but there is that oneness. Not the oneness of something up there called God, who alone is one. But the oneness of self, the oneness of being, the oneness of reality—that is Draupadi. And let variety be married to unity. And I hope to see that play when it comes—I don't think it's been to California yet, I hope it does.

Well, so many things—yoga, meditation, chanting, mantra, *chakra* [energy centres in the body], siddhi, guru, *bhava*, sex, freedom, [Acharya] Rajneesh, X, Y, Z—it is very difficult, really, to, how does one handle all of this without making two kinds of mistakes? Getting lost in the details of the performance of one or another group or individual, that is a terrible mistake. And [on the other hand] of having no sense of detail at all. So, I have had to struggle with this lecture, really, and I am still not sure how I can actually, really, deliver it. But I do think that we need to ask a few fundamental historical and philosophical questions first. Why is Indian spirituality coming here? One of the boasts, and I think legitimate, proud boasts of India has been that we have not been proselytisers at all. We've not tried to convert people to our religion. This has largely been true. And there is both a bad reason for it being true and a great reason for it being true. The bad reason, I think is this, has been this: that the conservatism of Indian spirituality in this regard has been to the great advantage of the established priestly order, because if you take new people into your fold, they are not always willing to go into the lower castes. So you have to change your caste system if you want to convert people. And this was not going to be very easy for the priestly orders, so often they did not.

So this is a bad reason, and I don't admire Indian non-proselytisation for this reason, of course not. But I do admire it for another reason. Because Indian spirituality at its depth is the spirituality of self, of you. And you are where you are. You don't have to find other yous. You are there. And everyone will find this. And the you and the I are one. So there is a deep confidence in Indian spirituality, of the greater [kind] that the self will reveal itself to everyone. We only have to manifest this in one part of the [world]. The kind of thing for which [Rupert] Sheldrake and others are finding scientific support. One self-realisation in one corner will, through an occult [process], assist self-realisation in all corners. And I think this is a great truth. And this is at the back of the reluctance of Indian spirituality to send missionaries out, to send preachers out, to hector, to impress, to convert, and to [keep], and so on. And not some kind of cultural desire not to influence others—Oh, no! We want to influence the world, so it's not that. You know, it's a bit like our, it is a fact that we haven't murdered our saints, although the murder of Gandhi is a terrible exception to this. But the reason for this is not that we are less prone to murder than anyone else [crowd reacts]—no! But because our spiritual texts prohibit this. Our spiritual texts proclaim that you are God in your essence. So when somebody says they are God, we can't kill them although we would wish to, because our scriptural texts don't permit us this. So all credit to those texts and none to our own natures. If those texts were proved to be fraudulent, we would be crucifying and murdering and stoning all the time.

Likewise, if Indian spirituality has not been proselytising, has not been soul-lusting, in that kind of objectionable way, it's not because we don't have a desire to do this. Scratch a sadhu and he would want to convert you, hmm? But because deep inside the sadhu is a conviction that this is wholly unnecessary and not only undesirable, because scriptures and sages have said this. They have preached more, all the way to Gandhi and Krishnamurti, that you manifest the truth, and that will attract the one if that is what's meant to be. You don't have to go out anywhere, the world will come to you if that's what's your karma. Ramana Maharshi never left Tiruvannamalai, this little [hill], the world was drawn to him. Every kind of world, every colour of the world, every race of the world. And he sat there. There are many who have travelled all over the world, many sadhus, but they have lost more pupils than they have gained. And they have lost a lot of time and money and energy and so on. So, that is the deep reason, the practice of Indian spirituality is the practice of self-realisation, everywhere. And by this anticipation of newly emerging scientific discoveries, it has had the shrewdness to see that is the deepest and the most fundamental kind of change that can occur—to wish for its radical and full occurrence in one place—in me. It's not the idea—oh, let me—it's not only the moral idea, mind you. Sometimes there is a merely ethical Christian-looking reason that's given for it: 'Oh, I better reform myself before I reform others', now that's good morality, of course, but it's not nearly enough as an explanation of Indian spirituality. There is the, the shrewder point is: 'And of course if I reform myself, and more than reform myself if I realise myself, that is a kind of explosion at the heart of the nature of things.' And that occult knowledge is absent when you find swamis and sanyasis and, I daresay, professors storming all over the place, and hectoring, and inviting you to change into this or that or the other. And that [is] what is wrong there. It's not, of course, they're being morally silly and objectionable. It's not only that but much more fundamentally than that, it is the violation of a very sacred and beautiful principle, not only [of] morality, but of physics and of metaphysics, of the nature of things. So next time you find any sadhu or lecturer being preachy, tell them that they are not preaching the truth.

Why is Indian spirituality coming to the West? There remains in me, although I'm a philosopher and a student of spirituality, something of the *bania*, the economist—I come from a caste of those who sell things—[I have] some shrewd sense of where the market is. There is a big market here. There is a big market for money, and for power, here. Not worse than any other kind of market, which of course people, I daresay, which traditional Christianity and other religions have exploited for centuries. But that's a sort of catchy thing you know. So that's what it is. And also because the caste system is breaking down in India for secular and political reasons. So conservatism pays poorer dividends now in India, okay? It's no longer in the interest of traditional Indian spirituality not to proselytise because there are no real gains by not doing, you're not really preserving the old social order by that, that is crumbling under the weight of history, okay? So that's one reason why new, new avenues, I'm not saying that this is necessarily bad in all cases, I'm trying to understand the social and economic reason for this. That, it is not that if a given sanyasin or sadhus were to stay on in India, he would have more followers, or that his old followers would stay with him, no. No, they wouldn't. [More] would want to come and they would find him not ready, not fit enough, and go away. So he's really looking, or she's looking, for competent pupils everywhere. This is why I maintain that the best way of regarding most of us who come here to teach Indian spirituality, is as teachers, as lecturers, as friends who have expertise in some area, and not as spiritually realised people, or unrealised people, for that matter. Offer them, and I suggested this during an earlier lecture, your love, and your scepticism, and your care, and your interest, and your need. Talk with them, take them to the pub, take them to the zoo. Like them, care for them, be liked by them, cared for [by] them, but the moment they affect superiority, laugh at them. And then you will get the most out of them and they will get the most out of you, which is human friendship, fellowship, a real giving and receiving of what they know, what you know. They would love to learn so much from you. And you have much to give. Do that. You may find that you are initially rejected by a given sect or ashram or order, especially by the new converts. They might find your attitude too irreverent. But I feel sorry for them, because they often will find their guru too inadequate and lynch him, or whatever, desert him, or burn his picture, whatever. So don't, you don't invite this kind of extremism at all.

I think your friend, Krishnamurti, has set a tremendous example here. Of course, he was so exceptional that it was very hard to see him as exactly like oneself, but he went on and on—he said, 'No, I'—if you tried to do namaste to him he would do namaste to you. If you tried to touch his feet he would try to touch your feet. A really very funny film should be made of Krishnamurti trying to touch your feet and you trying touch Krishnamurti's feet. But of course what we learn from this is that if Krishnamurti and Gandhi, say, could insist on this—and they were certainly men of realisation—this must be true. This is not false humility. They weren't saying, 'You know I'm really a little embarrassed, I'm, of course, what you think I am, but don't do this in public', they were not saying that. They were saying, 'This is totally unnecessary, if there is anything that we are teaching you, it is that this is false, don't do this.' So, I would suggest that that is the talisman that is the way of immediately relating to these exports. And of course, I'm not saying that one or more among them will not be realised sages, you will find that out in the process of ordinary loving and caring. Then you will have a quality of respect for them and love which will truly change you. When we meet with everyone with respect and then when we find somebody whom we can love, we really are able to do something better than merely respect. But if we have not treated people with respect, then even if we meet somebody whom we can love, we don't respect them. We bully them, in marriage, or love, or a relationship. So, the cultivation of a general attitude of respect and friendliness towards everyone is a good investment in the happiness of your partner, eventually, I think it's a good commonsense principle. Likewise, an attitude of ordinary respect and affection for every spiritual teacher who comes is good preparation for your special attitude to the realised one who may also come, or who may be born here, who may arise here, who may awaken here. But the cultivated ordinary enlightened attitude of equality and respect. I am not saying you're not doing this, don't get me wrong. I'm trying to identify types of thing, not enumerating them.

So, why is Indian spirituality coming here? It's not only the economic reason, I don't think so. I must tell you a spiritual story now. Lord Shiva, the Divine, understood as everything and also, of course, the Destroyer. We always think of the Divine as a gentleman or a lady, who will, of course, create and sustain but never destroy, hmm? But that is a poor tribute to the Divine. So, the Indian mind has conceived of its favourite deities, Gods or Goddesses, as doing everything. And the destruction, of course, is the destruction of the most recalcitrant thing, that is ignorance and ego, and not just the body, which time destroys. It doesn't take God to destroy the body. But the Divine destroys ignorance and illusion. So, the true

Destroyer, this Shiva, is the destroyer of ignorance and illusion, but a destroyer just the same. Shiva and Parvati, who are one, and not two, they are two in manifestation, in form. They have two sons, Vinayaka, Ganesha, the Elephant God—a little image of Vinayaka, who sits on a mouse, his vehicle. Every Indian God or Goddess of note has a vehicle, and this is deeply symbolical. Vinayaka has an elephant's head, and an elephant's trunk, which is the symbol of a powerful memory, the elephant has a very powerful memory, because the trunk is his nose; and memory here means he knows who he is, you know? A bit like Peter Sellers in that film *The Party* [1968], when he is being sought to be thrown out by this doorman. Peter Sellers is acting the part of an Indian, I have told this about a hundred times to you, but I like to tell it each time [audience responds] and there is a context for it. And the doorman is trying to throw him out, and he is trying to gatecrash this party, and he [the doorman] says to Peter Sellers 'Who do you think you are?', and he [Sellers] says: 'In India, we don't think who we are, we know who we are' [loud laughter]. So that's remembrance, memory, of who you are. Ganesha, the son of God, has the memory of who he is. He is really a key to understanding Christ, who is also described as the wisdom of God and the power of God. He knew who he was, the son of God. Ganesha knows this. Each one of us knows this, that we are imminent self-realisers—it's only round the corner. Each one of us has a sense of the self, but it's muddied, it's too limited, but it's like a scent and we can trace it to the flower. We have that knowledge.

Each one of us has that special scent to the flower, to the garden. We, therefore, have this occult symbolical elephant's nose, and he sits on a mouse because elephant and mouse look alike, structurally. They have big ears, and, also that Ganesha, although he is huge and big, is no bully. He can sit weightlessly on a tiny mouse. So next time you see a really fat sadhu, ask yourself if you are going to survive that weight [audience responds]. Maybe you will, maybe he will embody the true spirit of Ganesha, don't get me wrong. He is one son of God, and the other son is beautiful. He is youth portrayed in human form: Kumara, the youth. *Kumarasambhava*, Kalidasa's great play, 'the possibility of youth', it's a very great play. And he has a trident in his hand. And he looks like a tribal, a Dravidian, Jim.

And he probably is inspired by Dravidian life, so much the worse for theories that the north and the south are two different spiritual areas, which anthropologists insist on pursuing. Anyway, Kumara is this beautiful youth with a trident or a spear in his hand, and his vehicle is the peacock. The Divine is no discourager of adventure, or of obesity! Ganesha is the stay-put son. The parents ask their sons, oh, to measure the cosmos. Ganesha, the elephant-son, well, people think it's because of his overweight, laziness, he only goes round his Divine parents. And he says, 'I have measured the cosmos because I have gone round you.' That's a very smart thing to do, but still somewhat lazy. That's a bit like Indian spiritual teachers who never travel at all. They remain where they are, they go round their own deities and they are happy. Now, that's wonderful! But that's only one son of God! The other son, what does he do, Kumara? He gets on his peacock and goes away, shoots off into the cosmos. And of course, eventually, he also returns but he takes a much, much larger round. So the road to India is often through America, or through Europe, or whatever, through Africa. And the road to Africa, and to America maybe, by remaining in India. So there is a complementarity to the two attitudes: of staying where you are, of counting on the occult power of self-realisation to achieve transformation everywhere. But lest you become an idolater of this style of doing things merely, lest you confuse it with mere laziness, and comfort and complacency in your own priestly power, a corrective going-out is also needed. So, I entirely welcome this direction, don't get me wrong. I'm not saying, 'What a great pity, send these people back home', or, 'Don't give them visas', things like that. Don't give your bureaucrats power over these matters at all.

And I know in America you are less inclined to do that than we are in India. Because this is the Kumara. This is the other son of God, or other daughters of God. The other style of doing the same thing, the style of adventure. It is often said, especially by Indian sanyasins, and sadhus, and professors, I'm afraid, that India has no notion of linear time. This is not correct. India doesn't have only the notion of linear time. India also has the notion of cyclical time. Kumara, Subramanya, Kartikeya, names of the same second son, the younger son, represents linear time. Only linear in many directions:

all-encompassing adventurous time. And Ganesha, the more comprehensive cyclical time, of being. So, both are needed. And I don't think that Indian spirituality on the road is also important, but it should be a road of adventure and not of complacency, and it must lead back to the source. But these two styles ... [pause]. So, I am not, therefore, saying that all modes of proselytisation have been right in history. I think they have often been wrong because the sense of every religion being a son or daughter of the same Divine has been absent. Often, I'm afraid, when Islam or Christianity have ... [pause], I am not opposed to their having sought converts, at all, no! But often this was done under the misapprehension that they alone were the children of God, and other religions were not emanations. But if this is understood, then, converting is hardly the word, but loving, embracing everyone, taking the good news of Jesus to other sons of God. Hmm? Supposing I've lost my son, supposing I don't know that I have a brother somewhere in the world, and you come and tell me, 'Look! We have got news of another brother of yours!' That would be lovely and beautiful. But if you come and tell me that you are not the son of your father, only this other one is, that's not good news [laughter]. Okay? So the same energy of evangelism can be preserved for Christianity and Islam, and may I add for Buddhism, without the slightest embarrassment to others, without the slightest offence caused, if we think of the structural model of Shiva and Parvati—notice the absence of sexism here, Parvati means the Divine is not being conceived only as a male, but also as female. And if you might ask why is one child not a female, because strict parity is offensive to sacred art, or any art, and this is left to the imagination. There is indeed a notion of Ganeshwari, the female Ganesha, but you can make Kumara a girl if you like, a young woman, and 'Kumari' is a beautiful word in Hindi. And so, these two styles of movement should be represented by Indian spirituality, indeed by all spiritualities. In the end, if there is any truth in what I am trying to say, it would be valid not only for Indian spirituality, but for all spiritualities. I would like to see a Ganesha dimension of Christianity, and a Kumara dimension of Christianity. I would like to see a Ganesha dimension of Islam, which is happy to be in Mecca; and a Kumara, which is willing to go to Mars. And likewise, of Buddhism. And indeed in their true energies, all these traditions have been like that.

So I'm not trying to present a merely local, sectarian account of one kind of spirituality. I am a student of philosophy; my concern is to find universal truth. I happen to begin with what I know. But there I detect two ancient and powerful, and beautiful, styles of communication. One is what might be called the communication of silence, of saying nothing. That is more eloquent than speech. And you have Ramana Maharshi's explanation for that: a Westerner went to him and found him silent, he was not always silent, [though] he often was—[the Westerner asked,] 'Sir, what's the use of silence? It's so ineffective. Action is what is needed.' So, this question was asked, three times. And the master spoke and said, 'Well, the action is the child of language. You say something, and your servant does something. Language is the child of thought, you think something, and you give expression to it, in speech. Thought is the child of silence. So action is the great-grandchild of silence. How much more powerful silence is than action!' [audience responds]. I think that is a wonderful, powerful way of explaining the power of silence. And indeed, all of us know this very early on in life. When we ask our parents a question, they say nothing at all that communicates much more than if they say, 'Don't do this!' Hmm? That can always be disobeyed. But the terrifying silence cannot be disobeyed at all. Fortunately, it can be obeyed, you can take that as assent and do your naughty things, that's okay. I think silence is large-hearted enough to permit that. So, that is one kind of spiritual explanation of the Ganesha-path, the elephant-path, the large, heavy path of sacred inertia or laziness. I think that is blessed too. But there is the other path too: of activity, of energy, of not silence, but of song, and of dance, and of even continuous speaking, hmm? Of lecturing for eight days, or whatever, hmm [laughter]? There is room even for that—and not only for Indian spirituality, but for all spirituality, sacred or secular. So, I do think that the basic structure of the Shiva–Parvati–Ganesha–Kartikeya story will teach us a lot about how styles of spiritual [communication]—that's what it is, what is Indian spirituality in the West today? It is one mode of communication. As students of communication, we should ask if it is the only valid mode. I think it is one valid mode. But the other mode should also be exhibited. So there should be both an adventurous, whistle-stop tour that a sadhu should undertake here and also, an equally adventurous, stay-at-home, no telephone, nothing [mode]. Both should be encouraged, and if you find only the one or the other being manifested, be sure that something is being forgotten by these people.

So, what is it that we are meant to learn? Shiva—I just told you some Shiva stories and I will tell you some Vishnu stories. Now, I'm sorry to tell you, this is the first time I'm coming somewhere near criticising existing forms. There again, don't take this to be a criticism of some name and address, but of a possibility. Although, I daresay it is being fairly realised here and there. When I read of a Shiva movement here, which encourages criticism of Vishnu, or of a Vishnu–Krishna movement, which permits even the slander of other deities, divinities, I, my heart breaks. It is a bit like the worshipper of Shiva of whom Sri Ramakrishna tells. Sri Ramakrishna says there was this fanatical worshipper of Shiva, and he caused such great trouble to the world that Shiva himself had to appear before him, as Vishnu [laughter]. But he saw through it and said, 'I know you are Shiva, so that's okay, but the other fellow is no good.' So he appeared as half-Shiva and half-Vishnu. He said, 'Oh you are capable of anything; you are still Shiva. The other fellow can't do this.' Then he ... so he offered *puja*, he burnt incense. And the incense was going into the nostrils of Vishnu also. So he held the nostrils of Vishnu to prevent the incense from going into the nostrils of Vishnu, only the nostrils of Shiva could inhale it. So he was abandoned by Shiva, who said, 'You will be accursed upon the Earth.' It's a great story.

If we worship our God as the only God, God will curse us. Only when that fear enters our hearts, that we insult our God deeply, when we set him up against other Gods, only then can we be safe. The fear of the exclusively worshipped God should be the real fear of God. Not the fear of worshipping false Gods. But the fear of making God a false God by worshipping only him or her or it. So that is something that I find, this kind of false worship, and my heart breaks. And I do think that a great danger is involved here, the danger of the story of Ramakrishna. That we might punish God, we might suffocate the

Goddess. That we might, you know, because it did happen when our beloved loves only one part of us and not the other part, say, the beautiful part and not the human part? God too suffers like that, I think, when we worship only the oneness and not the variety; or the maleness and not the femaleness; or the humanness and not the animalness; the beingness and not the nothingness. So I do think that the whole spiritual task of humanity is to conceive of more and more comprehensive ways of envisioning reality: and Hinduism, and Buddhism, and Jainism, and aboriginal Indian religion, including the modern manifestation, are a wonderful introduction, not always a perfect one, but they are a wonderful introduction, of the possibility of comprehensive envisioning and worshipping. And I do think that this is what the West can learn from Indian spirituality. Likewise, what we can learn from the West—Christianity, and I include Islam, because from that which is not originally Indian—is the sense of adventure, this involvement in social change, this Kumara, possibility of the sacred, of shaking people up, of daring them to do certain things, warning them against doing certain other things, of engaging in real battle for the good, for God. We have something to learn, too. And often, we have been invaded and so on, because we neglected this part of our own sacred trust. And if Christianity and Islam and other kinds of the movement have been discredited, it is partly because they neglected the Vinayaka, the Ganesha part of the same communication. They didn't say, 'Well, it doesn't matter, we will be true Christians, and all of you will learn from us', 'We will be true Muslims, and all of you will learn from us'. Both are needed to be learnt by everyone.

While Gandhi was able to say, not out of sentimentality, that he is both a Hindu, and Buddhist, and a Christian, and so on and so on, he had only one minute to say this, so he did not produce a complete list of things, but he meant everything. So, there is maximalism, an insatiability, to Indian spirituality at its best ... which is good. And I do think that America, especially, is able to receive that message. It is that of which greed is a caricature. Greed is not everything at all. Greed is only a little more than what I have. But everything now, a total conception of everything, which makes me, which fills my heart with a sense of richness, already. That is, I think, a message which

Indian spirituality can communicate to the social and economic life of America. But if Indian spirituality makes the mistake of saying the richness is concentrated here, in Shiva, or there, in Vishnu, or there in Shakti—well, that's not enough. But, mind you, it's very important for the variety to be exhibited, so I'm glad that there is shaivite representation. There used to be a journal called *Saivite Hinduism*, now it is fortunately called *Hinduism Today*—progress! Okay? Not nearly enough, but moving towards comprehensiveness. And there are movements which represent Vaishnavism. But I don't think there are enough movements that represent Shaktism, the worship of the Divine as Shakti, as the mother. There ought to be many more, not in a sectarian sense but in a way of completing the list of possibilities and drawing from the rich storehouse of Indian spirituality. There ought to be more temples to the *devi*. And I have talked of the statue of Aditi, as a gift which Indian spirituality can make to this land but that is my last and most telling point, so I will come back to it.

There must be a greater representation of Shakta spirituality, of the energy of the Divine conceived as a woman ... the Divine as the magician. There is a wonderful movie which [I] saw called *Bagdad Café* [1987]—I wonder if you saw this [audience responds]? You know, I ought to get some kind of commission for selling these pictures [audience responds]. But there, there is a circus artist-woman who is a Christ-figure there, and I like that—who is a magician. So, the Shakti Devi, who is a magician in the way in which every mother is a magician, you don't see the baby, and there it is [audience responds]! It really is like pulling a rabbit out of a hat, giving birth to a child. It is pure magic, it's not biology and sociology and so on, or not only those things, those are dull things, without the magic! So a tribute to the magical aspect of the Divine, of nature, which produces the magic of the species, the magic of the elements, the minerals, and then also humour, all these are needed.

So, and you will find this in the greatest women spiritual teachers of India, a great sense of humour. Mirra Richard, whom we should regard as Indian, of course, Sarada, Alagamma, and all these, a tremendous sense of humour. And so, a conception not of a solemn female deity who's only out there to prove that the Divine is both male and female, but a laughing goddess, *attahasa*, devi is described as the one who laughs in that roaring way to confound everything, especially the *asuras*, the powers of resistance. So we need the Shakta, we need the Shaiva, we need the Vaishnava, and we need the tantra also—but tantra not to be understood as that which has been forgotten by the other traditions, that's a complete mistake, forgive me, many friends of mine I address directly in this regard. There is a tantra which is at the heart of Hindu spirituality. What is tantra? Tantra is the basic art of converting adversity into advantage. The fact that we are able to stand on our two feet by pedality is tantra. This was a tremendous handicap when we first started doing it presumably, but humans converted this into a supreme advantage. We are able to discover the human face for a start. We were able to discover the stars, for a start. We were able to discover language because it could carry, we could produce sound. We could discover hands, and hold hands. It is the conversion of an apparent—if you looked at a child learning to walk you would know what I mean—real disadvantage. But that is, if you like, to my mind, that is the biggest revolution that has occurred so far. Not the other ones, the agricultural, the industrial, the American, the Russian, no. But the bipedality is, remains, the biggest and the most outstanding revolution that has occurred. And I think it is rather being lost by succumbing to the motor-car. I think we do need to walk much more I think, and exercise our legs so that our basic self-image is no longer that of sitting like that but of standing up [audience responds]. And if we lose that self-image, I'm afraid we will lose—it is very difficult to carry on a conversation in a motor-car I find. You can't look at anyone. It's just impossible. So bipedality, walking, is tantra. And that root-meaning, don't forget! So tantra is not some special, esoteric practice which restores to spirituality the neglected sexual dimension. Of course, it is at least that, because sex is feared, shunned, avoided, renounced, often prematurely, by spiritual seekers. So great sages said: No! Sexuality is a perfect symbol, is perfect energy, perfect manifestation of the love of the self for the apparent not-self, of God for Goddess, of the One for the Many, that's wonderful, but that's not the only tantra. There is the tantra of Vishnu, there is the tantra—Shiva, who destroys also creates, by destroying ignorance everything falls into place. How does the day dawn? When the night is destroyed, a day comes. There is a tantra of creation, there is a tantra of destruction, there is a tantra of preservation—all are fully tantra. Don't think tantra is a special thing, especially tantrics tend to forget this; they often teach that theirs is the true way, implying that something else is a false way. Whenever we have the idea that we have the true way, we should think, maybe this was hidden everywhere and we failed to notice it. That is a good way really of spreading anything that you think is especially important by saying, 'Oh! I want to look for this in you, I bet it is there! Let's look at your scriptures, and find advaita there. Let's look at your scriptures and find theism there.' Let's look at your scriptures ... for the tantric to tell the Vaishnava, 'Let me find tantra in you, let me help you find this.' For the Indian to tell the American, 'Let me find the sage in you.' For the American to tell the Indian, 'Let me find the adventurer in you.' That's the way of love, that's tantra. Don't forget this, and you will not be deceived.

What is the basic lesson of Indian spirituality, of a deep kind? Which will affect not only lifestyle, not only worship-style, not only eating-style—all of these things are important enough. Speaking style, singing style, these are glorious things. When I hear chanting, the other day when I saw Shantibaba lead the chanting, when I looked around and saw American, young men and women, old men and women chanting the Sanskrit mantra, I was moved to joy and tears. It sounded so beautiful, wonderful. Of course, all this is great. But I do think that fundamental change occurs at the level of concepts and ideas, at the level of ideas where there are revolutionary inputs. The notion of individuality in the West is profoundly challenged by Indian spirituality. That, I think, is the conceptual revolution, that's the time bomb which Indian spirituality at its best places here. It is a totally non-terrorist bomb. It is more revolutionary than any bomb that any terrorist can place. The Indian notion of the self is the notion of you and of me, and of everyone, and of everything. But it is not the notion of you or me confined only to this, but it's the notion of you or me as both this form, all forms, and all forms of together, it's the notion of that which is at the back both of individuality and collectivity.

Now, I've been a student of Western philosophy for many years. The most powerful part of your tradition is the moral and political part; from Plato to Bertrand Russell, to John Dewey and others. You will find that these philosophers, although they have paid a lot of attention to metaphysical, and epistemological, and logical problems, they have also written and talked about moral and political matters. That has been an ongoing, wonderful, powerful tradition of Western philosophy. Now, what you have to ask of Indian spirituality is, do you deeply contribute to this or not? If you contribute only to our lifestyle, that's wonderful, but we are not shaken, because what really shakes us, whether you like it or not, is a moral or a political revolution. Have you anything like that to offer? And I would say Indian spirituality does, via its notion of the self. The old contrast, which you find in the Oedipus plays, which you find in Karl Marx and beyond, which you find in Freud, which you find in Jung, which you find everywhere: the contrast, the contradiction, between the individual and the collective. The collective unconscious, not only the individual unconscious, as though these are different! So the notion of the self is the notion of that, namely you, which manifests both as a collectivity and as individuality. I am this audience, and I am the speaker. This is not a mad, sentimental idea, it is a very economical idea, because if this is understood, that there is no numerical superiority which the collective has over the individual, this is a matter of fundamental importance, which I have to draw your attention to.

What has always embarrassed the two parties in this debate, between the collective and the individual, is the individual has always—look at Hobbes, look at anyone—felt threatened. He or she is the minority, and the majority is the majority. The majority oppresses the minority. And the most dramatic manifestation of this logical, spiritual fallacy is the murder of six million. You might say that's something that occurred in history, Ramchandra Gandhi, I would say yes, but history draws out the implications of bad theory. The notion that these are minorities and minorities are, of course, a nuisance. We are the majority. At the back of this notion is a false view of the individual and the collective—the view that the collective is numerically big, and the individual is numerically small, no. Or, alternatively, the view of the individual, of the individualist, that he or she alone is coherent and one, and the mass is dispersed and chaotic, that is equally false. The tyranny of individualism rests not merely on some powerful eccentricity or madness which seizes individuals, although clearly, this happens, but on the false view, nourished by bad theory, bad philosophy, bad logic, that the individual alone is coherent, that the crowd is not. Culture is a very coherent thing, and the individual can be a very broken-up thing. You know this, but not the, the West does not know this at a theoretical level, only at a moral level. And ultimate changes in Western thought occur, not because of spiritual realisation—so far—but because of theoretical innovation.

Moral and political thought should enrich itself by the notion—sanyasins and sadhus and others ought to be invited to departments of moral and political philosophy, not as a favour, not as sudden interest on the part of these academics in chanting and mantra, no! But as the curiosity regarding a notion of self, a notion of you or me, which may heal the troubles of Western thought at their source. So, I do think, when I take a long view of it, when I look over the next 100 years, and how Indian philosophical thought might become part of Western culture, which is now global culture, mind you—when I talk about Western culture I, of course, talk geographically, but also globally. What you think today, good or bad, true or false, even about India, India will think tomorrow. China will believe what you think about China. Africa will believe what you think about Africa. Such is your attractiveness, and not only your power. I am paying you a compliment. Therefore, the responsibility is very great, on you, to think deeply and correctly, about India, about China, about Africa, about Native America. Don't set up convenient self-images for us. Set up the true self-image which will explode like a time-bomb of goodness and beauty, and will transform at the very root, because India and Africa, if you look at official debates about socialism and individualism in India, or in China, look at the Cultural Revolution, it springs: why did it occur? Because China alone took seriously what the West was teaching it. We are poor learners and so we were spared the Cultural Revolution [audience laughter]. China took you seriously and believed you when you said the collective was more powerful than the individual, and they preferred more power. So don't do that again [audience laughter]. And don't swing to the other extreme and say, 'Of course the individual is more important', because Chinese learn very, very truly, they might become rank individualists. Bring to them a Taoist notion of the same thing.

All mystical traditions have the same notion of the self, including Buddhism: doctrinaire, no self-theorists ought to read the Buddha again. Wordlessly, through silence, the same thing is taught, not through words. And likewise through speech: there is a partnership between Buddha and Ramana in the way in which there is a partnership between Kumara and Ganesha. One adopts the way of silence, say, the Buddha. And Ramana Maharshi adopts the way of speech. They are a partnership in the way in which male and female are a partnership. So, that I think is the deepest contribution that Indian spirituality can make to the West, and therefore to the world, today. And that's the deepest love that you can show us.

I am very grateful for the other kinds of love that you show us, for what might be called the spiritual forms of our culture, and that's part of a global phenomenon. We, oh, I remember when the comic books arrived in India, oh, I loved them! They looked like stories from mythology [audience laughter], Tarzan and all kinds of figures of my childhood. I remember, oh, spending hours and hours neglecting my studies. And so, when you read the Puranas, I hope you will be as excited, as we were and are by your ... the comic strip is a tremendous contribution to consciousness. I think it is far more important than television, or even the movie. So, likewise, the chant, the mantra, the rebelliousness of thought which you find in Indian spirituality, embrace all these things, make them, and then take the thought, the fundamental, I don't mean details, don't say, ' Aha, there is a theory that anticipates Freud here', or ... don't say things like that. But that which does not anticipate Freud, but contradicts him, take that seriously. Not that which looks like Jung, but which looks totally unlike Jung, take that seriously. Not that which echoes Marx, and ignore what Indian Marxists are saying, they will say, 'Of course, Indian philosophy is an anticipation of Marx'—rubbish! Absolute rubbish! It's something of its own kind, which is a contribution to world thought, and not only world culture. Discover that with all the energy with which research occurs in these parts of the world. And then you might, at a very deep level, invite change.

I tend to go on, and on and on, but blame the subject also, not only me. It's an ongoing thing, Indian spirituality in the West today. I have drawn attention to some dangers, I have offered some explanations, and I have offered some suggestions—not only of a moral kind—don't do this, don't do that! I hope you won't go away saying that here's a fussy old lady who told us what to do and what not to do. I have been a bit fussy, I know, but I hope that I have also spoken more philosophically. And if there had been time I would have tried to speak more scientifically also, about the new science. There isn't time. I think that that's a great new field, but I watch with certain scepticism what's going on there. Because there is in the new science not yet a notion of self. There is discovery within the logic and idiom of physics of some new and exciting things, but maya, we know in India, is very tricky. Today physicists think this, tomorrow they might think something else. This world of manifestation, if you ignore that which is behind it, and that which is before it, namely the magician that you are, will play tricks with you. And it might play tricks, and physicists 20 years from now will contradict everything they are saying today. So those who have put all their eggs in the basket of the new science will have to, what? Eat those eggs? I don't know, whatever [loud audience laughter]. So, that can give you a stomach ache. So, well, be careful, and be careless.

Do let me repeat, therefore, my request, that you do all these things, and especially take the Shakta, the neglected tradition of Indian spirituality which celebrates the Divine, the Universe, as a woman, seriously. And do meditate on the notion of Aditi, she is the Goddess who is the creator of all Gods and all Goddesses. It literally means the indivisible. And take seriously the vision that I shared with you, of a massive statue of Aditi, to be set up in, perhaps, the desert parts of this country. But in my vision, she looked like a Tahitian woman, very powerful, remember those women that Gauguin painted? And very powerful, and very beautiful, in that strong muscular way of the current self-image of women, which is good. She looked powerful and beautiful, and strong, enough to put fear in the heart of Mike Tyson, I think? But she looked all that and he said there is no man who can beat me, but he didn't say no woman, huh? He was probably thinking of his wife [audience response]! Anyway, this statue of Aditi, indivisibility, set up in some desert area of this country, looking like that—powerful and beautiful and muscular, with eyes though, more compassionate than the Buddha's, yes, that's how I saw her. In one hand, it's a massive statue in bronze-gold of some kind—Maitreya will tell you, she had a fuller version of what I'm saying to you—and in one hand she holds a broken upturned arrow, symbolising the end of the way of war, and in the other hand a flute, half-raised to her lips, symbolising the way of music and of love. And, I'm convinced, in my vision, I was convinced, that when this statue is set up as the very essence of Indian spirituality, with full scriptural authority, mind you, then planes with bombs, when they fly overhead, will at least dip in salutation, even if they don't return to base, but they probably will, eventually. I think on that note, I want to thank all of you again. And this is the concluding lecture, so I want to thank you very profusely for your patience and for the wonderful energies that you have sent me. And I want to thank, finally, again, the person to whom these lectures have been dedicated—Dr Haridas Chaudhuri, and his wife, Bina Chaudhuri—I thank them, and I thank you [applause].

So many people have contributed to the creation and the sustenance of this institution, not only the great founders but, as I have discovered in the nine months that I have been here, faculty, staff, students, everyone. And so many of them have helped with these events. And I wish I could thank them all by name, but it's a long list, and I know they'd be embarrassed if I mentioned them by name, but so many people contributed to this wonderful place, including you, those who have come and participated in these events. And there is a special power to this area, the Bay Area, and all of this is very deeply mysterious, that we are situated in the Haight–Ashbury area is, again, I think of great significance, because a certain movement started here with, certainly, whatever may have been its failures, embodied a spirit of seeking and adventure. And that can never be abandoned; one has to build on it. And I do think that, therefore, all kinds of coincidences and accidents, and not only plans and visions, helped this place and the Bay Area. So we are meant to be very deeply grateful for all this. And who knows, this new meeting point of the east and west may contribute significantly to the future of our Earth.

I wonder if Deborah is here. There she is! One of the audience; ran into me in a restaurant when I was preparing my lecture, and I invited her to sit with me for a while, only, and she asked a question which reminded me of the most powerful image of Catholicity in India, and I forgot to mention this during the talk, and I am glad I am reminded of it again. It is the image of the Aswattha tree in the Bhagavadgita. Sri Krishna, the Divine, says to Arjuna that there is a tree, an inverted tree, whose roots are in the sky, and branches are down below. That is a powerful image of true rootedness, where our roots are in the infinite sky, not some local Earth; and where the fruits are on the Earth, they spread all over. If we are rooted up there, we will bear fruit down here. It is a marvellous image. So, if you want one image of rootedness and universality, at the same time, you have to—that is a tantric image. Tantra is an inversion of the existing order of things. So, this image of the Aswattha tree—I've forgotten the etymology of Aswattha, but it is a tree, it is not inverted like [that], but there is an occult tree, which is upside down. So, that is a powerful, wonderful image. So, if you want me to answer in an image, not in words, I would say contemplate the inverted tree, which has its roots in the sky—that is the true self, which has its roots in the infinite sky above, and its head here. It is like a *sirsasana* in yoga, where you draw your, where you are supported by the sky, and you touch the Earth with your head—rather nice. So, I do think that the current Earth-consciousness would also think of the feet which are supported by the sky, and then the head will serve the Earth better, I think. It is a difficult thing, sirsasana, don't practise it without advice. But many do that, and it is the king of the *asanas* [yoga postures]—the ultimate inversion of all regimentation ... the turning upside-down. Marx is not the only one who talked about the turning upside-down of history, the tanrics have done it all along and overdone it, I think. It's a, so you know that they are, it's the same thing, it's the upside-downing of everything, so you know what it is. It's about time that the true tantra of remaining what you are is also discovered.

So the old something about, 'Don't just do something, stand there!', or something you know, inversion of [laughter]. I think we've had a very rewarding evening, speaking for myself, and I'm really touched by your, not only the number of people who come, but the quality of your attention, and your speaking, and your curiosity. And this whole series has been for me, believe me, a very, very instructive experience; because it is only when you are in conditions of such matchless love as this institute provides, only when in these conditions you speak and lecture that you discover many things yourself—and discover how little you have discovered, at the end of it. So, I am very grateful to everyone who has made this possible: the Department of Philosophy and Religion, the Institute as a whole, the president, his staff, my friends amongst the staff, so many of whom are present here, and others, my friends, and Kusum, and Diana and Peter, who've made tea, and Kusum's mother, Faustin and Brian, who've done this recording with such attention, and every one of you who has both spoken and remained silent, and to this wonderful room, with all the presence, which the pillars and the walls represent, and for those who have not come [laughter], and with a volume of thanks, I want to say how wonderful this experience has been for me, and thank you very much [applause].

— *four* —

NIRMAL SMRITI VYAKHYAN*

Gagan, you placed this responsibility on me. I do not consider myself fit for this. I do not believe that I would be able to discharge this responsibility well. But, Nirmal [Verma] wrote that letter to Ram, and from that, I feel that I would converse with Nirmal. In that way, and looking at all these postcards, it feels ever more possible when someone is not embodied. When a person lives in the body, sometimes he is in the north, and not in the south. If he is in the east, he is not in the west. It is difficult to ascertain the address, and sometimes the letters do not even reach. But when the person is not in the body, he is in our hearts and it is easy to speak to the person. Although this is something akin to a lecture, I do wish to speak to Nirmal about quite a few things and, of course, with you and with myself as well. Gagan bears witness to the fact that Nirmal and I would talk about myriad subjects, very strange our talk used to be and filled with laughter and jokes. Sometimes when he would meet, he would say 'first tell me all the jokes, we shall talk later'. But the biggest joke is that despite the presence of so many learned people here, I have in their place accepted the

*Talk delivered in Hindi at India International Centre, New Delhi, 3 April 2007. Translated into the English by Tridip Suhrud.

responsibility of standing before you. If Nirmal were here, he would say, 'You can turn back even now.' But, I am not willing to do that. Gagan, your memory is special. You would remember that period when Nirmal and I shared silence—there was friendship, but there was silence. There is no reason to go into its causes, because if such silence were not possible we would not have the experience of Sri Ramana Maharshi, beloved to us both, in our hearts. Hence, that was necessary. I had begun to understand something of that. One day I was here (at the India International Centre); Nirmal would come to the bar and sit someplace away, further away. And both of us would silently abuse each other. One day, he got up from his chair and came towards me. I thought to myself, what new folly have I committed, what scolding would I get and how I would be able to rebuke him. He came and sat in a chair beside me. I said, 'Hello, Nirmal.' He said, 'Ramu I have not come to talk with you but I have come to be with you.'

I shall never forget this. I still experience togetherness with him. This story 'Kavve aur Kala Pani' [Crows and the Exile] is a story of togetherness of being and living together. I did not know that Sahaji Baba, a character of that story, is also a character in history. But to believe in this historicism or not, is to me secondary. Gagan, the way he enters the story and later within us, is not only a fact of history, it is a thing beyond time. It is higher, of a different order, it is magical. It is not merely a thing of true and false, it is something altogether different. I do not know about things that Gagan said. I would speak about the story, its characters, a story that is written in the 1980s. I have had an earlier occasion to speak about it. But I shall not repeat myself.

Today I read my old notes and placed them away. I have brought something new to share. What I am about to recount is true. Many years ago I reached Nirmal's Barsati, his home. There was no one else there, and my mind was melancholic. I hope that you would laugh at what I have said and what I am about to say. I told Nirmal, 'Today I am depressed.' He asked, 'Why so? Ramu, see how cool the breeze is!' Gagan also got some similar response; she recounts this in her memoir. One day Nirmal asked Gagan, 'Would you want *moksha* [liberation/salvation] or rebirth?' Gagan replied, 'Moksha.'

Gagan writes, Nirmal's large eyelashes closed and opened and said—Nirmal would ask a question to others and also to himself—'Why? How beautiful the world is! Why don't you want to return?' Nirmal said something similar to me, about cold breeze. That night I had a strange dream. And this is not something that I have made up. I was with Nirmal and was also depressed. Nirmal had a cooler in his hands and its cold breeze came up to me, and Nirmal said, 'Ramu, how cool is the breeze.' And just at that moment a crow came and sat on the cooler. We find this in many of Nirmal's stories, a sudden turn, an unprecedented phrase, a new idea, or to think over the same matter again and again. Ashok Vajpayee said that it was quite picturesque, and that is true. But it is also cinematographic, sculpture-like, very magical. It is possible only for a very accomplished writer like Nirmal, a writer who has written a great deal. But the world of his conversation is something else; it is not something that could be recorded. We can hear him, recall it. A special kind of laughter, it had a special kind of absurdism. And, of course, quarrels and rapprochement were all part of it. That is no longer possible. But Nirmal, this story of yours, 'Kavve aur Kala Pani', when I had the opportunity to speak to you about it, I told you, Nirmal, yesterday you asked for one glass *kala pani* and the nectar of two crows for breakfast. But, no, this story is serious, sombre. I had said something about it in 1989. Ashok had invited me to Bharat Bhavan. When the story was published, I was unable to measure its depth. One word is kala pani and the other is *kavva* (crow). It is a beautiful word, the moment you say it, the heart begins to crow. 'Kavve aur Kala Pani'. I would make no attempt to trace the history of this word. Kala pani is a form of punishment, a kind of imprisonment, which takes us to a place from where it is not easy to return. This has been a recurring thing in history: during the freedom movement, so many were imprisoned at the Andaman. This was considered the punishment of kala pani. But there is always a possibility, even when one is imprisoned for life, that one would return, that events would take a different course, that power would change and he would return among us.

But this is not the kind of kala pani that Nirmal alludes to, even while trying not to do so. In this story, in our philosophical culture, there is much on this subject, and I would try and speak about it. Take death for example. The letters that we heard, the letters of Ramkumar. Nirmal died, a friend died. But what is death? One always has this feeling that death is a form of punishment. But ultimately, what is death? It would be considered a form of punishment if takes us to a place from where no one returns. In Nirmal's story, this is one of the meanings.

The story begins with the truth of death; this is, of course, not meant in a literal sense. [Jean-Luc] Godard was asked whether a film necessarily needed a beginning, a middle and an end, to which he had said, yes, but not necessarily in that order. So the story begins thus.

The death of the father. Death is a grave idea in our age and I feel that the significance of the film also lies therein. In this age, each culture experiences the death of the father. Tradition has a voice, an injunction—do this, do not do that. I imply no criticism here. The voice of the father, or that of the mother, which told us things. My mother always told me (never an injunction that do this and not that) do anything, but do it with thought and understanding. Thus, she always had this apprehension that I would lag behind both in thought and in understanding. But we are not prepared to accept that everywhere the father has died. It seems that he has been killed. Then, what is this death? It is a punishment, if we were to accept that we would never return from that place. This thought does occur, and it occurs to everyone, but if that thought were to become a philosophy, a mode of thinking, it would create a certain kind of pressure in the world. And I feel at times that some such thing is indeed happening. Many persons, under these circumstances, would believe that death has to come someday or another, why not invite it. What is the difference between death today and the one 50 years later? I am not speaking of individual death, death of a person, but of collective death, death of the human race, and that is to happen at some point. And if death is a punishment and if it takes us to a place of no return, why not have that death today?

So there is this burden of consciousness or of false consciousness. Today, it is a force. There are those who believe that death is not a punishment, it is not the end, it takes us someplace else, to some Heaven where we already have a place reserved for us. Such persons would also be very eager to get to this place, to invite death and to award death unto others. Thus, the world today is ready in every sense, the modern world is ready for the incarceration to Kala Pani and to take all others there. This story recognises this temptation, and yet seeks a resolution from it, a resolution that we must attain. We must find this resolution because this Earth does not belong only to humans, there are beings other than humans, seen and unseen, to whom the Earth is home. And just as Gagan said a while ago, Nirmal used to say that no country subsists only on the living. Let us count the dead; so that we can decide who has the majority and who is in the minority? Let us count the dead, no matter which classifications they are of. If I were mature, if I were capable of speech, I would have said to Jinnah Sahib that you say that Muslims have died and so have the Hindus, give us a list of them, who is in the majority? And put the humans aside, can partitions ever be decided in such a manner? Have only the living served and cultivated this Earth? And this is not confined only to India, it is all-pervading. And not only with respect to religion, but this method of calculation, of making collectivities; this story seeks to fight that, or so I feel.

And something that just came to me. The story that Gagan narrated, Nirmal asked Gagan, why do you not desire rebirth, why wish for moksha? Look at the world, how beauteous it is, and that cold breeze; why would you not return? Gagan has not written as to what her response was. But I feel that this return, continuous never-ending birth, rebirth and death, again and again, is something that our culture has reflected upon. But this reflection has been found wanting, unsatisfactory, because each time we take birth, we would have fear of death and even eager aspiration for it as well. Many years ago when I was a college student, this assertion of Indian culture seemed very strange to me. This idea that I am free from birth and death is a selfish thought. Come, return many times! And Swami Vivekananda has said that I wish to return countless times and each time be born as the poorest of the poor. So then I felt that there was some confusion in this thought. But as I get close to death, my faith in the truth of this thought increases somewhat. And that faith is that if we were to be born again and again, leaving aside fear, this is a selfish idea. We reserve a body for ourselves every 100 years or so. I feel that this is a very narrow idea. This idea of seeking freedom from both birth and death, an idea that is also part of the story, suggests a possibility wherein we are with those who are alive and also with those who are dead. We do not desire a special body for us, a body specifically for our birth and death, this is a grand idea and Sahaji Baba understood this. And other characters aspire to this state; they wish to rise above themselves. In the story the father, the father is dead, but in another story, there is a severe conflict about the death of the father.

Nirmal has struggled a great deal with this idea of the death of the father. The other story that I referred to is a frightening story. We spoke of the hospital; it could be heard in Ram's letters. In this story, there is a father, a father in hospital—it used to be very difficult when I spoke to Nirmal about this. But he is no more here and we speak to ourselves, talk with Nirmal who is in us all, Nirmal, in that story there is a father and his son who nursed him, served him. That could be you, or someone else; I am not attempting to be autobiographical. The father scolded him, berated him, but he nursed with passion. These days it is not easy to nurse in the hospitals; even the doctors and others are unable to nurse fully. We have to try making an attempt; the father becomes sour. Father, mother or brother; in that story in the hazy light of the hospital, in middle of an argument one of them departs. The story says that who lives and who goes away, we do not know. We have seen fathers die, both in life and in this story. You must read it ['Beech Bahas Mai' (In the Middle of the Debate)]; I feel that it is essential to understand 'Kavve aur Kala Pani'. But, in this story there is no debate, the father is gone. There is a kind of silence, a silence which does not tell us that the father is gone and that he is not to return. There are all those concerns of a householder immediately after the death of the mother and father. There is this wealth, how is it being to partitioned, the division of assets. Many years before the death of the father, a brother, not the eldest, but elder to the brother who is the narrator of the story, leaves the house. There are sisters, children too, that brother has left home. But why did he leave? This is not told to us in the story. They have a conversation at the end. I am narrating incidents that took place later in the story first and the beginning towards the end. Baba is asked by the younger brother that if you are staying here or there [it] is the same, why did you come here? He says my staying there had no meaning for others, and here since there are no others, find your own answer. This is a great truth of advaita. We find our true purpose when there is no other. He left the home for this reason. Something similar with Sri Ramana Maharshi. He obtained moksha at the age of 16. And what moksha that was! He obtained it by fighting death, by defeating death, Nachiketa-like. He realised that there is consciousness. Death tells him this body of yours, give unto me, it belongs to me, and you stole it from nature. And Ramana Maharshi would have replied, take it away. And Death would have told him that this mind of yours, this Brahmin intellect, that you believe to be growing deep, subtle, this too you have stolen from the sky. The child Raman [would have] replied, take it away. And then perhaps Death [would have] told him that this *janeu*, this sacred thread of yours, you have stolen it from history, take that away too. And then a thought arouses in Ramana Maharshi's heart: Everything is gone and would I not survive when this body is burnt away? And this question which did not need words, gave rise to a deep consciousness within him, that consciousness perturbed him, caused turbulence, all bodies are his and so are all births. This is a story about that.

But to attain this truth, one is required to climb higher, but the life of a householder is centred around other humans. Family is located at its centre. This life is very small, narrow. And Chhote likes this very much; he lives in Delhi in a house of his own. There is a wife, there are children and there are others, friends, and a brother. He works in a newspaper and he also writes something. And after the father's death, he has a notice issued in the newspaper that father is no more, do come back. His brother responds, ten years after he left he sends his whereabouts, and says, come, meet me. The family says to Chhote go and meet him. But they do not say, go and bring him back. When Ramana Maharshi left the home for years, his mother tried to get him back; this is not there in the story.

This is most certainly not in the story, what it has I would recount after sometimes having thought about it. But Chhote travels to a hamlet in the hills by a bus. The letter had come from here, the letter of the lost brother. The first scene is so picturesque; if you were to make film, the screen would appear damp. It is raining. Chhote who has undertaken this journey under duress, against his own will, has three pieces of luggage. One holdall, one trunk and one briefcase. He is flung out of the bus with these three belongings. He stands alone and he feels, what if I were to have the bus stopped and ask it to take me back. In this story, nothing is accepted because it should be. It does not say accept this because it is true, this is our duty, the brother has sent a letter, and it is not so. The story allows us to think at every step, to ask a question at each step. These three things are very attractive; the things that Nirmal talks about. Like the paintings that [Vincent] van Gogh made, paintings of things: shoes, a chair. There was a chair here. I have placed my things on it. A chair should not be empty. Thus, many things inhabit Nirmal's stories, things they have a place, an entire life of their own in Nirmal's stories.

What is 'holdall'? Many years ago I travelled to Prayag with my mother's ashes and from there to Varanasi with a friend, Arvind Krishna Mehrotra. My mother had gone to Varanasi to study. And it was my deep desire that her ashes should also be immersed there. So we were walking about after having immersed the ashes. The architecture of Varanasi is that of Heaven, but its sanitation belongs to Hell. Both these coexist in Varanasi. A friend from Varanasi used to say, Banaras means Bana-Ras, where all *rasas* [fundamental qualities of classical Indian music, dance and poetry] are present. So we were walking about. There was a cavernous hole in a wall, where there was a bulb, and therein sat a man, who looked like a *munshi*, a chronicler, and he was writing something. We saw him, Arvind and I stopped. We wondered what he must write and why? And the red covered notebook, to me, he was certainly a munshi. He was writing accounts of our actions, of all those who had died; what they accomplished, what remains to be done, he did not even so much as look at us.

I had another question. Even then I was a servant of Ramana Maharshi. I like the images of Gods and Goddesses in our calendars. And in each image, the *vahana*, the vehicle of each God or Goddess, is given; like Nandi of Shiva and lotus for someone, a mouse and a peacock for someone. And I wondered that Satguru Ramana was no less than a God, what should be his vehicle? And we saw that there was a holdall hanging in the hole where the munshi sat writing. And I told Arvind, I now know that the vahana of Sri Ramana Maharshi is a holdall. Sitting astride on the holdall, he travels in the sky over the holy Arunachala. Arvind felt that in the sadness of my mother's death I have truly become somewhat mad. I had to explain to him that no, that is not the case. This holdall is an English word. It is a loose object, it has no defined shape; and it is everywhere. And the bus has to climb those heights, the entire experience of being in the bus, the bus grunts and labours, the bus driver has an image of the Goddess facing him and the bus is like her vahana, the tiger. And it climbs up with certain effort. And it threw out all four in the pouring rain: holdall, trunk, briefcase and Chhote. The holdall is this search, the search for truth, the search for the meaning of life and of death—if that is to come, why should one not die at this instance, and if there is indeed rebirth, what that is? One has to keep dying, why should one not go at this very instance? I feel that this question is in many hearts; we should accept that. Chhote has set out in search of this answer. The father is already dead. No one heard him. There was some talk but it remains unsaid. Holdall is a support, support of our traditions and the trunk is modernity, we carry in it books, good clothes, shoes, some photographs and I do not know what all we carry, including food, and we carry the tin trunk. This tin trunk is an accomplishment of modern India, while the holdall is age-old, comfortable, open it up and go to sleep, go beyond time, open the trunk and become selfish; keep buying, keep stuffing. Keep carrying it. But what is this briefcase? The briefcase in this story contains documents, all the papers are legal documents, and so long as they are unsigned, how will the house be sold? Let me say what comes at the end towards the beginning. When they meet, Sahaji Baba and his brother, he is told everything, that the father has died and we are required to do such and such; Sahaji Baba asks, when a person dies, what was his, does it become ours? It is a very deep thought; and why such a hurry? Baba had spent his entire pension on this, and where does the mother stay? Where does the mother stay! Of course, she lives downstairs alone. Why alone? A renunciate asks such minute question to a householder. Such is Sahaji Baba.

But let us return to that briefcase; it has all the papers, it has our photograph, our identity; a person like us who is distant both from tradition and modernity, and that makes India of today. I wish to say something about all three things. I studied here, I studied there, and I have this photograph, this identity card of the India International Centre, you can see all that and there is other luggage. But, he wants to return, to turn back because when we set out on this search in the quest for truth, how often we feel that let's give this up and return, let's sit down, live with the families, gossip with friends or let us do some work good or bad, but do something. This search for truth is very difficult. It requires a climb up, I am panting, out of breath, it is raining, how is it to be done! We delude our heart with such and similar arguments and at that instance they see an umbrella coming towards them in the rain; they cannot see very much.

An umbrella is a kind of crow. The umbrella approaches and then a person, he places half the umbrella over Chhote's head, thus Chhote is half-covered and so is the other person. That person is Masterji. Who is this Masterji? Nirmal, I think that Masterji is that person of modern India who has not lost his tradition, but has not had much success within the modern world. Nirmal, you are a writer living in Delhi, they are not like you. In villages and cities, there are people like that, they are different from us, we who live in the cities and have attained average or even above-average success. But these people are not such, they have not obtained a big job in a large city, they have a job in a small school, they have a deep affection towards tradition, Mahatmas and Sadhus; they understand them well. Someone had once asked me, no that was an interview with Raja Rao, and I asked him, 'Raja Sahib, is it not a matter of pain that so many false, untruthful gurus are going abroad from our country?' And he replied in English, 'Ramu, it is easier to detect a false guru than a false doctor.' We are acquainted with the languages, the mode of thought of false Gurus, and people of our country are very intelligent, they know in a short time, these are filled with straw, there is nothing to be gained from them and they go somewhere else. But we do not know what the trick of a doctor is; what knowledge, what science backs them, thus, Raja Rao was correct. But Masterji is that person who can know them, and know them closely. And he knows the Baba. Chhote wonders if he should send the documents with Masterji and turn back. But somehow his destiny keeps pushing him forward, upward and takes him to Masterji's house. And Masterji is very strange. What does his room have? These are many novels and all of them in English, not one of them with a name that you would recognise. Where does he get them from? Why does he read them? He too wants to know English and most significantly he is acquainted with the Baba. He says I do not know why you have come here, but earlier I used to fetch water and wood for Baba, I also told him that I would cook for him, bring him some food. But he declined. And what kind of a Baba is he that he does not know how to make use of other people, how would he know God? There is this belief in our country that so long as you do not have around you servants from whom you take work, you cannot be a Mahatma. This one was disqualified on the first ground itself. But Chhote, who has been listening to all these, suddenly asks Masterji, 'Where is the hotel?' He laughs and says, 'What is a hotel?' And he takes Chhote home. It is a very beautiful passage, you should read it, and we do not have the time for it. But do read it, the ambience of it, drink in its water, enjoy its rasas. This conversation takes place in a small room, there is a lantern; somehow Chhote manages to sleep, he does not wish to talk at all, but Masterji wants to talk, talk a lot about all kinds of things. Somehow Chhote manages to sleep, and next day, early morning, he goes to a tea shop, a *dhaba*, to have his tea, as he does not wish to trouble Masterji.

There is an Aghori Baba there. He asks, 'Have you come for the darshan of the Baba? How is he these days? He is unwell these days, I am told.' There are such Aghori Babas in our country who would not consider anyone a Mahatma, lest that person so much as sneezes or has some common ailment. One can be a Baba, a Mahatma only when one is stout in body and perfectly healthy. Thus, the Aghori Baba is disappointed. He asks for a tea and then another, well even he has needs. In this story, there are needs, the necessary conditions for arriving at truth, for reaching far, of understanding others, which would then help resolve all problems. There are necessities and conditions for meaning in life, for a fulfilled life, which cannot be set aside. Chhote asks him, 'Where is he?' And the Aghori Baba signals; for a moment Chhote thinks that he is pointing towards the sky, as if he is saying go there, like your father; Father is there, you would meet Baba also there. This is very beautiful; the brother is on a height, not face to face, but higher, waiting for you. And he is not high above, but at a slight incline. Such persons have many needs. And even persons like Masterji have needs, persons who have had darshan of the Mahatmas, of the realised and the knowledgeable—they have needs. It is likely that their faith is somewhat less than what it used to be before, but they hope that someday they would receive something. Masterji says, Baba gives neither discourses, nor does he conduct initiations. He is a renunciate of his own kind; sometimes I feel that his renunciation is not true. Having said this Masterji laughs; and yet they require such Babas. In modern India, there are thousands, crores of persons who cannot go to the university; for them, such proximity to a Mahatma is essential and they know a great deal about the Mahatmas. Older ascetics like Aghori Baba also welcome them. When Ramana Maharshi reached Arunachala in the early years, some naughty boys used to harass him by throwing a stone at him. He was protected by a Sheshadri Swami. Sheshadri Swami was robust and a stout person. He drove away all the boys and protected this child of 16 who sat in samadhi in a cave. As the child sat in samadhi, Sheshadri Swami stood at watch above. Later, when Ramana Maharshi went into the hills of Arunachala and an ashram was built at the foothills, people from across the world came there. When they came, the first person to meet them was Sheshadri Swami. He would ask, 'So you are looking for that householder, isn't it? He is there. Go a little further.' He is a householder! That implies that he still had doubts; so many people come to him but the family remains. Something similar is said to Chhote by Baba: that if you are under the impression that I have come here to escape the life of a householder, you are mistaken. What is the difference between living here and living there? Many come to see him, Masterji and Aghori Baba are of course among them, but there are many, they stand in a line and Baba walks away. Among them is a mysterious presence. There is a young woman, who has wrapped a black shawl around her. And I am extremely grateful to Meena Alexander who found this reference for me. van Gogh and Theo—the relationship between Ramkumar and Nirmal is in many respects is like that of van Gogh and Theo; they were brothers, and van Gogh lived on the support of the letters he received from Theo. And I feel that similarly, Ramkumar also gave support to Nirmal, and in one of these letters to Theo, or to someone else, Vincent writes about a new painting in which there is a woman with a black shawl—I liked this fact a great deal. This story of Nirmal, 'Kavve aur Kala Pani', takes us close, very close, to a great painting of Vincent van Gogh, *Wheatfield with Crows*—this was painted around the 1890s. There is a golden field in it, if you look closely at this golden field there is grass, the kind of grass with which the Yadav clan killed each other, it is very sharp, pointed. It is golden universe; over the grass there are clouds, somewhat displeased they appear and the sky above it, which seems unsteady. And I have looked at this painting for hours on end, and in that, and not only in the sky but deep within the field, there are cows, deep black crows. The shadow of [the] crow is present everywhere; no matter how prosperous we become, but so long as humans do not know the answers to the riddle of death, all else is futile. In the Isopanishad, the Rishi says to the sun, and he calls it the golden lid: Lid, go aside so that I can glimpse the face of truth. Whether Vincent van Gogh says this, or whether Nirmal wants us to understand that or not, but it is a mysterious presence, the presence of a young woman. There we see the first female character, we see a child-woman. I understand what Nirmal would have thought about that, which is a problem in our country, the problem of a female child. We, in our country, kill the female child in the foetus. And this woman is seeking protection of the Baba. Protect me, or else nothing will survive here. Only death will prevail, there would be no limits. How would life subsist? This door is ajar and from that slit Nirmal watches us. Nirmal has said this very serious idea in just a line. That among the people waiting to see the Baba is a very young woman who has a black shawl—a crow in the form of a black shawl. She has wrapped death around her, and her prayer is to let this not be done. And we have to reach those heights; the Aghori Baba has pointed in the direction, Masterji has spoken in tones of disappointment. And when Chhote told Masterji that he wished to meet the Baba, and asked Masterji to accompany him, Masterji seemed somewhat afraid, reluctant, and replied, you go, anyway I live here and can go any time I like. And there were people who would go for some time to Almora, make a family there and return. We, in our country, have such renunciates. Even they have permission that they experience the proximity of the state of renunciation, but it is not necessary that they are called ascetics.

But the possibility of living in proximity of the learned, the *jnani*, is a great thing. So Masterji says to Chhote, I can go any time, you have just come, you should go. And the Aghori Baba says, that straight path, keep to it and climb higher, to your right you will see an ancient temple. And to the right [of] the temple, there is a path which would take you to a hut, made among boulders, where you would find Baba. It is possible that he might be seated outside, but on some days he does not come out at all. Chhote climbs up to the temple clutching his documents close to his chest. Therein lies his identity, part moksha, part society, and some sense of nirvana, therein lies his identity, therein is his father's name, the names of his brothers and sisters, and his world is there in these documents. He climbs up clutching them close. As he reaches up to the temple, he sees that the temple is very old, quite ancient, but later when he talks to Baba, he is told that the temple was not all that ancient. But an old idol of Shiva was found here. There was no temple, no priest, no singing of bhajans, but just wilderness. Suddenly, a noise is heard, a monkey jumps from the tree and gets onto the roof of the temple. This is the first lesson for Chhote that religion, spirituality does not only belong to humans. Like always, beings other than humans would continue this tradition. This monkey is the priest and also the devotee. The monkey is all. You have hitherto learnt nothing. So long as we think only of human life, our desire to destroy all life other than human life, our desire to destroy all stems from our fear of death. We have to reach up to the temple, the mosque and the church. Nirmal used to get very angry when believing ourselves to be secular, we turned our backs to all of them. I know this. He left in the middle of the argument; otherwise, I too wanted to say some things to him in anger. But there was no need for it, as when I read his story again, I felt very good that he says that we cannot turn our back to the temple, the mosque, the church, to the gurudwara.

Whether your faith be higher or lower, you would have to go there, you have to go to Ayodhya. I have said this before. There was a memorial meeting held here for Nirmal. As soon as the pyre would have been lit, he would have sat up and called for Yamraj and would have chastised him, and when he chastised you, he spoke in English, 'Mr Yamraj, you kept Nachiketa waiting for three days, you must be a secularist.' Having said this he would have left, which implies that the doors of the temple, the mosque and churches should always be open.

You cannot go higher than this. Aghori Baba, who is on a lower level has already pointed out that there is a temple. You are required to go there. Our tradition has created many spaces for it. It might even be higher than the sky, but without the map provided by tradition, we cannot go any higher. He walks slowly upwards and meets Baba. Baba comes out on the steps. He meets his brother, a brother who was elder to him but not the eldest among the brothers. This is a remarkable aspect on the story. If he were to be the eldest brother, it would have become quite hackneyed as it appears in so many stories. The eldest brother is not present; the two brothers talk about the eldest brother, though not for long. The younger one has been sent, and that is good. He has a family of his own and he is quite attached to the life of a householder, to his children. When, after all these years, he receives the touch of his brother, it is as if [it is] magical. He receives the touch, not of the parents, but of the brother, who though devoid of attachment is both attractive and capable of an attraction. It is his touch. In this excitement, he drops the briefcase and it falls open, the papers scatter, fly away. And who gathers them! Baba. He asks, so these are papers; to which Chhote replies, yes, there are some papers which you would have to sign. Oh! That I will. Is everything alright? Yes, it is. Then why are you here? What difference does it make? I live here just as I lived there. Ramana Maharshi had said the same thing. When people asked him as to why did he not return to his family, he replied, 'Look, my family is here, there are thousands of persons, and not only humans, there are monkeys, tiger, panthers, peacocks, snakes, I have such a large family, who says that I am a renunciate?' Baba says the same thing. What difference does it make? At this point, Chhote is somewhat angry because the absence of ten years is a long time, the love between brothers creates dependencies, the brother is needed, absences are felt, and that was not available. The brother was lost, there were no replies from him, and they had searched for him in hospitals, in mortuaries, where for years there [were] dead bodies laid out on blocks of ice, and there you [would] go looking for the dead body, and the manager of the place [would] ask you to hurry up as there are others also searching for their dead. And there are people waiting outside for the darshan of the Baba, and just as you were from one block of ice to another looking for the dead body, Baba moves from person to person. And what is he searching for? Not a dead body; he is looking for that soul that is neither born nor dies. Even Ramana Maharshi continued to have darshan of people one after another, till the very end. And people believe that till the very end Ramana Maharshi allowed people to have his darshan. This is only a partial truth. Ramana Maharshi was thirsty for darshan; he wanted the darshan of the different forms through which the soul manifests itself. This is found in Sahaji Baba as well. And Chhote likes this. For the first time, he lies down unburdened. He finds Baba's body warm. There are these small details, which only the Aghori Babas of India can tell us—that the body of the seeker is warm to touch. Those who attended to Ramana Maharshi used to find his body warm, feverish. Chhote asks, do you have a fever? No, just some discomfort, why don't you stay here for some days? No, no, I must return. Well not here, but there is a rest house below and I know its manager, I would speak with him, he would make arrangements for you to stay. Who is this manager? What is this rest house? I feel that this manager is God and the rest house is Heaven. The realised one rises above Heaven and Hell. But, he has good relations with the manager of the rest house, which is God. The realised one knows that there would be a moment when we have to go there, but this is so easy. Yama says to Nachiketa, go to Heaven. Nachiketa replies that is far too easy, you may keep it. I wish to rise higher; I wish to know the mystery of immortality; who better than you to teach me that! The Baba's words are mysterious. I do not think that here Nirmal wishes to remind us of the colonial period and the rest house built by the British and its manager. It is not appropriate for the content of the story. What can the Sahaji Baba gives us? He has no money to give, but he can get for us Heaven if Heaven is what we desire. But like Nachiketa before him, Chhote rejected this. Perhaps Masterji would have accepted this, and perhaps Aghori Baba would have rejected it. But who knows! And then they talk. The Baba is deeply pained at the loneliness of their mother. The realised ones deeply long for their mothers. When Ramana Maharshi left home, his mother continued to search for him, from place to place. But this is not narrated in the story. There is a mother, the character of a mother. I feel that she should have been dealt with in detail. But Nirmal writes about so many other things. Why should Nirmal tell us about everything? The reader must also play some part. When Ramana Maharshi left home, his mother went across the world looking for him. And she went to this place in Kerala. She saw a boy in a circus who was like her son, she felt that he was her son, but the boy turned his back to her. I believe he must certainly have been her son. Ramana Maharshi, at two places at the same time! For him, it must have been a very easy thing. But he said, this circus that the world is, I would not be found here; it is not me that is in the circus. The mother said, come back, but Ramana Maharshi was not persuaded. But a son has a duty, and that duty is to serve the mother and father; this duty Ramana fulfilled. Sahaji Baba gave to Chhote the love and affection of a father, the father is no more and Baba is not the eldest brother, but gave the love of a father; something that Chhote needed. Just as Kafka needed his father. Ramana Maharshi did not go home with his mother from Madurai. But she came and stayed with him after some years, and thus he could fulfil his duty. His younger brother also came, so they experienced togetherness and proximity. Ramana Maharshi served his mother, and I feel that by giving his love, Sahaji Baba also served his family; at the same time, he tried to convey that there was no difference between 'here' and 'there', if the two were distinct and I were there, my presence there would have no meaning for you. There is no one else here and I think about myself. Masterji had asked him, don't you meditate upon God? Sahaji Baba replied, how can we meditate upon something that we do not know of? People would ask Ramana Maharshi if God existed and he would say, you know nothing about God, you know that you are, so search yourself. Sahaji Baba is saying something similar. In doing so he is not expressing any disrespect for God. But he says, 'Know yourself.' We are here and not there, we have this human body or is it something else; all this exists, it is not nothing; first, we must rid ourselves [of] all these dualities—that is the lesson. Chhote receives the love that he had not had, and also this knowledge, this knowledge cannot be had either from Masterji or from Aghori Baba, but it cannot be obtained without them showing the path.

Now let us return to the crow and the question of death. In our country, everyone has this faith, in some form or another, in rebirth. Because it is not proper that a being who has so many desires, aspirations, should get only one life. We do have faith in rebirth. The father is dead and if someone were to tell us that he shall be born again, this is a very powerful idea because let us try and understand this idea of rebirth; a person who dies could be born anywhere and for this reason, it is in our interest to serve the entire Earth. But anything that is predicated upon self-interest does not have the power comparable to the truth. The idea of rebirth has a lot of strength; it is not an idea to be discarded easily. But it does not do away with or in any way reduce the sense of otherness. We are born again, once again we have a father who would die, we have a brother, once again a wife and even children, a new father; this circle is endless. And only the idea of rebirth would not stop our march towards *pralaya*, the great dissolution. If we were to say to the world, all of you shall be reborn, you are all stupid to fight, so stop it, throw away all nuclear weapons because you will be reborn; they would laugh at us. The greatest scientist of our times, Professor Stephen Hawking, what intelligence he has, he knows about the Universe in its eternity. He does not say anything at all about himself. He is disabled; he speaks with the aid of a computer. What is his advice to us? He says the time is near, the Earth is certain to be destroyed, either a large meteor would destroy us or the war that we have embarked upon shall destroy us or a massive earthquake would bring about our end, and for this reason the human race should settle on a new planet, in a different constellation. Now tell me what this idea is! It is below the Heaven and would some new meteor never come there? Would there be no quarrels about caste and creed? Would there be no fear of death there? There would be the fear of death there as well, and it would take no time to destroy that small planet. Professor Hawking, what is this that you advise us to do? I respect you. Nirmal, he is a great scientist, perhaps you do not know his name. *A Brief History of Time*. I feel it is now time to write *A Very Brief History of Time*. Only a little time remains. If that is all that we can do, why should we do it? The depression that we experience today, the dejection that envelopes us, cannot be removed so easily. And the idea of rebirth can help us to a little extent. But I feel that the scientific mind of today would not accept this at all, [it] would not like such a thing at all. It is clinging on to this body or to another soul that has lost the body and waits for us in the Heaven. The otherness is not only with respect to the body, it could be with respect to souls also. If we were to believe that you are a soul and have nothing to do with this body, that does not make you a Mahatma. You would still scold your neighbour, you would be jealous, just as the Gods are jealous of each other. The Upanishads have these wonderful stories. And for these reasons, all roads are blocked. And let me take you back to van Gogh's painting. Imagine a golden field, not just a field, but much more, a slightly displeased sky and crows, many, many crows. There are three roads through that field. One to the left, a leftist road, and a road to the right, a path to capitalism, and a road in the middle, the middle path. But friends, van Gogh has barred all the three roads. And we would, therefore, not be able to cross the world, this field. The shadow of the crow is present there as well. And therefore the matter is not easy. If you were to call it a rebirth, people would not be convinced. Even if you were to prove it scientifically, they would remain unconvinced, and they would say that science is a specific kind of ideology. Science will not accept this. But science is a branch of a particular kind of philosophical system [of] our times. Let us assume for a moment that our philosophical-religious thought were to issue a commandment that those who do not believe in rebirth will be killed. But how many will you kill; all of them would be born again. What is the gain, in any case, such tricks would not work? What is the third way? Live with amity and love for all beings, protect and care for beings other than human. Keep them in your midst, but how long would you keep them and why? This death would not disappear even then. Thus, Vincent van Gogh closed the middle path for himself. This is a very heart-wrenching thing. I cried for hours while looking at it. It is not as if that by taking the middle path you would be able to walk away, the shadows of the crows [are] there as well. And he closed the green-outline as well. And that path has been made with thumb impressions. In the Upanishads, the thumb has been considered a marker and identity of the soul. Thus, in that painting, you would find the writing of van Gogh's soul. You must see the painting.

And in this story 'Kavve aur Kala Pani', the middle path is not the easy path. What is being pointed out is the path of the soul, the way to reduce the otherness, whether it is the middle path, or the leftist or rightist way, would depend upon the context. You could be anywhere, whatever be your morality, be it the allegiance to the nation, to science or to the entire Universe, so long as you maintain this sense of otherness, they would carry no meaning for you. If we forget otherness, our interest would be the interest of all. Nirmal has used the word '*matalab*' [meaning], and is the most apposite term. And the Baba says, stay here in the guest house; but, no, he wants to return. My narration of the story is also coming to a close. Nirmal, just as Ram also finished his letter to you, this lecture is also over and you must be laughing, and when you laughed you lost your voice as it were. I see you laugh, and ask, 'Ramu, what all have you said?' But Nirmal, I am saying what your story tells me to do.

Now he prepares to leave. The Baba has signed all the papers and documents. He is to return the next day to Delhi. The bus awaits, there are clouds and who are those running towards the bus? They are Masterji and Aghori Baba, who wish to say something to Chhote. I remember this story of [Leo] Tolstoy about three sages, deeply knowledgeable and realised sages, who lived on an island. The church in Moscow came to know of their existence and also the fact that they had no knowledge of theology, and hence sent a bishop to them to instruct. They were well instructed by the bishop in matters of theology, and having done his work, the bishop set out in his boat to the other shore. Meanwhile, the sages forgot the lesson of theology and ran after the bishop to ask him again. The bishop from his boat saw them run over the water towards him.

Similarly, Masterji and Aghori Baba wish to know from Chhote as to what was said, what truth was revealed. They could not hear the truth from Baba, but Chhote could tell them. They tell him, you are going away, going to a big city. You are very fortunate, we would be left behind and no one would care for us. Do tell us what did you hear, what did you learn? Chhote is unable to respond. And what happens when the bus leaves? The same snorting of the bus, the same cloud overhead and crows, thousands of crows.

Namaste.

— five —

The Peacock and the Sage

*Reflections on the Advaita of Architecture**

Thirty-seven years ago Ramana Maharshi lay dying in a hut in his ashram in Tiruvannamalai. Perched on the roof of the hut was a white peacock who shrieked through the night as life drained away from the sage's cancer-devoured body, the blessed body through which for more than half a century Sri Ramana had transmitted the saving truth of self-realisation to a self-forgetful age steeped in the delusion of otherness, the powerful uncaring, enveloping otherness still with us as the century—and doomsayers would quip, humanity too—draws to an end. Who is this peacock, and what is the significance of his shrill lamentation? And what does all of this have to do with architecture?

The peacock is an intimate disciple of the sage, one among numerous non-human creatures—lucky leopards, monkeys, dogs and cows, sparrows and squirrels and snakes and at least one golden mongoose—who had sought the proximity of the sage and no doubt received confidential Upanishadic instruction from him. The disciple cries because he fears that his beloved master will soon be

*Originally published in *India International Centre Quarterly* 15 (2), Summer 1988: pp. 27–30.

dead, but this cannot be the whole message of his wailing. From the 'rooftop', that is, to the whole world, the peacock announces the impending calamity and summons a spiritually starving world to the sage's feet while there is still time. Cosmic weatherman is this creature! But even this is not all that he is communicating, not the whole truth of his torment.

The peacock is a prophet who foresees the crisis of survival all life on Earth faces today, the dark fantasy of world-annihilation having been converted into grim probability by runaway militarisation and unecological industrialisation, mindless reproduction and heartless fanaticism. Imploring the sage to postpone his passing sufficiently to enable humanity to grasp his message of advaita—non-duality—more adequately, the prophet stridently demands of us that we ensure the survival of the world by learning to love it as ourselves.

Expressing its environing power, architecture fashions worlds within the world. Indeed on reflection, it becomes clear that architecture is *avataric*; it is the Absolute incarnate as ambience; it is the perfect image of the world teaching us silently and yet ceaselessly, as do sages, that we and it are one. Architecture is Guru. Is it surprising that Sri Ramana's peacock-pupil should draw attention to the connection between architecture and advaita by choosing as his pupil the roof of a piece of sanctified architecture, the sage's hut? But the peacock is panicking. Without Guru's grace, he is afraid that the sky will fall down upon him. So he howls. (He need not have been anxious, for it is on record that one of the Ramana's last utterances was a solicitous inquiry regarding the plumed *muezzin*'s dinner. Grace is unfailing.)

The sage himself is untroubledly happy inside the hut even as he is dying. For he knows that the hut's diminutive interior is continuous and identical with the infinite sky above and around, the contours of the hut dramatising—not denying—this truth. The hut does not imprison Ramana, the sky does not overawe him. The Earth is rich and large enough for our growth, not for our greed. And we need not succumb to existential anxiety in relation to the apparent nothingness of the cosmos, for it is not other than ourselves; it is self-consciousness itself symbolising the limitlessness of its sphere of manifestation. Life on Earth need neither be deprived nor desolate.

Architecture is the incredible realisation of enclosure as disclosure, and while this may well be regarded as proof of its profundity, the essential *divinity* of architecture is revealed in the following morally and metaphysically extraordinary feature of it: Even the meanest architectural form, say a dungeon, which permits only a trickle of light and air to come in from outside, intensifies for that very reason the contrast between outer and inner space and all the more poignantly, for the same reason, suggests their continuity and identity, and holds out the hope of freedom not only from incarceration but also from ignorance, duality. No architectural form can wholly seal off the inner space it fashions without ceasing to be architecture. A coffin or a tomb may be a sacred construction, but it is not architecture. Barely unsealed torture chambers are shockingly still architecture, but they ought, of course, gallantly to suffer the metamorphosis even of destruction in atonement for their desecration and attempted annihilation of the truth that interiority and infinity of space are one! (Nuclear winter is the condition of the Earth as unredeemable torture chamber, sin unexceedable against architecture and advaita.) Architecture is a Zen master, liberating and scandalising at the same time.

The inner space, interiority, fashioned by architectural form symbolises intimacy and inwardness, the warmth and security of unembattled life. Interiority cannot, self-evidently, afford to be so small and oppressive as to frustrate or distort this sacred task of symbolisation. Architecturally unsanctified smallness can batter intimacy into desperation and, out of warmth, ignite incendiary frenzy and hatred. There is clearly a limit to the economy of inner space—whether of individual dwellings or of neighbourhoods—that architecture can truthfully fashion. Likewise, no architectural form can be so extravagant of size as to bury its suggestion of infinity under the weight of its own gigantic finitude, be it skyscraper or metropolis. Such bigness of indulgence mocks the idea of authority and nourishes tyranny. The idolatry of big and small in architecture or in any other sphere of art or life can only be overcome with the aid of the image of a crying bird, an unceasing sky, and the thatched roof of a sage's small hut. Realisation, not reification, is what is needed for the unfurling of truth's many-splendoured plumage, says the peacock.

It is appropriate here to recall Christ's saying that 'in my Father's house', that is, on an *advaitin view, within the matrix of the unity of self-consciousness*, 'there are many mansions', an inevitable creative variety of forms of manifestation of truth. It is only in self-realisation that we attain to a true love of variety and faithfulness to unity, as opposed to anarchy and authoritarianism, whether in art and architecture or in politics and society. Also of profound importance for a philosophy of architecture is Christ's remark that while birds have their nests, and the fox his hole, the 'Son of Man' has 'nowhere to lay his head upon'. It is only in civilisation and realisation, and not in the barbarism of dualism, old or new, that the troubled spirit of humanity can hope to find rest beyond uncertain lodging and unquestioned belonging, beyond mere nesting and digging in. Resurrection is entrance into the architecture of self-realisation, beyond the imprisonment of womb and tomb, beyond the duality of birth and death.

The advaita of architecture is illumined by the architecture of advaita. Indubitable ultimate reality is the pure reflexivity of self-consciousness, that which *we are*, essentially; that which whatever *is*, is, essentially: *atman*, selfhood, heart, centre, matrix of all manifestation. Self-consciousness is not the consciousness of this or that inner or outer object, grand or subtle, concrete or abstract, but our *sahaja*, spontaneous, uninstructed, consciousness of ourselves as ourselves; and *it* [is] thus formless, *nirakara*, not being the consciousness of any object whose form it might acquire or represent. *Pure being*, it is perfectly symbolised not only by the concentrated catacomb intimacy of the shrine of Lord Vishwanath at Varanasi imaging formless creativity, soul, but also by the extra-mural all-inclusive university of the sky over Sarnath imaging formless compassion, under the banner and within the architecture of which, more than 2,500 years ago, Lord Buddha took his stand and turned the wheel of *dharma* [essential principle of the natural law]. Formlessness is one. Lord Vishwanath and Lord Buddha are one; creativity and compassion are one; inner and outer space, soul and sky, are one; atman and Brahman are one. Singular formless self-consciousness, intimate infinity, Atman-Brahman is creative and compassionately inclusive of all forms, natural and cultural, archetypal and architectural, concrete and abstract, static and dynamic, and throbs with an infinite reserve of creativity, as *AUM*, *AUM*, *AUM*! Sacred Symbol and substance of ultimate reality, *AUM* is also the structure of the universal experience of architecture as *indwelling*, comprehending—and exceeding—wakefulness, dream, and the reserve power of deep sleep; blessed gifts of home. *AUM* is home.

The deepest truth of architecture is the truth also of our embodiment. Analogously to architecture, our bodies open out through the senses [to] the outgoing mind into the vastness of space and time and circumstance suggestive of the infinity of godhead or Brahman. And again, strictly analogously to architecture's disclosure of interiority, the inwardness which our bodily life makes possible in its poise of yoga or contemplation reveals the truth of self-consciousness, atman. And like Lord Vishwanath and Lord Buddha, the limitless space within which we situate our bodily life and the interiority of self-consciousness where we situate ourselves are continuous and identical, in the way the *angan*, inner courtyard, of a traditional Indian house, is continuous and identical with the visible sky above it. (It is the angan, heart-centre of domesticity, that initiates Indian family life into the advaita, non-duality, of immediacy and infinity, samsara and nirvana, destiny and freedom.) The body too like architecture and angan is Guru. *We cannot honour our body and not want to honour our environment. But who cares? Besides the peacock on the roof, who cares?*

The fixity of architecture powerfully images being, the autonomy of self-consciousness, finality of Atman-Brahman. Architecture *is*; like God, it is *that* it is. But architecture is also an unfurling and environing power, *spider-power*, drawing out from its existential stillness, and yet situating within itself, all the rhythm of life's action and imagination and renunciation; work and play and rest; wakefulness and dream and sleep. Most singularly advaitin among the arts, architecture unalienatingly dramatises being *and* power, reality *and* its circumambient manifestation, the spider *and* his weaving, the peacock *and* his wailing, the sage *and* his teaching.

Who knows what the architecture of existence will unfurl in the years and century and millennium ahead? Who besides Sri Ramana and the screaming peacock on his roof?

— six —

THE FIREFLY'S PRAYER

*A Parable of Sri Ramakrishna Paramahansa**

An old fort stood on a hill which had once been covered with thick grass and flowering trees. The grass on the hill had withered and the trees did not bloom because there had been no rains for a long, long time. Without flowers and leaves on their branches, the trees looked like ghosts on moon-lit nights. No one dared to live in the fort any more.

A wandering firefly found a shady nook in the outer wall of the fort, a hollow space between two slabs of stone. 'It is so hot even in the shade!', the firefly moaned. 'May it rain, may it rain, may this land be green again!', it prayed.

As the sun set behind the hill in the evening, clouds gathered in the sky and a gentle breeze began to blow. The firefly leapt into the current. Gliding high and low left and right, the little acrobat glowed with pride as it traced loops of light against the darkening sky.

'I am the light of the world, I chase the darkness away!', thought the firefly, humming like a top. The breeze turned into a gale and the firefly was lucky to find its way back to its shelter.

As the gale swept the clouds aside, stars appeared in the sky.

*Originally published in *First City*, April 2002, p. 37.

'Fifty, sixty, seventy, eighty,' counted the firefly, but lost count as hundreds of stars filled the sky. 'We are the light of the world, we chase the darkness away!', they thought, glittering like cities in the night.

Lightning flashed and thunder brought back the clouds to hide the stars.

A round and radiant moon now pushed its way out of a huddle of clouds and stood high without a rival in the sky. 'I am the light of the world, I chase the darkness away!', thought the moon.

Hungry clouds devoured the moon, swelling and spreading across the sky. 'We shut out the light of the world, we are the darkness!', they thought.

The sky and the Earth trembled as lightning and thunder tore the clouds apart.

'Is this the end of the world?', wondered the firefly, falling deep into sleep.

And then it poured and poured with rain.

The rain stopped a little before dawn.

The first rays of the rising sun stretched out like hands of friendship towards all beings.

'In the midst of darkness, there is light,' the sun seemed to say. 'The moon shines when I rest at night. And on a dark night when the moon does not appear, travellers are guided by the stars. And when even the stars are hidden by the clouds, we are led by the light which shines within us, the light of hope, the light of happiness.'

The firefly became aware of its own light and woke up.

Soft grass and wildflowers had sprouted all along the wall of the fort. Water flowed in the river-bed below the hill. The firefly's prayer had been heard.

— *seven* —

Is Our Heart On the Right Side?*

Preface

Sri Ramana Maharshi tells the story (I have taken the storyteller's liberty of embellishing it) of a king who had conquered the world, but who was terrified of his own shadow. Whenever he stepped out of the safety of his palace into the real world, his shadow would fall across his path, coiled around his feet like a snake, as he thought. He hated his shadow, it slighted him, mocked his majesty.

So great was this king's hatred of his shadow, Ramana tells us, that he ordered his security guards to throw it into the palace moat to be devoured by alligators. When they failed to carry out this order, the king had the guards thrown into the moat! The king now rarely stirred out of his palace.

One day, however, Ramana says, the king walked out of his palace in the hot sun and was inevitably stopped in his tracks by his shadow. But the emperor had a smile on his face as he encountered his dread enemy; he had found a way of getting rid of his shadow, or so he thought.

*Originally published in *First City*, January 2003, pp. 36–39; reprinted in *Postcolonial Studies* 6 (1), April 2003: pp. 57–64.

'Shadow!', he thundered, 'say your last prayers. I shall soon be free of you forever.' 'Give me a spade!', he commanded, and his prime minister gave him a spade. And the conqueror of the world worked like a common labourer at midday under a merciless sun, digging and digging, digging a grave for his shadow, a pit to bury it in. As the pit deepened, the king's shadow went down and down and was soon at the bottom of a very deep pit indeed, trapped like a hunted animal.

'Shadow!', the tyrant roared, 'I shall now fill up this pit and you will sleep in your grave till eternity. May your soul rest in peace, and may I rule my kingdom in peace!' The king started filling up the pit and his shadow came up and up and up and was soon staring at the king again.

Ramana does not tell us what the king did next, but he tells *us* something to think about. 'If you are afraid of your shadow falling across your path, and think of it as a curse, take your mind off it. Turn towards the sun, and your shadow will be behind you, ready to follow you like a friend, not confront you like an enemy,' says Ramana Maharshi.

We try to bury our unalloyed anxieties and unappeased hatreds and unfulfilled desires into our unconscious minds, hoping, like the king, to give them a decent burial. But they do not go away. They surface in our dreams to torment us, they intervene in the events of our waking life like bad omens, and they rob us of our sleep. So we become obsessed with them and never stop thinking about them. If only we do neither, that is, neither repress nor revive them, but turn all the energy of our consciousness towards the depth of its own centre, self, and the limitless vastness of its reach, symbolised powerfully by the sun and the sky, our fears and hatreds and desires will become transformed into energies of work, play and rest; and we will see and treat the world as ourselves and be at peace with it.

However, this miracle of transformation is not possible if we remain attached to the idea of ourselves as being exclusively our bodies, driven by the biological heart on the left side of our chest. Our true heart, Sri Ramana teaches, is on the right side where there is nothing, only a depth and vastness which holds everything in its embrace of compassion, including our bodies!

I

The austerely advaita teaching of Sri Ramana Maharshi is enlivened by what looks like a quaint insistence on his part that atman's seat in the human body is on the right side of the chest, corresponding almost exactly to the biological heart of the left side. Of course, Sri Ramana makes it clear again and again that this anatomical identification of atman is only for the benefit of those who are unable to be rid of the false identification of themselves with their body and mind, body for short; that in truth atman had no physical location at all.

Yet, reading through all of the master's conversation and writings, one gets the impression that this relegation of his doctrine of the spiritual heart on the right side to secondary importance is also a concession to those who, imperfect advaitins, shun physical analogies even as they fear the world. Again and again, the master reverts to the doctrine of the heart on the right side, refers to an obscure Ayurveda text and also to the Sita Upanishad in support of it, and also sometimes impatiently dismisses requests for authoritative support of his novel doctrine on the ground that his experience confirms it and that he is not in need of any external authority for his doctrine.

Experientially, it is on the right side of the centre of the chest that Sri Ramana's Koham (Who am I?) *sadhana* [disciplined and dedicated practice] yields a powerful current of awareness as is testified by a number of *sadhaka*s [practitioner/seeker], and indeed the metaphor of the heart on the right side is a profound one. The biological heart on the left is the seat of all our anxieties and partial, fleeting arrogant pleasures connected with *dehatmabuddhi*, the I-am-this-body orientation of *ajnana*, ignorance.

Ruthlessly corrective of this delusion, this tragic investment of all worth in the biological heart, is the heart on the right side of which the master speaks, the heart which is biologically non-existent and yet the power of which is felt in sadhana and even the contemplation of the very idea of which at least weakens considerably the hold of dehatmabuddhi. There appears in thought and imagination the idea of an alternative centre of our being, a non-corporeal reality mysteriously lodged within our body which rivals in power and benevolence the fickle pump on the left, a very simple and secure foundation for faith. (Needless to say, in those rare cases where the biological heart is on the right, the spiritual heart will have to be and will be able to be imagined as being on the left side, although Sri Ramana has not said so; but in our reflections, on his teaching, we can continue to think of the spiritual heart as being on the right without qualification.) But is there any other kind of support for Sri Ramana's doctrine besides the corrective role of it and the authority of his declaration?

Ramana Maharshi often used to say that everybody knew that he or she was most fundamentally centred on the right side of the chest because whenever we wish to point to ourselves we touch the right side of our chest with our forefinger. Why do we do this?

There is, of course, the convention of pointing to people with our forefinger when we wish to refer to them ostensively, and the ritual of pointing to oneself by touching our chest with our forefinger or pointing the forefinger in the direction of our chest is an obvious imitation of ostensive reference to others, but this cannot be the whole story.

That this cannot be the whole story is shown by the fact that when I point to myself in this way and ask you if you really mean me, which is the standard occasion of employment of this ritual, I simply do not need physically to point to myself at all. I could merely utter the words, 'Who, me?', and omit the pointing gesture and still be perfectly understood. It cannot even be the case that apparent ostensive pointing to oneself takes place when speaking is for some contingent reason difficult, as when you are too far away to hear me or when I have lost my voice or do not wish to be heard, etc. I apparently ostensively point to myself, point my forefinger towards the right side of my chest normally when you are well within hearing distance from me, and when my vocal cords are quite unimpaired and I wish to underscore in a special way the force of my clearly uttered words, 'Who, me?', that is, by way of pointing my forefinger towards my chest.

What is then the real communicative thrust of this ritual of the inverted forefinger? It wordlessly explicates the words, 'Who, me?', as follows: I am pretending that my forefinger is the forefinger of a third person who is answering a fourth person's question about you, the second person, the question, 'Who does he mean?', and the third person physically points to me in answer to this question, indicating that you mean me. Do you? And this explication is put across to you not in some uncheckable irredeemably private occult way, but by means of the visible, although imaginative, employment of all the paraphernalia of multiple endorsements which the hinted third and fourth persons of the ritual represent.

Thus far, the ritual is a tribute to the power of ostensive reference, the hold of *dehabhava*, the physicalist orientation of our ordinary consciousness. Yet it is precisely *dehatmavada*, the 'I am this body' illusion, which the ritual repudiates at a deeper level. For as a manifest fantasy of ostensive self-reference, the inverted forefinger dramatises the impossibility of such self-reference, something which should not be impossible if I were merely a body. What a pity [Ludwig] Wittgenstein never met Ramana!

Suppose by *atmavichara* (self-inquiry), by *sravana*, *manana* and *nididhyasana* (hearing, reflecting and meditating on the teaching), and by the grace of a guru, I reach intellectually the conclusion that I alone am real, that all else which appears to be not-I is really I, myself, the appearance of not-I being illusion and not reality. Suppose further that this conclusion, although strong, is nevertheless quite definitely this side of advaita siddhi—so that at the most I regard the conclusion as only the intellectually and somewhat insecurely understood statement of my guru that I alone am reality. Would I not in imagination then turn to my guru and address to him the words, 'Who, me?' Would I not be driven in imagination even physically to point to myself as I utter those words?

Indeed there remains always about self-consciousness this wondering about itself, not wondering that it is this or that, but wondering just that it is, whether or not one is deliberately engaged in atmavichara. This self-wonder, this combination of amazement and certainty that one is, is just what is more grossly also involved in what occurs communicatively when I physically point to myself and ask you, 'Who, me?', in connection with some possibly quite trivial matter relating to you and me and our world.

The foundation of all human communication is addressing, the vocative identification of one another by human beings, that is, their identification of one another not as being of this or that kind, possessing this or that kind, possessing this or that characteristic, but as themselves, *nirguna* [without form or tangible attributes] centres of self-consciousness. It is in consequence of vocative identification, of addressing one another, and subsequent to it, that we go on to communicate to one another a variety of things about ourselves and the world, but in vocative identification, we essentially merely stir one another to a nirguna conception of ourselves.

We do not, of course, easily always or even much or at all notice this, but in a variety of situations, and not merely through philosophical analysis, this is brought home to us in the thick of our worldly communicative life as the essential truth of ourselves and as the essential message of that life when all that has to be said is said and there remains a bare nirguna indication of ourselves as that, that we are. Love, aloneness, joy and peace also bring this insight.

At a deep level, therefore, we may regard everyone who addresses us as a guru, like the innumerable gurus of Dattatreya, drawing our attention to our nirguna absolutist mode of self-consciousness. Because our wonder at our own real status remains always, we would wish to ask anyone at all who in addressing us necessarily restores us to our atmic status, the rhetorical question, 'Who, me?', and we might cause these words to be accompanied by the magic ritual of pointing with our forefinger to our heart on the right side of our chest.

Thus, the act of pointing to the right side of our chest with our forefinger to which Sri Ramana draws our attention to remind us of the fact that we do really take ourselves to be centred there, is indeed full of mystery, is the oldest ritual of human communicative Veda. It is the aboriginal ritual of *ascharyam* (wonder) of Atman-Brahman, its eternal wonder at being all that is, one and only reality. Interestingly, *advaitin uttara mimamsa* [a school of Indian philosophy] teaching becomes involved in this magic *purvamimamsa* ritual, witnessing to the unity of Vedanta.

Our self-wonder is never a doubting, except in a mysteriously fallen condition. It is play and it is in play that Atman-Brahman unfurls itself as an apparent plurality of subjects and objects, subjects pointing to one another and the world or aspects of the world in ascharyam and, as it were deeply always to say, 'He, me, you, this, that and that other, are all one, all me,' *sarvamkhaluidam brahma*.

II

It has been recorded that in a dream or vision a devotee received *sparshadiksha* (initiation by touch) from Sri Ramana which consisted in the master pressing with his forefinger the right side of the devotee's chest. (Wittgenstein was struck by Luther's remark that faith is under the right nipple.) Could it not be that in touching ourselves with our forefinger on the right side of our chest in mock ostensive reference to ourselves we imagine ourselves to be the recipients of such *diksha* [initiation]? Do we not indeed in and through that ritual proclaim, however disguisedly, that we are *dikshita* [one who is ordained], even that we are self-realised Atman-Brahman?

All are jnanis, and each human being who speaks to another is a secret guru initiating the other into advaita sadhana. But for an unshakable realisation of that, we need the grace of Ramana Maharshi, who had until as recently as 53 years ago physically pressed upon us the truth of ourselves. May we all at least in dream receive his sparshadiksha, be touched on the right side of our chest by him.

The doctrine of the heart on the right also bears a tantric interpretation, tantric in the fundamental sense of involving a transformation of adversity or handicap into a supreme spiritual advantage. Symbolically one can regard the situation of the biological heart on the left as the original sin, a deviation leftwards from the centre of our being, in consequence of which all our attention is fixed on questions of bare physical survival and well-being, important though these are, although exclusive concentration on physical survival and well-being is not even the wisest way of ensuring these things.

Avidya or primal ignorance and obscurity can also be seen as symbolised by this leftward shift and centring of our concerns. So powerful is this shift that a mere concentration of our attention upon the centre of our being, that is, as symbolised by the centre of our chest, the *anahata* centre, does not suffice to correct it, to bring us back to the centre of things, the truth of incorruptible satchidananda [absolute consciousness-bliss]. Only the powerful symbolism of the spiritual heart on the right can redeem us, annul the error of our samsaric leftward shift. In view of the samsaric naturalness of the leftward shift, the *dehatma* [body-soul] obsession, the idolatrous exclusive nursing of our physical individuality, the violence of the corrective rightward shift to which Sri Ramana calls us, is properly describable as a tantric *tapasya* [austerity], a reversal of the inverted order of our fallenness, a putting right and a setting upright of ourselves.

Tantra is not in its essentiality offensive rebelliousness and disregard of normality in shocking ritual, perversely important though even such abhorrence can symbolically be as a corrective to our more fundamentally unnatural worldliness. A shifting of attention from the biological heart on the left to the spiritual heart on the right is *sahajatantra*, a general and yet supremely powerful atonement of our imagination, our attention.

What a marvellous upsetting of conventional samsaric anatomy this is! It rivals the image of the Aswattha tree in the Gita, interpretable readily as the inverted tree whose roots reach out skywards and whose fruits transform the Earth, the image of illumined life which draws its real sustenance from above and gives all in transformative power to what is below.

The heart on the right is the saving absurdity of which also Kierkegaard ought to have spoken, the absurdity which alone can save us from the insanity and delusion of avidya. Obsession with the biological heart on the left and the worldliness which such obsession fosters is the most deeply ingrained *vamamarga* [forest-path/glade] of our nature, more offensive in what it entails for the whole of our lives than the most shocking irresponsibilities of deluded tantrikas.

The doctrine of the heart on the right is the true foundation of all tantra of the *daksinamarga* [right-hand path], lovely, auspicious, supremely powerful, *mangalamaya* [aupicious, prosperous]. (Political left and right are both spiritually left, biology-obsessed and life-denying.)

A human being is a tantrika, a converter of apparent handicap into supreme advantage, if only and powerfully symbolically because (s)he is a biped and transforms the apparent handicap and awkwardness of two footedness into the supreme advantage of a stance without which there would be no human love and communication as we know these things, no interface in human life, no looking upwards, heavenwards, in prayer and aspiration, no fear of falling which symbolises our heightened awareness of possibilities and responsibilities towards these possibilities. Symbolically and substantially Sri Ramana's doctrine of the heart on the right is no less revolutionary and tantric a step forward in the evolution of human consciousness than bipedality, and if only we were to live the doctrine fully, it could even transform human life in the way that bipedality has done.

It is characteristic of the absolute harmony with the most developed existential and aesthetic sensibility of our age with which one associates Sri Ramana, that he should indicate quietly, unstridently, with the innocence of a Paul Klee drawing, and yet with all the Shakti or Shiva, the true way of sahajatantra and future evolution represented by his doctrine of the heart on the right.

On the right side of our chest, corresponding to the biological heart on the left, there is nothing like a pump or any organ, sensory or motor, that we can identify, and yet there is there a nothingness, not the nothingness of despairing nihilism or absurdism, but the nothingness of *chidakasha* [consciousness-space], either of infinite consciousness. Can there be greater faith than this, that we should invest our all in a biologically non-existent heart whose mystical location on the right side of the chest tantalises and transforms the harried and fickle muscle on the left?

What a pity Simone Weil and Albert Camus did not visit Tiruvannamalai!

That the advaitin path of Sri Ramana as a whole is tantra and not merely his doctrine of the heart on the right, is even more important to discern. What is a more persistent obstacle and handicap and embarrassment not only in the spiritual life, but in all higher social and cultural life than the divided and limited and divisive and limiting ego, *ahamkara*? Transforming this apparently insuperable disadvantage into omnipotence by stirring it to a depth of self-consciousness, advancing it on a self-sacrificial journey of self-knowledge in search of the true 'I' of which it is but a shadow, is supreme tantra, is the path of Sri Ramana.

Sri Ramana often said that *Aham* ('I') was even greater as a mantra than *AUM*, not separative shadowy ahamkara but the supreme I-am-that-I-am, *soham*, the very meaning of 'Jehova', the very *purusha* [man/pure consciousness] whose sacrifice as described in the Rigveda is the foundation of all that is.

If the ego is a heart-breaking obstacle in the way of all higher human life, the answer is not to indulge it or stifle it, the answers of individualism and collectivism, but to hold it to its own true form, soham (I am that) which is the form of the reality of all that is and can be and thus links all in community without sacrificing the individuality of any, thus harmonising the truth in individualism and collectivism, the twin impulses of our age. Can there be anything more satisfying to the tantric imagination than the discovery that salvation lies in the true form of that satanical non-starter and tyrant illusion, ego, in self-sacrificing atmavichara, self-inquiry?

The ego is not to be indulged or stifled, it demands unmasking, a task for which our age has a special genius but which refuses in its psychology and sociology and medicine to interrogate the ego, except as in panicky collectivism or despairing nihilism by drowning it or drugging it, whereas what we are meant to do in the light of Sri Ramana's teaching is to look it in the face and thus sacrifice it and resurrect it at the same time, as soham, I-am-that-I-am, unfettered consciousness.

In connection with tantra, true tantra and not the self-advertising caricature of it with which we are in these flaunting times so overburdened, we cannot fail to think of Ramana Maharshi's contemporary, Mahatma Gandhi. It may be regarded as unusual to think of Gandhiji as a tantrika, and yet there is no way other than the tantric of understanding his sadhana of *satya* [truth] and *ahimsa* [non-violence].

Telling your adversary what you think of him and what you plan to do in relation to him is foolishness, a supreme handicap, by ordinary non-tantric standards of worldly battle. But the sadhana of truth which Gandhiji practised and taught on an unprecedentedly massive scale holds the opposite to be the case; it maintains that nothing disarms the adversary in a global moral and spiritual struggle involving exploiting masters and exploited slaves than telling the masters that you are going to cease to obey them in all the wrongdoing which they have so far compelled you and bribed you into participating in, provided a vital condition is observed, the condition of ahimsa which was the other arm of Gandhiji's tantric sadhana.

Can anything on the face of it be more of an impediment in the struggle of millions of Indians for a dignified autonomous existence than their reluctance, springing possibly from malnutrition and centuries of servitude, to take violent physical revenge upon their numerically weaker alien rulers or alienated ruling class? Yet, this very apparently cowardly reluctance can become transformed into a species-saving spiritual weapon of our times as ahimsa, as courageous refusal to perpetuate the violence of exploitation as authors of it or participants in it and facing faithfully all the consequences of this great refusal for the sake of the truth, that without sacrifice truth cannot spread, which is the very fundamental teaching of the Vedas.

Thus, we have in Ramana Maharshi and Mahatma Gandhi two practitioners of authentic tantra. Sri Ramana teaches the way of transforming the ego into Atman-Brahman without destroying its true form, which is true ahimsa, and Gandhiji demonstrates the large-scale possibility of transforming the cowardice and selfishness of exploited humanity into the unbeatable spiritual power of love which does not seek to harm but also does not obey bullies and cowards.

It is amazing that Maharshi and Mahatma never met. Sri Ramana remaining rooted in Tiruvannamalai and Gandhiji restlessly, and yet always godwardly, moving all over the place in the hectic first half of the twentieth century. The tantric truth of the former and the courage of the latter must combine if there is to be not only Indian but even human survival in dignity.

The ritual of mock ostensive self-reference is rivalled in its power of repudiation of dehatmavada by another omnipresent everyday ritual—the unavoidable 'looking at one another's eyes'. Which is our way of 'looking at one another'. Why do we do this, and what does the ritual say? Why do not we look at one another's hands when we look at one another? Because we would self-defeatingly regard one another as objects, things, hands, merely, if we were to look at one another's hands to 'look at one another', to realise the utter reciprocity and unity of awareness—*sambodhana*—suggested by that phrase.

In looking at one another's eyes, in the simultaneity of that magic extensional realisation of self-consciousness, we don't look at eyes as an ophthalmologist might; we simultaneously deflect objectivist looking back and forth between one another, causing its consumption in the sacred fire of self-consciousness, revealing the divinity of advaitin seeing, *divyadrishti*, however fleetingly and reversibly, but indubitably. What else are *divyachakshu* (Divine eye) but our own eyes unburdened of the dross of objectivist delusion, hauntingly beautiful in that awakening like Sri Ramana's eyes?

Teri ankhon ke siva duniya mein rakha kya hai!

In looking at one another's eyes in this way we realisingly affirm our utter simultaneity, our *ananyatva*, non-otherness, for perfect simultaneity is only of self with itself in the *spanda* (vibrancy) of self-consciousness. Simultaneously, with that realisation and affirmation, we repudiate dehatmavada, the idea that bodily separativeness is the essence of ourselves. Looking at one another's eyes in that uncovetous glancing way of oneness is a complete Upanishad, a recurrent Vedic mantra in *mauna* [silence, reticence] of our everyday life.

Holding hands is an equivalent realisation of the unity and spanda of self-consciousness, especially for the blind.

— eight —

FOREWORD TO THE ENGLISH TRANSLATION OF *HARILAL GANDHI: A LIFE**

Less than 20 years younger than his father, *satyagrahi* in South Africa at the age of 15, devoted to his mother and brothers throughout his life, Harilal Gandhi was yet a fierce critic of his father.

Harilal could not understand Bapu's conviction that one should love other people's children as much as one's own; more if their need was greater. Like Nathuram Godse could not understand Gandhi's special concern for vulnerable Muslim minorities in India after partition. Harilal, of course, did not ever want to kill his father. But the comparison is instructive.

The education that Gandhi's ashrams provided was one of India's greatest experiments with truth. No caste restrictions, obligatory manual labour, no gender discrimination, the development of religious tolerance—all that the great ashrams of antiquity lacked. The uniqueness of this experiment seems to me to have hardened Bapu against the good that conventional education could provide, and Harilal was too dazzled by modern education and lifestyles

*Originally published in C. B. Dalal (2007), *Harilal Gandhi: A Life*, trans. Tridip Suhrud, Orient Longman, Chennai, pp. *xi–xii*.

(as his father had been for a while) to take seriously the alternative education that Bapu was experimenting with.

A clash of fundamentalisms seems to me to characterise the conflict between father and son regarding many matters.

Harilal gave himself up to alcohol, even as Gandhi gave himself up to Ramanama. The son suffered privations, the father won martyrdom and, possibly, moksha.

There are greater similarities between them than we would care to notice.

On one point Bapu seems to me to be theologically wrong. He thought that his own carnal nature as a youth was punished by God in the form of a bad son. Surely God must have more things to do than punish fathers with recalcitrant sons!

Harilal's rebelliousness must have tempered Bapu's ego by the realisation that he could not control everything.

Harilal's role in the spiritual growth of Gandhi cannot be overestimated.

Nor can one withhold criticism of Harilal's moral failures.

I had the privilege as a child to see Harilal Kaka during his visit to my father's home in Delhi and observe the great affection that my father, Devadas, Gandhiji's youngest son, had for his older brother.

I am myself an old man now. It seems to me that in Gandhiji's life Harilal was a morally non-conformist angel whose alcoholic stupor indicated, by way of caricature, the complete renunciation of ego which is the *svaraj* [self-rule] of moksha.

Some of the rambling wisdom of Gandhiji's addresses after prayer meetings in Delhi towards the end of his life is suggestive of inebriation which is greater than the sanity and worldly wisdom of teetotallers and enables me to see Harilal Kaka's self-destructive alcoholism with more compassion.

May this English translation of Sri Chandulal Bhagubhai Dalal's Gujarati biography of Harilal Gandhi by Sri Tridip Suhrud urge us to think beyond the clash between son and father, and see a deeper mystery which united them.

— *nine* —

Whitehead on the Distrust of Speculative Philosophy*

Whitehead's most straightforward account of speculative philosophy is to be found in *Process and Reality* (1957a: *viii*). In the preface to that book, he lists nine 'prevalent habits of thought which are repudiated [in that book] in so far as concerns their influence on philosophy'. The first on this list of repudiated habits of thought is 'the distrust of speculative philosophy' (ibid.). This distrust is a feature of much twentieth-century philosophy, and it might be instructive to try to appreciate Whitehead's reasons for disregarding the suspicions with which speculative philosophy has been viewed generally, and especially in our own time.

I

At the level of popular opinion, the distrust of speculative philosophy is hard to distinguish from the distrust of speculative thinking as such, so that it might be useful to examine first the nature of the distrust of speculative thought in general in order to understand better the

*Originally published in *International Philosophical Quarterly* 12 (3), September 1972: pp. 389–414.

special misgivings which people have regarding the usefulness and legitimacy of speculative philosophy. The most obvious example of speculative thinking is imaginative literature. No philosopher or scientist has any serious quarrel with imaginative literature so long as it does not claim cognitive significance. But it often does, and that is when it lays itself open to the charge of encroaching upon the territory of exact knowledge. And this charge is often justified. The scientific falsehoods and half-truths of literature are legion. And yet it cannot be denied that great literature often succeeds in disclosing in flashes of insight the ultimate nature of things, unsuspected by science and common sense. Whitehead takes this penetrating quality of literature seriously and assigns to it an important place in philosophical discovery. In illustration of this power of literature he quotes: '... the line and a half of poetry in which Euripides compresses the main philosophical problems which have tortured European thought from his day to the present—"Zeus, whether thou art Compulsion of Nature or Intelligence of Mankind, to Thee I prayed"' (Whitehead 1933: 291–92).

[David] Hume, says Whitehead, would be able to find no 'impressions of sensation' from which to derive 'Zeus', 'Intelligence', 'Compulsion' or the would-be persuasiveness which we call 'prayer', and yet the line expresses the profound spectacle of life passing into religious emotion.

It is unnecessary to multiply examples to appreciate the profound philosophical perceptiveness of great literature. Not even the most hardheaded sceptic can fail to notice this. Nevertheless, there is something about imaginative literature which we deeply distrust, something which is disruptive of the straightforward common sense and scientific procedures of obtaining knowledge. What is this disruptive element? An answer is provided by Whitehead in his discussion of speculative, as opposed to practical, reason. His answer is that while speculation as such is inherently disruptive, 'speculative reason' is not; in fact, speculation as controlled by reason is the very foundation of all progress in life and thought.

It must not be forgotten that the speculative capacity of literature has its roots in anarchic imagination, running wildly beyond all limits of credibility. It is this anarchic character of imagination which lays all speculation open to profound distrust. There is in Whitehead's book, *The Function of Reason* (1929), a highly generalised account of the role of anarchic imagination in the development of human mentality, to which it would be useful to turn at this stage. Whitehead there develops the thesis that history discloses two tendencies. One tendency is exemplified in the decay of physical nature: 'With stealthy inevitableness, there is degradation of energy. The sources of energy sink downward and downward. Their very matter wastes'. The other tendency is exemplified by the recurrences in nature, 'by the yearly renewal of nature in the spring' (ibid.), and by the upward course of biological evolution. This is the 'originative element' in history. It appears as appetition for a novel experience in all life and in mankind as imagination. The reason is the 'self-discipline of the originative element in history' (ibid.). Apart from such self-discipline, this element is anarchic. But apart from anarchic appetition—in mankind's unbridled speculative curiosity—there is a mere repetitive experience which reduces life to non-entity by divesting it of all novelty and zest. As Whitehead puts it, 'Apart from anarchic appetition, nature is doomed to slow descent towards nothingness. Mere repetitive experience gradually eliminates element after element and fades towards vacuity' (ibid.: 27). But, of course, 'mere anarchic appetition accomplishes quickly the same end' (ibid.).

Thus, Whitehead's view on the question of the usefulness of speculative thought as exemplified in the more extreme forms of poetic fancy and imaginative literature would seem to be this, that while left to itself, such speculation stultifies life and thought, it is nevertheless the very basis of the emergence of more advanced types of life and thought when it subjects itself to the discipline of Reason. The reason is able to accomplish these advances because it 'civilizes the brute force of anarchic appetition' (ibid.). Describing the appearance of Reason on the scene he says,

> But when mentality is working at a high level, it brings novelty into the appetitions of mental experience. In this function, there is an element of sheer anarchy. But mentality now becomes self-regulative, it canalizes its own appetitions by its own judgment. It introduces a higher appetition which discriminates among its own anarchic productions. Reason appears. (Ibid.)

This is really the appearance of speculative reason, the self-discipline of imagination, no longer anarchic but ordered, and yet retaining the speculative boldness of its wayward beginnings. Such rational, or at any rate in some sense 'orderly', speculation first appears in the history of human thought in the shape of prophecy, and as inspiration. 'Seers, prophets, men with a new secret, appeared. They brought to the world fire, or salvation, or release or moral insight. Their common character is to be bearers of some imaginative novelty, relevant and yet transcending traditional ways' (ibid.: 52).

But there is another kind of reason, practical reason, which is much older. It does not seek to transcend the 'traditional ways'. Its function in the art of life (the function of reason according to Whitehead is to promote the art of life) is the discovery and enforcement of successful methods for achieving the purposes of survival. It is the 'discipline of shrewdness' (ibid.)—the discipline of technique and method. The speculative reason, on the contrary, questions all methods, but is in its essence itself 'untrammelled by method' (ibid.). 'Its function is to pierce into the general reasons beyond limited reasons, to understand all methods as correlated in a nature of things only to be grasped by transcending all method' (ibid.: 51).

Out of the conflict of these two functions of reason arises the distrust of freedom of thought. It is the triumph of practical reason when such distrust assumes the form of ideological impatience and repression—religious, moral or scientific. Whitehead points out that the passionate demand for freedom of thought is an ultimate moral claim of the speculative understanding, and the perennial struggle between Reason and Authority is 'tinged with bitterness by the intrusion of this sentiment of an ultimate moral claim' (ibid.: 30). Part of this demand is for the right to revise the successful symbolism of society, symbolism which expresses its hitherto successful methods of survival and continued existence. Commenting on this right elsewhere, Whitehead (1928: 104) says, 'Those societies which cannot combine reverence to their symbols with freedom of revision must ultimately decay either from anarchy or from the slow atrophy of a life stifled by useless shadows'.

II

Keeping in mind these general observations of Whitehead on the nature, limits and scope of speculative reason, we can now set the present discussion of the distrust of speculative thought in another light. In the fields of science and philosophy, this distrust takes two concrete forms. In science it expresses itself as the distrust of speculatively arrived at theories which transcend the limitations of the procedures of observation and induction. In the case of philosophy, the suspicion chiefly falls upon speculative metaphysics.

The classical expression of the distrust of speculation in science is [Francis] Bacon's stringent requirement that scientific investigation should confine itself to the careful observation and accumulation of particular facts, that its generalisations should be strictly based on these observations. In violation of this requirement the history of scientific discovery shows how successful speculative reason has been in discovering scientific principles. Indeed, scientists and philosophers of science are beginning to repudiate the Baconian conception of the nature of the scientific activity. In his book, *The Logic of Scientific Discovery* (1959: 169), Karl Popper expresses this sentiment in the following words: 'I don't see any reason why these conjectures [speculative scientific theories] should be inspired only by the accumulation of a large mass of inductive observations'. Also, he quotes in support of his view the following extract from a letter written by [Albert] Einstein to him: 'Altogether I really do not at all like the now fashionable "positivistic" tendency of clinging to what is observable ... and I think that theory cannot be fabricated out of the results of observation *but that it can only be invented*' (ibid.: 458).

Whitehead expresses the same thought much more forcefully in *Process and Reality* (1957a: 7). Talking of the approach of rigid empiricism in science and philosophy he says,

> In natural science, this rigid method is the Baconian method of induction, a method which, if consistently pursued, would have left science where it found it. What Bacon omitted was the play of free imagination controlled by the requirements of coherence and logic. The true method of discovery is like the flight of an aeroplane. It starts from the ground of particular observation; it makes a flight in the

> thin air of imaginative generalization; and it again lands for renewed observation rendered acute by rational interpretation.

Now examples of the success and demonstrations of the necessity of speculation in science would not satisfy the critic of speculative *philosophy*. He would feel that speculation in science, howsoever bold it might be, nevertheless constantly justifies itself by appealing to the facts of experience; indeed, its sole purpose is merely to further our understanding of these facts. It is, therefore, a purely methodological supplementation of the Baconian conception of scientific inquiry. Speculation does not make science less fact-oriented and empirical than it has always been supposed to be. Speculation in philosophy, on the other hand, goes beyond all bounds of actual and possible experience; it has no contact with the every-day world of common sense whatsoever. In the name of ultimate reality, strange entities are invoked which no one encounters in experience. This is the belief not only of people who have no intimate acquaintance with the work of speculative philosophers, but also of many professional philosophers. In the history of philosophy, speculative thinking has been deeply suspect at least since the time of the British empiricists. What is the basis and justification of this suspicion?

There is one curious feature of the professional philosophers' distrust of speculative philosophy which throws light on this question. Philosophers who have doubted the legitimacy and usefulness of speculative philosophy have differed greatly amongst themselves as to the proper function and aim of philosophy. Hume distrusted speculative philosophy and suggested his own view of what philosophy should do. [Immanuel] Kant distrusted speculative philosophy and prescribed a different procedure for philosophy. And in their own ways, [Bertrand] Russell, the logical positivists, the linguistic philosophers—all of whom distrust speculative philosophy—recommend very different ways of doing philosophy. There is also, of course, [Søren] Kierkegaard, who distrusted speculative philosophy and, in the process, founded existentialism.

Leaving aside Kierkegaard and the existentialists for the moment, it becomes obvious on reflection that what these philosophers have rejected or failed to appreciate in different degrees is the central problem of speculative philosophy, the problem of conceiving the nature of 'ultimate reality', 'substance', 'being', etc.—the problem first clearly stated by Aristotle in his definition of metaphysics. It is hard to believe that these philosophers have been opposed to speculation in philosophy as such. Indeed, the work of Kant, Russell and Wittgenstein, for instance—to pick three names arbitrarily—is characterised by great inventiveness. There can be no doubt at all that at the bottom of their distrust of speculative philosophy there is the suspicion that the classical subject matter of philosophy, the nature of ultimate reality or 'being as such', is illusory. This has resulted in the feeling, more or less honestly acknowledged, that philosophy has no subject matter at all. This vacuum the anti-speculative philosophers have tried to fill by suggesting different preoccupations for the philosopher—suggestions valuable in themselves, but nevertheless tinged with the fear that philosophy has probably no permanent subject matter of its own.

Whitehead is profoundly convinced of the legitimacy of the classical metaphysical concern of speculative philosophy. 'The final problem is to conceive a complete fact' (Whitehead 1933: 203), he says, the term 'complete fact' being his equivalent expression for Aristotle's 'being as such'. Among writers on the philosophy of Whitehead, it is Leclerc (1958) who has most clearly perceived the frankly metaphysical—and metaphysical in the Aristotelian sense—character of Whitehead's philosophic endeavour. Leclerc aptly quotes in this connection Whitehead's remark (mentioned above) that 'the final problem is to conceive a complete fact', and compares it with Aristotle's statement, 'And so we must consider chiefly and primarily and almost exclusively what that is which *is* in this sense'. Leclerc arrives at the conclusion that Aristotle's meaning and Whitehead's meaning are the same, namely that the metaphysical task is to find out what that concrete, the individual, reality is which exists in the full sense of the word 'exist', and not as an abstraction. He quotes the following passage from Gilson's book *Being and Some Philosophers* (1949), which corroborates his own interpretation of Aristotle's meaning:

> Whatever other name it may bear, reality always is for him (Aristotle) a particular and actually existing thing, that is, a distinct ontological

> unit which is able to subsist in itself and can be defined in itself: not man in himself, but this individual man whom I call Peter or John.

Whether or not this is exactly what Aristotle meant when he defined metaphysics as the inquiry into 'what that is which *is* in this sense', it is certainly true that for Whitehead, at any rate, the 'final real things of which the world is made up' are 'actual entities'. 'There is no going behind actual entities to find anything more real ... The final facts are all alike, actual entities; and these actual entities are drops of experience, complex and inter-dependent' (Whitehead 1957a: 27–28).

However, it is obvious from the last sentence of the above passage that Whitehead would not agree with Gilson and insofar as Gilson's interpretation of Aristotle is correct; with Aristotle, that reality is an ontological unit which is able to 'subsist in itself'. His is a powerful protest against the notion of self-sufficient existence. Actual entities are inter-dependent, not self-subsisting. But it is true—and Leclerc points this out too—that Whitehead, according to his own statement, maintains the general Aristotelian principle that 'apart from the things that are actual there is nothing—nothing either in fact or in efficacy' (ibid.: 64). Also, Whitehead maintains with Aristotle that the fundamental metaphysical question is, 'What is it to be an actual entity?' (ibid.: 218). Whitehead's choice of the expression 'actual entity' to describe the 'that' of Aristotle, 'which *is* in this sense', in place of the familiar expressions 'being' and 'substance', is dictated partly by the ambiguity of these expressions, and also partly because of their historical associations with doctrines which he repudiates.

III

There is, however, no doubt at all that Whitehead stands clearly in the classical metaphysical tradition of European thought. What are his answers to the sceptical questions that have been asked in the past and in our own time regarding the very legitimacy of the metaphysical enterprise?

There is, to begin with, the Kantian objection that traditional metaphysics makes the impossible attempt to discover the nature of things-in-themselves—impossible because things-in-themselves are inaccessible to human experience and fall outside the scope of human knowledge. So much was also hinted at by Locke in his view of the inscrutable nature of 'substance', the something he knew not what, which underlies the appearances of things, the 'ideas' as he called them. Now it takes very little reflection to see that such a view clearly rules out the possibility of metaphysics in the sense of an inquiry into the nature of 'being'. What things are in themselves, the nature of that which can be said to *be* in the fullest sense of the term, is of primary concern to metaphysics. To shut experience out of any interchange with the ultimate nature of things is to deny the possibility of metaphysical knowledge. Kant, of course, believed that our practical reason, as opposed to theoretical reason, provides us with a basis for metaphysical belief, though this is not the same thing as having metaphysical knowledge. Now quite apart from the question whether or not our metaphysical presuppositions are most clearly revealed in the moral life, there is no doubt that metaphysics historically has equally, if not primarily, been the product of *theoretical* curiosity. Kant is undoubtedly anti-metaphysical in his confinement of the activity of theoretical understanding to the world of 'phenomena'. Is his view justified?

All doctrines of the unknowability of the ultimate nature of things lend an air of illusoriness to the world of our experience, for the question of the ontological status of what we in fact experience becomes impossible to answer if the intrinsic nature of things is held to be impenetrable to human understanding. The experienced world gets reduced to the status of 'mere appearance', a mere shadow of the reality which always eludes us. Also, even if the doctrine of the unknowable 'things-in-themselves' is rejected as a piece of unwarranted speculation, and mere 'appearance' or 'impressions' or 'sense-data' retained, the difficult question of the ontological status of these data remains, of how and, in particular, 'where' they can hang together. They are literally left hanging in the air. The metaphysical question can only be meaningfully raised in the context of a realistic epistemology which recognises that in our experience we encounter real, concrete things, which exist in the same sense as we do or, at any rate, in a closely analogous sense.

The lack of metaphysical suggestiveness inherent in the sense-data analysis of experience becomes most apparent in relation to its interpretation of the nature of human existence. We experience ourselves as concrete existents and naturally come to ask the general question as to what it is for anything to exist in the concrete sense in which we do. The sense-data theory has no access to this basis of metaphysical inquiry in our experience.

Whitehead repudiates two doctrines to which can be ascribed much of the lack of metaphysical interest in recent and contemporary philosophy. These are 'the sensationalist doctrine of perception' and the 'Kantian doctrine of the objective world as a theoretical construct from purely subjective experience' (ibid.: *viii*). Kant inherited Hume's analysis of experience into 'impressions of sensation', which, possessing no ontological foundation, have merely a subjective and accidental validity. Experience discloses no principles of connection among them, and Hume traces such principles of connectedness as we find ourselves presupposing to 'custom', while Kant held that they exist *a priori* in the mind and endow subjective experience with objective validity. This is, of course, an over-simplification of the doctrines of Hume and Kant. But the important thing to observe is that their doctrines leave no room for the fundamental metaphysical curiosity which springs from the awareness of actualities in the world which are actual in the same sense as we are, leading to the general question—the central metaphysical question—what is it to be an actual entity? The sensationalist doctrine of perception subscribes to the view that the primary data of experience are the clear and distinct *sensa* such as colours and sounds.

Whitehead holds that these are among our more superficial experiences. These are also the most variable elements in our experience. On the other hand, '[t]he necessities are invariable, and for that reason remain in the background of thought, dimly and vaguely' (Whitehead 1938: *vii*). Sensa considered in themselves are abstractions from the total process of experience. There is always in the background of our consciousness the 'sense of realities behind abstractions' (ibid.: 170). Whitehead's doctrine of perception is complicated and this is not the place to discuss it. What is important here is to observe that the sensationalist doctrine identifies experience with sense-perception—the perception chiefly of the clear-cut sense-data of sight and hearing—and this, according to Whitehead, is a misreading of experience. It is also the reason for the indifference to metaphysics of those schools of philosophy which subscribe to the sensationalist view of the experience.

IV

Perhaps Whitehead's defense of metaphysics could be seen in a clearer light if we consider his attitude to the kind of view of metaphysics which Kant held, the view according to which it is not the task of metaphysics to delve into the nature of things as they are in themselves, but to uncover the structure of our actual thinking about the world, including ourselves. This is what [P. F.] Strawson (1959) calls 'descriptive metaphysics'. [R. G.] Collingwood (1940) also subscribes to a similar view of metaphysics in his theory of 'absolute presuppositions'. Strawson's being the most recent exposition of this view of metaphysics, let us first compare Whitehead's conception of metaphysics with his.

Strawson divides metaphysics broadly into two kinds: descriptive metaphysics and revisionary metaphysics. Descriptive metaphysics is 'content to describe the actual structure of our thought about the world, revisionary metaphysics is concerned to produce a better structure' (Strawson 1959: 9). On the basis of this classification, the metaphysicians of the past can be seen either to have been 'revisionary' or 'descriptive'. Descartes, Leibniz, Berkeley are revisionary; Aristotle and Kant descriptive. Whitehead is certainly a revisionary metaphysician, although he has also done a great deal by way of describing 'the actual structure of our thought about the world'. Further describing the nature of what he means by the phrase 'descriptive metaphysics', Strawson says,

> ... there is a massive central core of human thinking which has no history—or none recorded in histories of thought: there are categories and concepts which, in their most fundamental character, change not at all ... It is with these, their inter-connections, and the structure that they form, that a descriptive metaphysics will be primarily concerned. (Ibid.: 10)

Also, he does not dismiss revisionary metaphysics as a pseudo-activity. 'The productions of revisionary metaphysics remain permanently interesting, and not only as episodes in the history of thought. Because of their articulation and the intensity of their partial vision, the best of them are both intrinsically admirable and of enduring philosophical utility' (ibid.: 9).

But Strawson feels that this merit can be ascribed to them only because descriptive metaphysics requires no justification at all beyond that of inquiry in general. And revisionary metaphysics is at the service of descriptive metaphysics.

Whitehead would have no objection to this programme of descriptive metaphysics provided it did not rule out the possibility of metaphysics in the classical sense. Kant, an advocate of descriptive metaphysics, rules out this possibility. Also, Strawson does not make it quite clear as to what he expects revisionary metaphysics to do. Metaphysics is not just any sort of thinking about the world. It is an inquiry which seeks concertedly to arrive at a satisfactory conception of the nature of actuality, of a complete fact. Our ordinary thinking, and even specialist thought, can be frankly unmetaphysical and even anti-metaphysical. Uncovering the structure of this kind of thinking would not be metaphysics at all. Metaphysics is a self-conscious activity which utilises the categories and concepts of ordinary and specialist thought, and also imaginatively arrived at principles of explanation, in order to formulate a satisfactory conception of the ultimate nature of fact or actuality. The uncovering of thought-structures is relevant to metaphysics only to the extent to which it discloses such conceptions or contributes to the production of more adequate conceptions of the nature of actuality.

Collingwood's conception of metaphysics as an inquiry into the 'absolute presuppositions' of the knowledge of a particular age is closely related to Strawson's conception, although unlike descriptive metaphysics, it is an essentially historical inquiry. Collingwood extracts from Aristotle's metaphysical programme two propositions about the nature of metaphysics: that it is the science of pure being and that it studies presuppositions. Regarding the first, he holds that '[t]here cannot be a science, nor even a quasi-science or pseudo-science, of pure being' (Collingwood 1940: 20). The universal of pure being is the limiting case of the abstractive process, and abstraction consists in taking out something. 'But science investigates not what is taken out but what is left in. To push abstraction to the limiting case is to take out everything; and when everything is taken out there is nothing for science to investigate' (ibid.: 14).

Now if Leclerc's interpretation of the phrase 'what that is which is in this sense' is correct, namely that it signifies what exists in the fullest sense of the term—not as an abstraction at all—then Collingwood is mistaken in interpreting Aristotle's conception of metaphysics as the science of pure being, the highest universal which is devoid of all content. Leclerc (1958: 18) points out that the Greek word *οὐσία* combines the abstractness of 'being' with the concreteness of a particular individual.

However, let us consider Collingwood's positive view of the nature of metaphysics. Metaphysics is for him the science of absolute presuppositions, by which expression he means those presuppositions of science at different stages of its development which are not relative, in the sense that they are taken for granted and in terms of which other relative presuppositions are justified. The question of the truth of these absolute presuppositions does not arise precisely because they are absolute presuppositions. For instance, that every event has a cause is an absolute presupposition of Newtonian science. The question of its truth or falsehood does not arise for Newtonian science. It is taken for granted. Metaphysics is concerned with uncovering such absolute presuppositions in the history of thought. It is thus properly a historical science.

Now Collingwood is quite right in holding that absolute presuppositions cannot be explained in terms of anything more general than themselves. But the question arises as to what exactly constitutes the significance of absolute presuppositions and how this significance is to be judged. The most general assumptions of thought ought to be explanatory of the most general nature of things, that is, their metaphysical nature. It may be that the criteria of truth and falsehood do not apply to them in an unqualified sense. But this does not imply that they cannot be evaluated in terms of *any* criteria. Absolute presuppositions, the fundamental, unquestioned assumptions of thought, can be seen to be more or less adequate in conceiving the fundamental nature of things, more or less useful in ordering the diverse data of experience into an organised whole.

That the fundamental notions of science are in constant need of metaphysical appraisal is a lesson which Whitehead drew from the fate of Newtonian physics. 'The fate of Newtonian physics warns us that there is a development in scientific first principles and that their original forms can only be saved by interpretations of meaning and limitations of their field of application—interpretations and limitations unsuspected during the first period of successful employment' (Whitehead 1957a: 15).

Whitehead witnessed the development of Newtonian physics into something like a rigid orthodoxy in his own lifetime. He was as convinced as anyone else in the late nineteenth century when he studied and taught science and mathematics, that the physical world was adequately interpretable in terms of the Newtonian cosmology. Then, by the turn of the century, literally at his doorstep, the entire edifice of Newtonian physics blew up, and that was an experience which conditioned all his later thinking. 'The exactness is a fake': the last words of his last philosophical writing reflect the powerful influence of that experience (Whitehead 1948: 74). In the essay from which the above sentence is taken, Whitehead talks of the alleged exactness of the statements which form the basis of the special sciences, their 'absolute presuppositions,' and the error of basing one's final philosophic outlook on them (ibid.).

The point at issue here is that metaphysics cannot be a silent spectator of the rise and fall of scientific first principles, content merely to uncover them whenever science is in a self-questioning mood. Scientific first principles are half-truths which philosophy must question. Also,

> [t]he systematization of knowledge cannot be conducted in watertight compartments. All general truths condition each other: and the limits of their application cannot be adequately defined apart from their correlation by yet wider generalities. The criticism of principles must chiefly take the form of determining the proper meanings to be assigned to the fundamental notions of the various sciences, when these notions are considered in respect to their status relatively to each other. The determination of this status requires a generality transcending any special subject matter. (Whitehead 1957a: 15)

The generality sought by metaphysics necessitates the analysis and critical evaluation of scientific presuppositions with reference to other general ideas of civilised thought, moral, religious, sociological and aesthetic, so as to arrive at a satisfactory conception of the most fundamental character of all that we encounter in our experience.

V

Now the reduction of metaphysics to undeservedly modest proportions is perhaps not the most serious challenge it faces. It is the understandable reaction of a critical age to centuries of seemingly fruitless rancor and rivalry between metaphysicians and schools of philosophy. What is more serious is the attempt, probably quite old in the history of thought, but receiving fresh impetus and logical respectability in our own time, to show that the language of metaphysics is meaningless, that it does not satisfy the basic condition of meaningfulness which other kinds of language claiming cognitive significance satisfy, namely verifiability. Thus, on this view, associated chiefly with the logical positivists, metaphysics lacks cognitive significance because its statements are unverifiable, because they cannot be ascertained to be true or false. The truth of this view obviously depends upon the adequacy of its conceptions of 'metaphysics', 'meaning' and 'verification'. Also, verification, that is, the procedure of ascertaining the truth of a belief, has value to the extent the view of experience on which it is based is adequate.

The logical positivists' doctrine of experience is what Whitehead has called the sensationalist doctrine of perception—in his opinion a completely erroneous view of the nature of our experience. This doctrine misconceives, according to Whitehead, both the nature of the datum in experience, as well as the nature of the act of experience. It seeks to describe the datum of experience purely in terms of universals, in terms of clear-cut data such as colours and sounds. And it conceives the act of experience as the bare subjective entertainment of these data, 'devoid of any subjective form of reception' (ibid.: 239). It is impossible on this view to have an intelligible conception of a particular, concrete fact. Particulars cannot be extracted out of universals, nor even out of any construction or configuration of universals. And without a notion of what it is for a particular, concrete entity to exist, there can be no metaphysics in the classical sense. Also according to Whitehead, the true description of the act of experience is not the bare subjective entertainment of universals, but the active bringing together of particular existing things into the concrete unity of subjective experience. This concrete unity of experience, also called by Whitehead an 'actual occasion', is the final metaphysical reality which he recognises. '"Actual entities"—also termed "actual occasions"—are the final real things of which the world is made up. There is no going behind actual entities to find anything more real' (ibid.: 27). The basis in experience of this conception is the vague and massive feeling, somewhere in the background of awareness, of our derivation from the immediate past into the present concrete unity of experience in which we find ourselves. The sensationalist doctrine of perception fails to take into account this experience not supplied by the clear-cut data of sense-perception—of derivation from the past. Thus, on Whitehead's view, the epistemology of logical positivism denies itself access to the most concrete basis for metaphysical generalisation in our experience. Consequently, it cannot but be anti-metaphysical.

What is Whitehead's specific response to the charge that metaphysical propositions are *meaningless*? According to Whitehead, every proposition 'refers to a universe exhibiting some general systematic metaphysical character' (ibid.: 17–18). The complete analysis of a proposition proposing a fact must disclose the general character of the Universe which that fact requires. Verbal phrases are thoroughly inadequate as statements of propositions (ibid.: 16). It is for this reason that they allow of limitless expansion and analysis of meaning. The full analysis of the meaning of linguistic expressions discloses tacitly accepted metaphysical presuppositions respecting the 'universe of discourse' in question. It is credulous to hold that language, even of the simplest the-cat-is-on-the-mat sort, is free of metaphysical presuppositions. The truth or falsehood of such seemingly simple linguistic expressions depends upon the adequacy of the metaphysics they presuppose, not the other way round.

But linguistic expressions are never adequate representations of propositions. Whitehead believes that this distinction between verbal phrases and complete propositions 'is one of the reasons why the logicians' rigid alternative, "true or false", is so largely irrelevant for the pursuit of knowledge' (ibid.: 17). He is not, of course, suggesting that reference to the Universe in all its details is required by each proposition. 'A proposition can embody partial truth because it only demands a certain type of systematic environment, which is presupposed in its meaning' (ibid.). But the metaphysical reference is inescapable. The following passage sums up Whitehead's view on the subject fairly clearly:

> The technical language of philosophy represents attempts of various schools of thought to obtain explicit expression of general ideas presupposed by the facts of experience. It is, therefore, no valid criticism of one metaphysical school to point out that its doctrines do not follow from the verbal expression of the facts accepted by another school. The whole contention is that the doctrines in question supply a closer approach to fully expressed propositions. (Ibid.: 18)

Thus, it is no valid criticism of the statements of metaphysics that they do not follow from the verbal expressions of the logical positivist worldview. Analysis of the language of logical positivism would reveal a tacitly presupposed metaphysic as much open to critical evaluation as any other kind of metaphysic.

Finally, something ought to be said about the logical positivists' conception of metaphysics. Collingwood (1940: Chapters 14 and 16) takes serious objection to their putting metaphysical statements to an empirical test and finding them unverifiable and therefore meaningless. For him, metaphysical statements are about the absolute presuppositions of science, and these are not statements of fact which can be said to be true or false. Whitehead would not strictly accept this position, although he would certainly object to a simple-minded application of the criteria of truth and falsehood for the purpose of evaluating the worth of metaphysical doctrines. He would rather say that the sort of empirical test visualised by the logical positivistic epistemology is vitiated by its narrow view of experience, its misconception of the nature of the datum of experience in particular. The characterisation of the datum in the act of experience cannot be too carefully scrutinised. 'The whole philosophical system depends on it' (Whitehead 1957a: 238). As was pointed out earlier, this results in failure, on the part of logical positivists, to take into account just those elements in our experience which are most concretely suggestive of the metaphysical problem.

There is another reason for the metaphysical indifference of logical positivism. It is that the appeal to facts, while of basic importance, is never easy. There are no 'pure' facts. Experience is shot through and through with interpretation. 'If we desire a record of uninterpreted experience, we must ask a stone to record its autobiography' (ibid.: 22). The belief that the appeal to facts is simple is engendered by the fallacious doctrine that the nature of the fact of experience consists in the bare subjective entertainment of data, devoid of any subjective form of reception. In cognitive human experience, this form of reception is the interpretative framework of the mind. Whitehead sums up the importance and difficulty of appealing to facts succinctly in the following passage:

> All human discourse which bases its claim to consideration on the truth of its statements must appeal to the facts. In none of its branches can philosophy claim immunity to this rule. But in the case of philosophy, the difficulty arises that the record of the facts is in part dispersed vaguely through the various linguistic expressions of civilized language and of literature, and is in part expressed more precisely under the influence of schemes of thought prevalent in the traditions of science and philosophy. (Ibid.: 62)

The complexity of the seemingly simple appeal to the data of sense-perception becomes apparent when one faces the problem of reconciling the world of colours and sounds and odours with the world of atoms and electrons and quanta of energy in terms of which physics seeks to interpret the former world. It was precisely the perception of the great difficulty of this problem that led to the transition in Whitehead's thought from philosophy of science to metaphysics. This problem of reconciliation cannot be solved without an adequate metaphysical conception of the nature of actuality. Thus, it is not the case that logical positivism has an erroneous conception of metaphysics; it has no conception of metaphysics at all, for the simple reason that it does not perceive complexities inherent in our experience, which challenges our understanding to undertake the metaphysical task of conceiving the final nature of fact or reality.

VI

However, the discovery and formulation of metaphysical first principles is never an easy task. 'Weakness of insight and deficiencies of language stand in the way inexorably' (ibid.: 6). This brings us to another feature of the distrust of speculative philosophy, the complaint that speculative philosophy does violence to the ordinary, conventional meanings of linguistic expressions and that it introduces in their place a technical vocabulary which makes no literal sense at all. The method of speculative philosophy described by Whitehead largely arises as a result of the attempt to circumvent the two difficulties of the inadequacy of language and the deficiencies of our metaphysical insights. Something was said earlier about Whitehead's view that linguistic phrases are not adequate expressions of propositions. The meaningfulness of a proposition is dependent upon its reference to an environment exhibiting some systematic metaphysical character (ibid.: 17). This metaphysical reference is least required when the environment presupposed by a proposition is very special, not requiring any highly general knowledge of the nature of things. And within such limits, language can be said to be precise. To this class of 'precise' language belong those of our linguistic expressions which have reference to things obviously important to us for purposes of survival and enjoyment, for 'being' and 'well-being'. Whitehead also includes in this class—perhaps overconfidently—the language of the special sciences, because they deal with 'topics which lie open to easy inspection and are readily expressible in words' (ibid.: 14). Ideally, of course, 'a precise language must await a completed metaphysical knowledge' (ibid.: 18).

Language breaks down precisely at the task of expressing explicitly the larger generalities, 'the very generalities which metaphysics seeks to express' (ibid.: 16). The reason for this Whitehead holds to be the discrepancy between linguistic expressions and the determinate propositions which they seek to express, a point which cannot be emphasised too frequently. 'The position of metaphysics in the development of culture cannot be understood without remembering that no verbal statement is the adequate expression of a proposition' (ibid.: 20). As Whitehead explains elsewhere, the verbal disagreement of schools of philosophy is not an adequate measure of their metaphysical divergence. The question is one of the adequacy of their verbal formulations as expressions of propositions concerning the general nature of things. The whole contention of a school of philosophy claiming to be more adequate than others is that its doctrines supply a closer approach to fully expressed propositions (ibid.: 18).

And yet, 'the tool required for philosophy is language', because 'the general agreement of mankind as to experienced facts is best expressed in language' (ibid.: 16). 'Common sense' is an elusive term in philosophy, but to say that it expresses the general agreement of mankind as to experienced facts is perhaps as good a definition of it as any that has been proposed. And philosophy may not defy common sense beyond limits. 'You may polish up commonsense, you may contradict it in detail, you may surprise it. But ultimately your whole task is to satisfy it' (Whitehead 1957b: 110).

But language has to be modified a great deal for it to serve the philosophical purpose of expressing the fundamental character of things. Whitehead says, no doubt metaphorically, that it has to be redesigned much in the same way as physical appliances have to be redesigned for novel scientific experiments (Whitehead 1957a: 16), and for similar reasons. Speculative philosophy too is an experimental venture: it is an imaginative experiment which aims at the discovery and expression of the most general features of things which ordinary language fails to express by reason of their persistent exemplification in experience. The undoubtedly artificial character of the language of speculative philosophy arises out of this necessity of redesigning language so as to make it the vehicle of unusually general thoughts, and also because the success of the imaginative experiment depends upon successful generalisation of the meanings of familiar terms so as to make them relevant to areas of experience outside their customary field of application (ibid.: 8). Such generalised terms have an air of artificiality about them.

Critics have taken Whitehead to task for his highly generalised use of such familiar terms as 'feeling', 'satisfaction', 'decision', etc. The justification of this procedure of Whitehead's has to do with the requirement that speculative generalisation should start with notions whose applicability to a particular region of experience is familiar and established, so that the generalisation would certainly have some relevance to experience. The successful use of these notions in unsuspected areas of experience would then illustrate principles common to a variety of facts, thus assisting in the achievement of a synoptic vision of the world.

In the light of Whitehead's extensive, although generalised, use of expressions belonging to ordinary language, it would be unfair to say that he is pleading for the creation of an artificial language which has nothing in common with ordinary language at all. There is in Whitehead's writings a fair balance between novel technical terms and familiar expressions which are seen to possess unsuspectedly wider application and greater explanatory power than conventional language is willing to allow them. Also, it is unfair and in patent contradiction to the general facts about Whitehead's intellectual development to interpret this feature of his writings in terms of an alleged mathematical or scientific bias, as for instance, Urban does in his essay on 'Whitehead's Philosophy of Language' in the Library of Living Philosophers volume on Whitehead's philosophy (Schilpp 1951: 308–11). Urban reads into Whitehead's plea for the redesigning of ordinary language the 'external-tag' view of language, the view according to which language is external to reality and can never quite 'fit' the facts. Urban rejects this view outright. 'Language is not an external tag or mould. It is rather the necessary condition of the experience of objects as such' (ibid.: 309).

Now Whitehead's insistence noted earlier, that experience is through and through interpretative, that it is absurd to look for a record of uninterpreted experience, should be sufficient to discredit any such allegation. It is true that Whitehead does not describe interpretative elements in experience in terms of 'language', but rather in terms of such general notions as 'propositional feelings', 'subjective forms of reception', etc. (Whitehead 1957a: Chapter 9). But this is precisely because he does not conceive language as an external tag on reality, but as a species of symbolic functioning inherent in the process of experience itself (ibid.: Chapter 8). The 'necessary condition of the experience of objects as such' ought to be described in far more general terms than what is commonly understood by 'language'. On the other hand, if Urban uses the word 'language' in the passage quoted above in a highly generalised sense, he is not entitled to criticise Whitehead for taking similar liberties with other words of 'ordinary' language.

The point at issue is that for Whitehead, language—that is, words and sentences which have an established usage sufficiently adequate for the purposes of ordinary interchange of ideas—is a thoroughly inadequate instrument for the expression of metaphysical ideas in any systematic way. It is, of course, true that the language of great literature—and it is often the very simplest kind of language—succeeds in conveying these ideas. But it does so unsystematically and unpredictably. This erratic process of discovery cannot be made the basis of the method of speculative philosophy, although something of its anarchic character is an essential prerequisite. For the purposes of speculative philosophy, 'Words and phrases must be stretched towards a generality foreign to their ordinary usage; and however such elements of language be stabilized as technicalities, they remain metaphors mutely appealing for an imaginative leap' (ibid.: 6). However, there is no getting away from language, whatever the difficulties it poses. A way out of these difficulties—there cannot, of course, be an entirely satisfactory way out—is to operate in philosophical discussion not with isolated notions inadequately expressed by linguistic phrases, but with a set of interrelated notions which lend to each other clarity and make up conjointly to a point what in isolation they lack by way of adequacy. This is not to imply that they should be definable in terms of each other. What is important is to see that 'what is indefinable in one such notion cannot be abstracted from its relevance to the other notions' (ibid.: 5).

VII

Whitehead's scepticism regarding the capacity of individual linguistic expressions to express metaphysical ideas leads him naturally to a 'constructional' and 'scheme' view of the method of speculative philosophy. This is a basic tendency in Whitehead's thinking, a profound distrust of the metaphysical adequacy of our conceptions of isolated entities, whether they are individual linguistic expressions, sense-data, or ultimate ontological units like the 'substances' of medieval philosophy, which allegedly exist 'in and for themselves'. He substitutes for this concept of isolated existence his own notion of interrelated existing things: categoreal schemes of interrelated notions in place of mutually exclusive statements of fact; the concept of an actual occasion of experience as arising out of the 'concrescence' of other actual occasions of experience in place of the concept of a bare subjective entertainment of unconnected sense data; and the concept of a 'nexus' of actual entities, internally related to one another, in place of self-subsistent substances with merely external relations amongst themselves.

The inadequacy of language is not, however, the only obstacle in the way of metaphysical discovery. Although holding that there is no first principle which is in itself unknowable, not to be captured by a flash of insight (ibid.: 6), Whitehead points out that 'deficiency in imaginative penetration forbids progress in any form other than that of an asymptotic approach to a scheme of principles, only definable in terms of the ideal which they should satisfy' (ibid.). This ideal is adequate metaphysical generality and explanatory power. One cannot wait indefinitely for a happy insight of such generality and power to float into consciousness, although it is always welcome. There are limits—not absolute, perhaps, but impassable enough to bring progress to a temporary halt—to our imaginative power of penetrating into the depths of things. When this happens, the least one can do is to 'frame a scheme of ideas, the best one can, and unflinchingly to explore the interpretation of experience in terms of that scheme' (ibid.).

Perhaps Whitehead's clearest account of the importance and necessity of framing such schemes of ideas is to be found in *The*

Function of Reason (1929: 52), where he discusses the 'incredible' discovery, which he ascribes to the Greeks, that the speculative reason could itself be subjected to orderly method. This discovery is in the widest sense the discovery of the 'logic of discovery'. According to Whitehead, the use of Greek Logic as perfected by the experience of centuries can be said to consist in subjecting the content of any belief to the following criteria: (a) conformity to intuitive experience; (b) clarity of propositional content; (c) internal logical consistency; (d) external logical consistency; (e) status of a logical scheme with (i) widespread conformity to experience, (ii) no discordance with experience, (iii) coherence among its categoreal notions, (iv) methodological consequence (ibid.: 53). Whitehead points out that the application of the first four of these criteria presents great difficulties. The fifth criterion is really a procedure; but of that later.

By the expression 'conformity to intuitive experience,' Whitehead means the appeal to immediate experience for the verification of a proposition. This appeal is never a straightforward process. There can be no analysis or interrogation of experience without the introduction of interpretative elements which can always be erroneous. There are no 'pure' facts of experience which can be viewed without any bias of interpretation. Thus, the so-called verification of propositions by appealing to immediate experience is far from being final. Clarity of propositional content is again difficult to achieve in the absence of an adequate understanding of the metaphysical character of the Universe presupposed by the proposition in question. This point was dealt with earlier in connection with Whitehead's view that language is never an adequate expression of propositions. It is for this reason that the analysis of statements is always incomplete and ambiguous. Also, because of this incompleteness and ambiguity, the self-consistency of any statement—this is the third criterion of 'internal logical consistency'—can never be established beyond doubt. Factors disclosed in the subsequent analysis may render the statement in question inconsistent with itself. And for the same reason the fourth criterion of 'external logical consistency'—which consists in testing the consistency of a proposition with other propositions known or accepted to be true—is also difficult to apply conclusively (ibid.: 54–55).

The fifth criterion, which is really a procedure, is designed to remedy the difficulties of applying the first four criteria mentioned above: the difficulty, in general, of judging individual propositions. This difficulty is circumvented by having recourse to a system of ideas

> ...whose mutual relevance shall lend to each other clarity, and which hang together so that the verification of some reflects upon the verification of the others. Also if the system has the character of suggesting methodologies of which it is explanatory, it gains the character of generating ideas coherent with itself and receiving continuous verification. (Ibid.: 58)

Logical positivists should pay attention to these difficulties of verification which Whitehead points out. A single proposition is shrouded in vague notions about the environing world. Its role in clarifying experience is limited because of the unclearness of its analysis and the consequent uncertainty as to its self-consistency and lack of contradiction in relation to other propositions, and also its doubtful disclosure of the nature of fact. Whitehead does not illustrate this point with many examples, but his meaning seems to be that direct observation of facts, issuing in single propositions, seldom leads to any advance in thought, whereas '[i]t is by their emphasis on schemes of thought that the Greeks founded the various branches of sciences, which have re-made civilization' (ibid.). On the other hand, 'The comparative stagnation of Asiatic civilization after its brilliant development was due to the fact it had exhausted its capital of ideas, the product of curiosity. Asia had no large schemes of abstract thought energizing in the minds of men and waiting to give significance to their chance experiences' (ibid.).

The point is that if thought is to be relevant beyond the narrow focal region of immediate experience and thereby also further illuminate the character of immediate experience, observation must be preceded and accompanied by schemes of ideas purporting to be explanatory of the general nature of the sorts of things observed, so that in the event of successful interpretation, much more than immediate experience becomes illuminated. It is only in the rarest of instances that a novel observation results in enhanced theoretical understanding. It is generally wasted, for '... if there be no scheme to fit it into, its significance is lost. The way of thoughtless nature is by waste—a million seeds and one tree: a million eggs and one fish. In the same way, from a million observations of fact beyond the routine of human life, it rarely happens that one useful development issues' (ibid.: 57).

By a scheme of thought, Whitehead means a scheme of 'morphology', that is, a scheme of ideas concerning the 'forms' which facts illustrate; and the secret of progress 'is the speculative interest in abstract schemes of morphology' (ibid.: 58). The production of such a scheme is a major effort of the speculative reason.

> It involves imagination far out-running the direct observations. The interwoven groups of categoreal notions which constitute the scheme allow of derivative extension by the constructive power of deductive logic. Throughout the whole range of these propositions respecting the interrelations of the forms of things, some of them allow of direct comparison with experience. The extent of this conformity ... with observed fact can thus be explored. A scheme which for a time at least is useless methodologically is one which fails to yield these observable contacts with fact. (Ibid.: 56)

However, the methodological uselessness of an abstract scheme of morphology can never be conclusively established. Often time is required. Whitehead points out that the theory of conic sections had to wait 1,800 years for its practical application. The theory of probability, the theory of tensors and the theory of matrices are other instances of this curious feature of the history of science (Whitehead 1957a: 9). The question now arises as to what sort of scheme of ideas Whitehead thinks speculative philosophy should seek to elaborate so as to be explanatory of the nature of a 'complete fact', and thereby of the infinite variety of our experience. This question, however, falls outside the scope of this article, because I have confined discussion in this article to Whitehead's response to very general criticisms of the assumptions of speculative philosophy, ignoring the details of his actual procedure in metaphysics.

References

Aristotle. 350 BC. *Metaphysics*, trans. W. D. Ross, Z, I, 1028b, 5–8.

Collingwood, R. G. 1940. *Essay on Metaphysics*. Oxford: Clarendon Press, Humphrey Milford.

Gilson, Étienne. 1949. *Being and Some Philosophers*. Toronto: Pontifical Institute of Mediaeval Studies.

Leclerc, Ivor. 1958. *Whitehead's Metaphysics*. London: Allen and Unwin.

Popper, K. 1959. *The Logic of Scientific Discovery*. London: Routledge.

Schilpp, P. A. (ed.). 1951. *The Philosophy of Alfred North Whitehead*. New York: Tudor.

Strawson, P. F. 1959. *Individuals*. London: Methuen.

Whitehead, A. N. 1928. *Symbolism: Its Meaning and Effect*. Cambridge: Cambridge University Press.

______. 1929. *The Function of Reason*. Princeton: Princeton University Press.

______. 1933. *Adventures of Ideas*. Cambridge: Cambridge University Press.

______. 1938. *Modes of Thought*. Cambridge: Cambridge University Press.

______. 1948. *Essays in Science and Philosophy*. New York: Philosophical Library.

______. 1957a. *Process and Reality: An Essay in Cosmology*. New York: The Humanities Press.

______. 1957b. *The Aims of Education and Other Essays*. New York: The New American Library.

— *ten* —

Self-consciousness*

Who am I? Suppose I 'ask myself'[1] this question, and suppose I produce the following answer: 'I am R. G., father of L. G., etc.' Would this answer necessarily satisfy me? I don't think so, because I could go on to 'ask myself'[2] the further question: 'But who is this person of whom I have said that he is R. G., father of L. G., etc.?' Would the satisfactory answer to *this* question be: 'I, myself, the thinker of this as well as the preceding thoughts'? The really crucial part of this answer is the element 'I, myself', because with regard to the 'thinker of certain thoughts' I could 'ask',[3] again, 'But, who is the person of whom I say that he is the thinker of this as well as the preceding thoughts?' So what are we to say about the thought 'I, myself' as an answer—a clinching answer—to the question, 'Who am I?' Is it a clinching answer? To suppose that it is would involve the supposition that the thought 'I, myself', as thought by me, in some way uniquely indentified me. And this identification of myself by myself for myself would have to radically differ from the sort of identification of a person—even

*Originally published in *Indian Philosophical Quarterly* 1 (3), April 1974: pp. 167–81. For helpful criticisms of an earlier draft of this paper, I am grateful to my colleague, Dr Mrinal Miri.

if it were a unique identification—which depends upon the correct application, vis-à-vis the person in question, of a descriptive phrase or referring expression. The thought 'I, myself' would have to be supposed by me to identify me non-descriptively, non-referentially—in *principle* so. (Thus, this thought would have to be distinguished from anything analogous to an act of pointing towards a person in order to identify him for a hearer, an act which can always be replaced by an utterance employing a suitable descriptive or referring expression.) But can the thought 'I, myself' be said to achieve such non-referential identification? For only then could it be regarded as a clinching reply to the 'self-addressed' question,[4] 'Who am I?'

Another mode of asking the above question is this: Is there a notion of self-consciousness such that I may be said to be conscious of myself in a way which necessarily involved my thinking of myself *not* as being a creature of a certain sort, but, quite simply, as being 'myself', a unique but bare particular—a 'soul'? I am inclined to deny that there is such a notion of self-consciousness because I am inclined to think that it does not make sense to talk of non-referentially identifying oneself. However, I shall argue that it *is* possible to speak of oneself *imagining* that one was being non-referentially identified by another person because it *is* possible to be non-referentially identified by others, and that the notion of self-consciousness should be regarded as being, at least, the notion of oneself *imagining* that one was being non-referentially identified by another person. I shall also consequently be enabled to argue that this notion of self-consciousness can be regarded as being equivalent to the notion of *imagining* that one was conscious of another person being conscious of oneself in a way which necessarily involved his thinking of oneself *not* as being a certain sort of creature, but as being 'oneself', a unique but bare particular.

II

What do I mean by saying that it is possible for one to be non-referentially identified by another person? Suppose there are three persons, A, B, and C. Suppose A, pointing to C, says to B: 'That is C.' This would be a case of A identifying C for B. But not *in principle* non-referentially or non-descriptively. A's utterance can always be translated into some such utterance as: 'The person standing under the tree over there is C.' Suppose, instead,[5] that A merely *addresses* B, say by issuing the utterance 'B!' to B. Would A have *referred* to B in conversation with B? Certainly not! This is because the possibility of a conversation starting between A and B depends upon the success of A's act of addressing B. And yet A's act cannot fail to have the force of a communicative utterance of the form 'Attend to me!' Now insofar as A succeeds in addressing B, that is, insofar as a communicative utterance of the above form may be supposed to have been successfully issued by A to B, A can be said to have non-referentially or non-descriptively-identified B. For B would be brought in possession of the correct answer, 'He means me', to the question, 'Who does he mean?' 'He means me' is a thought which B would be logically necessarily brought in possession of as a result of A successfully addressing B. Clearly such non-referential identification is a necessary condition of communication. We could say, equally correctly, that *addressing* (which requires non-referential identification of addressee by addresser) is a necessary condition of communication.

Now I can explain why I said in the previous section that it did not make sense to suppose that one could non-referentially identify oneself. To say this is to say that one cannot significantly be said to 'address' oneself. It is because of this belief of mine that I put expressions like *ask* (in relation to the notion of *asking oneself a question*) and *self-addressed* (in relation to the notion of *addressing oneself a question*) inside quotation marks in the previous section. This is because if it doesn't make sense to speak of addressing oneself, it must also not make sense to speak of communicating with oneself in the literal sense of that expression in *any* form. However, we do have a use in our language for expressions like 'asking oneself a question', 'talking to oneself', etc. I want now to give an account of the basis of the use of such expressions. Take 'addressing oneself', for 'addressing oneself' in some sense or other must be the presupposition of all 'self-communication'. Why is the literal use of such expressions as 'addressing oneself' not significant? The reason for this is that it doesn't make sense—and with respect to the question in hand it is quite pointless—to suppose that the self—whatever it is—is non-unitary.[6] It doesn't make sense to speak of inviting oneself to attend to oneself.[7] One doesn't stand in need of being invited—by oneself—to consider the truth or falsity or obedience-worthiness, etc., of the utterances that one 'addresses to oneself'.

However, one can always *imagine* that one was being addressed by another person, or that some utterance or other was being addressed to one by another person. The imagined 'other person' here need not be anyone, in particular, he could be imagined as being quite anonymous. Thus, my thought, 'I, myself', which I believe uniquely and non-referentially identifies me for myself can be regarded as being equivalent to an imagined addressing-utterance issued by an imagined anonymous speaker to me. Thus, the thought 'I, myself' or, more briefly, the thought 'I' can be regarded *not* as identifying a bare particular—'myself'—but as an act of the imagination which puts me in the stance of an 'audience', thereby enabling me to 'weigh' utterances which too I imagine as being addressed to myself: that is, as an act of the imagination which enables me to think in accordance with the requirements of the logic of discourse which governs the audience–speaker relationship. At this point, one might ask: How do I acquire the ability to perform the act of imagination (which makes soliloquy possible) referred to above? I think the answer to this question must be this: I acquire the ability to perform the act of imagination in question *at the same time as* acquiring the ability to *listen* to a real speaker. When, in the course of the process of being inducted into a communicative form of life, I am first successfully *addressed* by a speaker, I must be supposed to be logically necessarily brought in possession of the thought, 'He wants me to attend to him'. Now being able to think this thought must involve being able to think the thought 'me' or 'myself' or 'I', that is, it must involve being able to perform the imaginative act of casting oneself in the role of an audience vis-à-vis an imagined speaker. Thus, the word 'I' need not be supposed to be the 'name' of anything. But it doesn't follow from this that it connects up with nothing. It connects up with our capacity for soliloquy, among other things.

III

In addressing me, you do not refer to me, although you may employ a referring expression for the purpose of addressing me. You may, for instance, say 'Mr Chairman!', which locution involves the employment of the referring expression, 'Chairman' (not to mention the undoubtedly referring character of the expression 'Mr'), and I may well be the Chairman. But you would not have, so far, *referred* to me as Chairman in conversation with me. Your utterance, involving the utterance of the word 'Chairman' would attract my attention to you, but also at the same time to the fact that you were not really trying to attract my attention to yourself in a purely causal fashion. (You were not producing the loudest noise that you could produce—something which would attract my attention to you in a much more straightforward manner.) It would become clear to me that you were *inviting, soliciting,* my attention—that is, you were addressing me. One could also say that your—successful—act of addressing me would make me conscious of the fact that you were conscious of me in a way which necessarily involved your thinking of me, in addressing me, *not* as a certain sort of creature, but as a bare particular—as 'myself'. (Of course, you would have to take me to be a communicative creature in order that you may be able, in addressing me, to think of me as a bare particular, as 'myself'.) It would follow from this that my thinking the thought 'I', or the thought 'I, myself', would involve my imagining that I was conscious of another (anonymous, perhaps) person being conscious of me in a way which necessarily involved his thinking of me as 'myself'—a bare particular—and not as a certain sort of creature. I suggest that this is the correct analysis of the notion of self-consciousness. But the notion of self-consciousness must also apply to the case where I am *actually* conscious of the fact that another (not anonymous) person is, in addressing me, conscious of me in a way which necessarily involved his thinking of me *not* as a certain sort of creature, but as 'myself'—a bare particular. Thus, I am self-conscious when I am actually in a listening-stance vis-à-vis a real speaker, and also when I *imagine* that I am in a listening-stance vis-à-vis an imagined (possibly anonymous) speaker. In both cases,

I am enabled to think in accordance with the requirements of the logic of discourse.

I think I could maintain that the account of self-consciousness that I have sought to give is not an eccentric one. Although I have followed different routes of argument, my conclusion is the same as the Kantian conclusion that self-consciousness is a necessary condition of thinking.[8] What I have emphasised is that thinking has to do with the taking up of actual or imaginative audience-stances vis-à-vis actual or imagined speakers. I have sought to relate the notions of self-consciousness and thinking to the public phenomenon of human communication.

I have also sought to give some explanation of the basis of the sense of deep self-acquaintance (not self-knowledge by description but, as it were, self-knowledge by acquaintance) which haunts our mental lives. I have implied that this sense of deep self-acquaintance has to do with our actually or imaginatively taking up audience-stances vis-à-vis actual or imagined speakers. This involves our being conscious, or our imagining that we are conscious, of another person being conscious of us in a way which necessarily involves his thinking of us not as creatures of a certain sort, but as bare particulars—as 'ourselves'. Of course, it doesn't follow from this that we are bare particulars. But the self-imposed illusion, which lies at the heart of the act of addressing, that one's audience is a bare particular, is a necessary condition of communication.

IV

There is a puzzle about dreaming which I feel can be sorted out with the aid of the account of self-consciousness that I have been trying to develop. The puzzle is this. Why is it that while we are dreaming, we are unable to ascribe our dream-experience to ourselves? The following reflection should help in answering this question: What is it for us to be able to ascribe experiences to ourselves? Surely our ability to ascribe experiences to ourselves presupposes our ability to soliloquise, that is, our ability to take up an audience-stance vis-à-vis an imagined speaker or a speaker-stance vis-à-vis an imagined audience (what is expressed in the last part of this sentence is not something I have alluded to in the previous sections, but it can easily be accommodated into my account of the imaginative mode of self-consciousness.) Now we don't *just* soliloquise, we soliloquise under pressure to transform our soliloquies into communications if it becomes necessary to do so. And this is not just a psychological matter. Soliloquising is preparatory, hypothetical, imaginative communication. It would follow from this that if we were under no pressure at all to communicate with others, we would not soliloquise. Now it is fair to assume that when we dream (as opposed to daydreaming—which can take place at night in bed also—and related phenomena) we are sound asleep, that is, not in a condition in which we can enter into a communicative relationship with anyone at all. Deep sleep unburdens us of the weight of the permanent possibility of communication. It would follow from this that when we are dreaming we do not soliloquise. The dream-thought 'I am dreaming', which often occurs to us in a dream, is not a piece of soliloquy. For if it *were* a piece of soliloquy, it would be possible, logically, for us to transform it forthwith into a communication. But the possibility of our being able to do this is *ex hypothesis*, ruled out by the condition of a deep sleep, which is also the condition of dreaming. This is why we are not able to ascribe our dream-experience to ourselves. But it does not follow from this fact that in dreaming we suffer no experiences. Being able to soliloquise is a condition of making our experience intelligible to ourselves, but it is not a condition, I am sure, of the possibility of experience as such. The notion of an unintelligible experience is not a self-contradictory notion. To return to dreaming. We can say that, because of the absence of soliloquising, dreaming constitutes an unintelligible experience. However, when we wake up from deep sleep, our capacity for soliloquising is restarted. We are then retrospectively able to cast our unintelligible dream-experience (of which we undeniably have memory-images) into an intelligible, soliloquised, narrative form. This does not, of course, enable us to say that at some point at night when we were fast sleep we were having so-and-so experiences in the sense that we could have ascribed these experiences to ourselves at the time of their occurrence. Dream-reports are, in this respect, quite different from ordinary memory-reports. What we can say is that it is only in the form of our dream-reports, and their soliloquised versions, that we can make our unintelligible deep-sleep experiences intelligible to ourselves and to others. I find myself able to say only the following by way of anything like a positive pronouncement about the nature of our dream-experiences: that they are a species of hallucinatory experiences which we suffer under a special handicap, namely the handicap of a total, although temporary, loss of our capacity for soliloquising, which is the same thing as our capacity for ascribing experiences to ourselves.

Postscript: In saying that dream-experiences are unintelligible to us at the time we suffer them, I do not wish to suggest that they are necessarily a medley of images or something like that. I do not wish to suggest this because, after all, even an experience of confusion is, in principle, self-ascribable. What I mean by saying that dream-experiences are unintelligible is that while we are dreaming we cannot seriously ask, or try to seriously answer, the question 'What is going on?' in relation to our dream-experiences. And experiences which resist interrogative scrutiny cannot be intelligible.

V

So far I have been concerned mainly with what might be called the ontological and epistemological dimensions of the notion of self-consciousness. But the notion of self-consciousness also has a moral and political dimension. I shall now try to explore this region a bit.

I have said that being self-conscious is a matter of being able to adopt an audience-stance, actually or imaginatively, vis-à-vis an actual or an imagined speaker. How does one acquire these abilities? One is clearly not born with an operative ability to adopt an audience-stance vis-à-vis speakers. One is *cast* in the role of an audience by others, by one's parents, etc. This activity of casting an infant into the role of an audience—and thereby initiating the process of inducting him into a personal form of life—has morally significant features. You can only seek to cast an infant into the role of an audience by going on trying to 'address' it, that is, by going on trying to solicit, invite, a communicative response from it and not by interacting with it in a purely causal fashion. This being so, attempts to 'address' an infant must be characterised by a *minimally caring* attitude towards it. Activity which is *less* caring than this would not be describable as an activity of trying to solicit, as opposed to trying to elicit, a communicative response from the infant. It would simply frustrate the infant, if not kill it off. The acquisition of communicative capacity, upon which the acquisition of personality is logically dependent, is thus the consequence of a *gift* from others, the gift of a minimally caring communicative attitude. Personality acquisition is not even *in principle* a case of contractually acquiring something. This fact puts one, insofar as one is conscious of the fact that one is a person, under an obligation to *unconditionally* adopt a minimally caring communicative attitude towards anyone who adopts a minimally caring communicative attitude towards oneself. Thus, the notion of self-consciousness and the notion of an (unconditional) moral obligation towards (some) others are logically connected notions. The possibility of altruism is rooted in the nature of self-consciousness.

But so is egoism rooted in the nature of self-consciousness if by egoism is meant an attitude of regarding oneself as valuable, and not simply an attitude of selfishness. How can this be shown in the light of the preceding discussion? Consider the statement, say, made by me, that I am not valuable in any sense at all. Now the making of this statement involves the thinking of the complex thought symbolised by the expression 'I', that is, it involves my imagining that I have taken up an audience-stance vis-à-vis an imagined speaker, that is that I am an object of an imagined person's minimal communicative care. But how can I imagine this if I don't value myself at all! To this question, I might reply: 'I can't help imagining that I am an object of a minimally caring attitude, but I ought not to.' But this will just not do, for this reply equally involves the thinking of the complex thought symbolised by the expression 'I'. I cannot *self-consciously* deny that I have some value, because I cannot, self-consciously, fail to cast myself in the role of an object of a minimally caring attitude. But this is a point in logic. Unqualified self-deprecation, mindless suicide, etc., are undertaken in disregard of this point.

Acknowledgement of rationality and pursuit of blind passion are not, unfortunately, incompatible.

Before concluding this section, I would like to draw attention to two important consequences of the conclusion that men cannot help regarding themselves as being valuable in some sense or other. The first consequence is that the existence of such concepts as those of injury, damage, harm, pain, etc., in our conceptual system becomes easily explicable. If I cannot help regarding myself as being valuable in some sense or other, then I cannot also help regarding myself as being 'vulnerable' in some sense or other. This connection between the notion of regarding ourself as being vulnerable can be seen more readily by reflecting upon the connection between the former notion and the notion of regarding oneself as being 'precious' in some sense or other. Regarding myself, as being valuable (and in some sense 'precious'), I must necessarily find in life actual or possible states of affairs which would be unacceptable to me. Words like 'injury', 'harm', 'damage', 'pain', etc., pick out such states of affairs. I am not suggesting that there must be some unique set of states of affairs which must be picked out by these words. What I am suggesting is that given that human beings necessarily regard themselves as being valuable in some sense or other, they must necessarily find in the world states of affairs—actual or possible—which they would find unacceptable, and that this is the general fact which explains our possession of such concepts of those of injury, harm, etc.

The second consequence of the fact that human beings cannot help regarding themselves as being valuable in some sense or other to which I wish to draw attention is that, given this fact, the 'problem of evil'—familiar to students of the philosophy of religion—arises for the agnostic as well as the atheist, and not only for the theist. Regarding myself unavoidably as being valuable in some sense or other, I cannot acquiesce in a merely causal account of my suffering and agony and pain beyond a certain point. (Here I am thinking of human suffering which is *not* the result of man's inhumanity to man.) But as an atheist or an agnostic, my protestations (regarding my suffering) would never be able to have an unambiguously literal force for me. But I would not, in logic, be able to refrain from protesting. It would always, *prima facie*, seem legitimate to me to ask the question, 'Why should I suffer so much?' I do not know how this form of the problem of evil is going to be resolved. I merely mention it here as a logical consequence of the conclusion that human beings cannot fail to regard themselves as being valuable in some sense or other, and the fact that they suffer beyond endurance.

VI

I have said that the acquisition of personality, of communicative abilities, of self-consciousness, is the consequence of the *gift* of a minimally caring communicative attention on the part of others. Now, these others need not be more than two or three persons. Also, the labour that is required for the task of casting an infant in the role of a person is by no stretch of the imagination of universal social labour. The acquisition of personality costs very little; it only requires a certain amount of love. It would follow from this that *the fact that I am a person* is not something which I owe to society at large. This is my ultimate theoretical safeguard against the tyranny of the crowd, the majority, *everybody*.[9] Now the facts of human language and personality acquisition may have been different, but the facts to which I have drawn attention in this connection belong to the category of those very, very general conditions of human life, acknowledgement of the existence of which is a necessary condition of our ordinary thinking about the world and ourselves.

Granted that the fact that I am a person is not something which I owe to society at large, and so also granted that an anarchist attitude of rebellion against 'mass society' has foundations in our condition, it still remains the case that for the full development of my personality, and for its sustenance throughout a lifetime, I have to depend upon (increasingly) universal social labour—including the labour of past generations of human beings. This being so, I am also under a deep obligation to contribute my share towards the creation of an equalitarian society. Why an equalitarian society? This is because *qua* human beings, human beings value themselves in a sense in which it is absurd to speak of value hierarchies. There is no *reason* for me to suppose that I can, in rational argument, convince another human being that he is, intrinsically, *less* valuable than myself. There is a notion of 'regarding oneself as valuable' which is connected with the notion of 'human personality' in such a way that there can only be an acknowledgement, and no grading, of the intrinsic worth of human beings: and this is only compatible with the ideal of an equalitarian society. This view is a secularisation of the religious theme that God values all men equally. To conclude this section, an anarchist attitude of rebelliousness against mass society is perfectly compatible with the socialist commitment to the task of creating an equalitarian society.

VII

I shall conclude this paper with some reflections on the notions of birth and death and their connection with the notion of self-consciousness.

I cannot conceive of my birth or death, nor, to put the matter slightly differently, do I possess concepts of *my birth* or *my death*. But don't I believe that I was born and that I shall die? Indeed, I not only believe, I know this to be the case. But this is a piece of *general* knowledge which I possess about any member of the human species in which I cannot refuse to be included. I do not come to possess this knowledge by a process of enumeration of the births and deaths of human beings, but on the basis of direct observation as well as information—both scientific and lay—about the nature of human being construed strictly under the category of 'the other' or 'the third person'. Under this category, a human being is seen as an animal organism of a certain type, an entity of which it makes sense to say that at a certain time it 'came into being, that is, became operative as an animal organism of a certain kind', and that at a certain time it will 'cease to be, in the sense of ceasing to be operative as an animal organism of a certain type'. Now I cannot refuse to acknowledge that I am construable under the categories of 'the other' and 'the third person' by others, and so I cannot refuse to acknowledge the applicability of the above truths to myself. But I cannot *conceive* of myself as coming into being at a certain time and as something which will cease to be at a certain time. This is because I cannot conceive of myself as 'the other', or as 'the third person'. Nor can conceive of you, while I am seeing you *as* 'the second person', the recipient of my communicative actions as well as the issuer of communicative utterances to me, as 'the other' or as 'the third person'. 'You' are the bare particular I must think of you as, and not any *sort* of creature, in order for me to be able to address you. And the thought 'I', as thought by me, is my act of imagining myself to be a 'you'—the recipient of an imagined speaker's act of addressing. Thus, you and I are in the following predicament. We, as members of the human species, know that we were born and that we shall die. But as reciprocally related by the communicative relation, we *cannot* conceive of ourselves as having come into being from nothing, at a certain time, and as being creatures who will cease to be at a certain time. We cannot help—logically cannot help—nursing the illusion of a beginningless and endless existence, but at the same time we cannot fly in the face of scientific as well as commonly observable facts as to the organic nature of oneself seen as 'the other'. I do not believe that this predicament can be dissolved by an increase in scientific knowledge. Of course, espousal of certain religious doctrines such as those of reincarnation or resurrection amounts to wishing away the predicament. But these religious doctrines bristle with insurmountable difficulties.

VIII

If what I have been saying about the notion of self-consciousness, and related notions, is at all sound, then there cannot exist what Stuart Hampshire commendatorily calls 'the perfect secular mind' (Hume 1963: 9). But this does not land us in the lap of religion. The religious attitude, like the attitude of 'the perfect secular mind', does not countenance the possibility that there might lie at the heart of the nature of human life an ineliminable sense of paradox.

Notes

[1] An explanation of the quotation marks here is given later in the chapter.
[2] Ditto.

[3] Ditto.

[4] Ditto.

[5] Of course, even in the earlier case, A would have to address B. Addressing in a necessary condition of communication. Here I am concentrating on A's act of addressing B for a special purpose.

[6] Suppose the self is divisible into two selves. Can either sub-self address itself? The same question reappears.

[7] If it did, would not the inviting self have to invite itself to invite the invited self? Infinite regression here.

[8] Here, as well as in the other places in this paragraph where the word 'thinking' occurs, I should like to qualify and say 'thinking which is conducted in accordance with the logic of discourse'.

[9] In the 'collective' sense of this expression.

Reference

Hume, David. 1963. *A Symposium*. London: MacMillan.

— *eleven* —

What We Do and Say in Saying and Doing Something

An Exploratory and Experimental Move from Austin to Advaita[*]

We are all familiar with [J. L.] Austin's (1962) useful and insightful notion of what we do in saying something, as opposed to what we bring about by saying something through the intricate causality of our linguistic utterances. To recall, my utterance of the words, 'I am sorry!', for example, may or may not intricately or coarsely causally bring about a state of mind of gratitude or irritation in you, my audience, and this may or may not be my intention: but my words, 'I am sorry!', are an act in doing which I apologise to you quite simply because of the meaning of the words and the appropriateness of our situation in the world and the nature of our relationship and conventions and rules that identify the utterance of those words as an apology in appropriate standard circumstances. Likewise, in standard felicitous circumstances, the

*Originally published in *Indian Philosophical Quarterly* 11 (2), April 1984: pp. 145–60. This chapter was read as a paper at a seminar at Jadavpur University in January 1983.

words, 'I promise!', 'I forgive!', 'I command!', 'I stipulate!', etc., constitute acts of promising, forgiving, commanding, stipulating, etc., whatever be the causal consequences of the acts of uttering them. Here, *in* uttering words, we *do* things, we do not merely do something by uttering them—the very utterance of them autonomously, in appropriate standard circumstances, constitutes the performance of crucial human actions. This notion of Austin's, the notion of a performative utterance, has rightly been much discussed in recent philosophy, and has rightly been well-made use of in diverse branches of philosophical and theoretical enquiry. However, there is, unfortunately, in Austin's own work, drowning of the general significance of the notion in a mass of classificatory and terminological detail, whatever be the importance of such detail to a systematic study of language. What tends to be forgotten often and remains underdeveloped theoretically is the insight at the heart of the notion of a performative utterance that human language is not only an ingredient, perhaps the most powerful ingredient, of ritual in human life, that it is itself ritual, not in the way of a piece among other pieces of doing in a complex ritual or ceremony, but internally, in itself, ritual; and not only when utterance constitutes the ritual of Austinian performative actions but generally, barring compromisedly voluntary emissions of linguistic noise such as in drunkenness, although something of the ritual of language unavoidably attaches even to such noise.

I do not wish here to enter into the rich classificatory world of Austin's own treatment of the notion of a performative utterance, fruitful though entry into that world always is in philosophical inquiry and linguistic cartography. I wish instead to ask heretically the un-Wittgensteinian and even un-Austinian question as to whether there is any one very general kind of non-trivial thing or action we do in saying anything at all, a substratum of necessary ritual performance which accompanies and even vehicles all specific illocutionary actions—the variety of Austinian things we do in saying something. I believe there is such a substratum of ritual performance, an abiding vahana of all meaning in communication.

II

Any linguistic action at all is a very self-conscious piece of intentional doing, self-consciously an exercise in freedom as opposed to the passivity of being merely grossly or subtly, causally pushed along and about by the past. Of course, often belief in freedom of choice and action is deluded, but such delusion itself points to the general possibility of undeluded freedom and action, even if the scope of these is far more restricted than we in our egoistic disavowal of our causal/vulnerability are willing to allow. The tiniest bit of linguistic action, a half utterance, or even a mumbled drunken linguistic noise, is proof of intentionality, a manifestation of our independence of causality in the narrow but humanity defining area of our lives where self-consciousness explicitly reigns. The incompletest linguistic utterance is such a proof, it is an announcement and celebration of self-consciousness in its aspect of independence from causality. This is very minimally what we do in saying anything at all and in all that we say: We pointedly and unambiguously taunt the purely causal power of the past, something we no doubt do in all intentional action but not explicitly self-consciously as in linguistic action. One might even say that language is at least the explicit self-consciousness of freedom.

There is no mistaking what might be called the general moral and political character of even a fragment of linguistic action, it bears the stamp of self-conscious intentionality. Linguistic noise-making may or may not in given cases prove causally efficacious in desired ways; it may or may not rhetorically or dialectically move men and nations; it may or may not achieve literary or colloquial significance and excellence. But unfailingly speaking establishes and celebrates the massive causal independence of self-consciousness by reason of its pointed confession of human authorship. The least that we can do in saying anything at all and in saying all things great and small is announce and celebrate human authorship, not merely activity, that is, our status, however partial and obscure, as creators and cause of ourselves, a Divine image. Man's linguistic communicative capacity is an unmistakable sign of his godlikeness.

But we do more in saying anything at all than celebrate causal independence; the substratum of ritual performance in all linguistic activity has another equally fundamental dimension. We establish or seek to establish a relationship of causal independence between ourselves. For the actual or imaginative communicative intention in all linguistic action is such that I necessarily seek in you, my would-be or fancied audience, a contemporary witness to myself in my linguistic stance or dance or act or whatever, and not a mere causal target of my action. In the absence of or in abstraction from your actual or imagined contemporaneity with me, my linguistic action cannot be described as a communicative venture; and your contemporaneity, actual or imagined, establishes or envisions you in causal independence from myself, immunising you utterly in your role of pure witness against my causality. All initiation of communication has this unfallenness, symbolised perfectly by the deity of initiation and inauguration, Vinayaka, who is imaged massively and yet as so causally uncoercive as to be able to ride a little mouse.

Beyond initiation, however, presupposing and yet perverting the purity of that rite of emancipation, the historical development of communication and its function in personal and social life exhibit every variety and weight of causality and manipulativeness, a fall from grace. And yet the two-fold grace of Sarasvati, Goddess of speaking, does not abandon us. The tiniest bit of linguistic action suffices to wrap intentionality in self-consciousness, and the timidest communicative venture in its vocativeness surrounds and suffuses with self-consciousness the sense of mutual causal independence which contemporary human beings enjoy in their deepest self-image, their root *ananda* [bliss] of a many-centredness of unexploiting selfhood. (Mutual causal independence in the simultaneity of vocative identification does not monadically isolate addresser and addressee from one another. Logically such a relationship of mutual causal independence can only be between secretly identical realities which therefore must affect one another in the profoundest possible way—by identity, via an eternally established oneness.) In saying anything at all to another, I victoriously celebrate my independence from the causal past, and gallantly establish causal independence also in the present between myself and fellow communicative beings, by holding them and myself in a framework of pure witnessing contemporaneity, at least in the main vocative thrust of my communicative action. If language is the self-consciousness of intentionality and thus an image of divinity in its aspect of power, as a framework of non-causal contemporaneity it is self-consciousness in plurality of centredness, and bears thus in its undegenerateness the stamp of divinity in its aspect of love which stimulates without coercing, hearkens without possession.

Thus, in saying anything at all and in saying all things great and small, I announce victory and confess love, both announcement and confession being an overcoming of causality, by transcendence as in intentionality and by disavowal as in contemporaneity—underscoring vocativeness. I overcome the world in Christ's sense and in the advaitin sense in both cases, world and worldliness. In causally impinging upon you I am worldly, I am in relation to you what the world is in its causal power in relation to me. In vocatively disavowing causal coerciveness in relation to you I disown my world like or worldly possible power over you. My self-conscious intentionality could hardly credibly and creditably be an overcoming by transcendence of the world as the causality of the past if my self-conscious relationship with you were essentially and unmitigatedly that of causal enslavement, that is, if I were to be in relation to you, or you were to be in relation to me, unqualifiedly and unalterably a world of causal power. I overcome the world in self-conscious intentionality and renounce worldliness in self-conscious, that is, characteristically linguistic, communication. Helpfully rhetorically, one could say that in saying anything at all and in saying all things great and small, we boast our transcendence of causality and avow our renunciation of it. And this is the substratum of ritual action which we unfailingly do in all speaking and linguistic communicating, the abiding performative Austinian action, which vehicles all the indefinite variety of illocutionary acts noticed and unnoticed by Austin himself. In drawing attention to such a ground ritual, I have not been partial to one among several performative actions of the same kind, which would indeed involve the kind of essentialist fallacy which Wittgensteinian and Austinian pluralism rightly pounce upon. The ritual of victory and renunciation to which I have drawn attention is related as ground to figures, whole to parts, system to detail, to all specific illocutionary acts and communicative interchanges; and it is not in competition with them.

In what follows, I develop the notion of what we say in doing something, the exact opposite of the Austinian notion of what we do in saying something. Also, I distinguish between what we say in doing something in the sense of some specific message or other which what we do contingently and contextually varyingly may convey, from what all doing necessarily says, a substratum of message which necessarily accompanies and underlines all communicativeness of doing, vehicles all specific messages explicit or implied in doing. There is an analogy here with the distinction between the variety of Austinian illocutionary actions which we do in saying something and the substratum of ritual performance which accompanies and vehicles all specific items of illocutionary doing.

Is doing always only pushing and pulling and bringing about and straining and winning and losing? Surely not, and the most effective argument against such an activist view of doing would be not an example or set of examples of quiet action or mild contemplation but that hard to acquire and strangely difficult to comprehend thing which is being absolutely still and quiet, not forcibly nailed to one spot but rooted massively and simply in one's own being. Sri Ramana Maharshi recommended this as the most perfect sadhana, and in support often quoted the words of God in the Bible, 'Be still and know that I am God', of course interpreting these words not dualistically and alienatingly but in an advaitin and liberating way to imply that when we are still, absolutely still, we know that we are God and that all is God and that there is nothing else. Being thus still is freedom from thought also, no attraction or temptation of cogitation disengages us in that state from stability and eternity of being, nor are we dislodged by any whisper or storm of feeling, nor hurled into whirling behaviour by desire or will. The condition is not necessarily that of physical immobility—the *sthitaprajna* [firm minded] sage can be in Kurukshetra or Vrindavana in battle or dance, he could permit the manifestation even of wailing as did Rama when he lost Sita in the forest. At all times and in all externality of situation, however, the sthitaprajna sage is absolutely still in the centre of his being. And this stillness is no inertia; it is infinitely vibrant in self-consciousness, the incessant becoming—conscious-of-itself-and-its-objects, which is self-consciousness, spanda of eternal creativity.

In self-consciousness, quiet yet intensely vibrant, what do we say? Suddenly emptied of *raga* [indulgence, attachment], *dvesa* [jealousy], and *moha* [infactuation, endearment], *bhaya* [fear] and *krodha* [anger], not as a result of deliberately executed sadhana necessarily, but by reason of that play of probability which is Divine grace, we are incredibly stilled and fill the Universe with the vibration of our still-centredness. What do we say wordlessly in that vibrant stillness? This: I am that I am, soham, I am all that as well, all is me and I am all, I am not separate from and do not separate anything or anyone. God and nature and beast and saint and sinner am I. In being still we speak the truth of advaita,[1] and when we are not still as in laziness, or as in activity clamorous with separativeness, we deny advaita, we say there is I and absolute others, that you and I and nature and God are precariously, contingently related to one another, manageably at times but mostly hopelessly. All men are others, not brothers, we imply. But none and nothing is other in the stillness of self-consciousness. We are false when not still.

And in speaking advaita sincerely and not merely professorially, in soliloquy or in earnest speech, what do I do? What do I do in thinking advaita? In imagining advaita? This: I love as myself all that is, even in its grossest camouflage of appearance as not-self. I love truly and not compulsorily, or self-deceivingly or limitedly, and conceitedly, altruistically and reversibly all others, because I see none and nothing as other than myself. But to live advaita is not easy. It requires a ceaseless holding fast to the image and idea and power and glory of the self and self-consciousness, one in all and as the sole central reality of all, hateful or harmful or hideous appearances to the contrary notwithstanding. Advaitin love is constantly threatened by dualistic doubt, but the gates of Hell do not prevail against it because it is founded on the indubitability of self-consciousness and is a flowering of it, a lotus of self-certainty springing out of unpromising self-doubting dualistic mud, pankaja.

Is it not ironical that in what appears to be minimum doing, that is, being still, we say the maximum, we claim the maximum, we claim advaita? Equally ironically, in what logically is the most economical speaking, the speaking of advaita, we *do* the maximum conceivable, love all that is and can be as ourselves.

We cannot think advaita and speak advaita without living advaita. The doctrine that we do something in saying something manifests itself as a necessary truth in the context of speaking and living advaita. If advaita is right, to think separatively is to try and separate, and to think unitively is internally simultaneously to begin to undo separativeness and separation. Likewise, to live advaita, that is, to be absolutely still in the self, is internally and simultaneously to make the most catholic claim conceivable. This thought should throw some explanatory light on Sri Ramana's declaration that mauna is the most incessant eloquent speech. For as we advance towards the perfection of mauna, what we say in our advance claims more and more of subject matter until it claims all in the Mahavakya *sarvamkhalvidam brahma* [all this Universe is verily Brahman]. Equally significantly, if we can imagine Arjuna asking Sri Krishna after the battle of Kurukshetra, after all that slaughter and agony and loss, what it all comes to, what it all means and says, can we not imagine Acyuta declaring that all says just this, inconceivably economically, that I (Vasudeva) am all?

Austin distinguished between what he called a *locutionary* act, which is the act of uttering certain words with specifiable meanings and standard force, and an *illocutionary* act, which is what we do *in* performing a locutionary act, such as promise, command, assume, etc., something, and between these and what he called a *perlocutionary* act, which is what we bring about as a result, as a causal result, of performing a locutionary and an illocutionary act. Putting to use the notion of what we say in doing something, we can say a locutionary act is what we minimally relevantly do *by* uttering certain noises intentionally;[2] an illocutionary act is the saying of something *in* producing those noises, the *language* we utter; and a perlocutionary act is what we minimally relatively do *by* our illocutionary act, a causal consequence of the noise-sequence and not merely its temporal realisation, the difference we make to the world relevant to our uttering of language and the language we utter. Since it is the illocutionary act in Austin which is a proper piece of communication, that is, a vehicle of meaning, it is helpful to regard it as the specific saying of something in doing the locutionary act. Thus, the notion of doing something in saying something, which is most clearly exemplified in the idea of an illocutionary act, becomes clarified by the notion of saying something in doing something because that is what an illocutionary act turns out to be.[3]

It may, therefore, be maintained that the notion of saying something in doing something is more primitive than the notion of doing something in saying something. Austin's theory of performative utterance importantly protects linguistic theory from behaviourism, by attributing to the heart of language, namely illocutionary meaning, a status not of a causal outcome of uttering semantic noises but of an accomplishment internal to and constitutive of such utterance in appropriate contexts and given undisqualifying backgrounds. But there remains the following difficulty or possible difficulty in Austin's general communicative theory. The saying remains locutionary and the heart of linguistic communication, namely illocutionary meaning, becomes a piece of doing or a class of doings. On the other hand, the notion of saying something in doing something both protects saying from behaviouristic reduction by making it not a causal consequence of doing but the inherent speaking of doing, and by retaining the notion of saying as characterising the essence of linguistic communication. An atomistic acts-oriented account of linguistic communication is avoided at the same time as preserving Austin's insight regarding the non-causal status of linguistic meaning. The notion of saying something in doing something has also many other dimensions of explanatoriness which I cannot here explore adequately.[4]

One chief *prima facie* objection to the notion of saying something in doing something could be that doing is crass, not a candidate for the status of vehicle of meaning at all. The most general overcoming of this objection that I can think of is via drawing attention to being still, doing nothing overtly and yet being intensely dynamic, the stance being the very heart of maximal saying, the saying of advaita in its all-claiming sweep. Considered in this light, doing is a very appropriate vehicle of meaning. Philosophy of language does not need to separate meaning from doing, it needs a more satisfactory notion of doing than behaviourism or voluntaristic activism permit. Self-conscious intentional doing, as opposed to process, is deliberately discontinuous; and deliberate discontinuity in behaviour is inescapably an invitation to interpretation and witnessing, hence a saying and speaking. Self-consciousness is a ceaseless beholding and upholding of itself in all things in ascharyam, mother-tongue of all speaking whose basic idiom is 'Am I this !', 'Am I not that?'

III

In being still we say everything because there remains nothing to be said once advaita has been found. When is it that we say nothing? If I see nature and the world as other than myself, and if I see you and him and her and God separatively and as essentially other than myself, and with my effort to overcome my alienation from all things and beings great and small consuming all my energy and life, how can I possibly have any time to say anything to anyone? Even what appears on a dualistic basis to be a piece of saying would really be a piece of the attempted overcoming of imagined others. All manipulation of human beings by one another is founded upon a failure a vision, a failure to see oneness, self, one in and as all things and everyone. And manipulation is not communication. So when we manipulate nature or man or the gods or God, we say nothing. And when we are still in oneness with all, we say everything that has to be said.

But is there not between saying everything and saying nothing a region of saying something as opposed to nothing which is inhabited by most human communication? What does human communication come to exoterically? In answer to this question let me summarise a consideration which I have developed at length in my book *Presuppositions of Human Communication* (1974). The heart of the argument is this: If I am to tell you something, tell you that something is the case or tell you to make something the case, I must not [do so] openly, and I don't have to at all try to get you to believe that something is the case or to make something the case, bring it about that something is the case. I must adopt a style of behaviour which has the *form* of an act of trying to get you to believe or do something, but manifestly not the *force* of such an action. And if my behaviour directed towards you is of a vocative kind, that is, if it involves inviting your attention to myself, as opposed to merely causally securing it, then and then alone can my behaviour be interpretable by you or anybody else as conveying meaning, as meaning that something is the case or that you are to do something or that I want you to believe that something is the case or make something the case of your own free accord. Indeed vocative action itself exhibits such a style of behaviour. In addressing you I openly pretend to be trying causally to attract your attention to myself, I unconcealedly simulate attention—attracting behaviour, in consequence enabling you to interpret what I am doing as expressing the *meaning*, as saying, that I want you to attend to me. Here we have the outline of just that region between saying everything and saying nothing which we wanted to locate. In openly pretending to be trying to get you to believe or do something, I make it clear to you in essence that I do not regard you as other, an another, who can be causally manipulated by me. My behaviour denies dualism. In a sense, it also like being still says everything because it implies advaita. But the specific way in which it denies dualism becomes a vehicle of less than total saying so that I am able to say quite humdrum things to you or important things even which are not the explicit sayings of advaita.

Thus, if by the use of an indicative sentence in communication with you I make it clear to you that I am openly pretending to be trying, by deploying the mechanism of conditioned response, to get you to believe the proposition indicated by the indicative sentence in question, I not only at the highest level of generality enunciate advaita, I also express the meaning that something more mundane is the case, let you know that I want you to believe something of your own free accord. The humdrum becomes possible in communication because of the profound and the total. Quite truly in communication we first seek the kingdom of Atman-Brahman and secure it, and all *vyavaharika* [pragmatic] meanings become available to us. This is how we are able to say everything and also something as opposed to nothing.

There is another way of looking at this whole question of saying everything, nothing, and something as opposed to nothing.

My unconcealed simulation or open pretence in communicative behaviour can be regarded as *niskama karma*, as an action done essentially for its own sake. This is because my action or behaviour involves a manifest surrender of efficaciousness to you, my audience. You interpret my action as expressing my wish that *you* believe or do something and as meaning something, and not at all primarily and identifyingly as an attempt to *make* you believe or do anything, the question of believing and doing having been left entirely to you. Indeed there would appear here to be not only niskama but also an absence of that sense of agency which we are asked by Sri Krishna to surrender to Him, the agency being surrendered by me to you in relation to the matter of your coming to believe or do something. And indeed in its advaitin insightfulness, communicative action must regard the audience as Atman-Brahman, Vasudeva, who is all secretive, and therefore communicative action appears to exhibit powerfully the teaching of the Gita interpreted in an open-endedly advaitin way. I tap you on the shoulder, making it communicatively clear to you that I was not in my action trying causally to turn you round to face me, that my shoulder-tapping action, in consequence, expressed the meaning that you are to attend to me where you and I could be anyone. Now it cannot be that you and I could be anyone but not one another! It would be a travesty of the idea of universality which goes with meaning if this were the case. Somebody may wish to make peace by saying that you and I could not be one another at the same time. But why not? If self or Atman-Brahman is regarded as infinitely and simultaneously many-centred, and advaita interpreted communicatively requires that we so regard Atman-Brahman, then you and I are simultaneously one another because of one. There is here on one view action without desire because although my action is interpretable as expressing a complex desire of the mind, it is also capable of being regarded merely as an expression of meaning, a universal possibility and structure of cognition and volition. There is also quite decisively a surrender of power to you, my audience. And there is the seeing of selfhood as one in you and me and all else. Is this not the heart of the Bhagavadgita? Thus, when we say something as opposed to nothing, we invoke the Gita! All is sacred in communication, the saying everything which is mauna or stillness and the saying of quite ordinary things also. The teaching of the Gita is not any specific thing that I say in saying something to you as opposed to nothing; it is rather what is involved in my saying anything at all to you, in the general structure and style of all communicative behaviour. The greatest message is truly the medium itself. For the medium is communication and communication is either saying everything as in saying advaita, or it is the manifestation of the total surrender of agency and egoity which is *bhakti* [devotion].

IV

Sri Ramana Maharshi insisted again and again that no one had to become a jnani, that all are already and eternally jnanis. Why then is it necessary for one like Sri Ramana to speak to others, to teach others, and why is it necessary for others to listen to one like Him and to receive the truth from Him? One classical answer, a powerful answer if also a much-misunderstood answer, is that our seeking of *jnana* [knowledge], or the imparting of jnana, by a teacher to us are both illusion, not reality, because when we realise that we are Atman-Brahman, we will realise that we were always so and that we never needed to seek or receive jnana. But for those who are unable easily to see the truth of this, it should be possible to point out that the heart of even mundane communicative seeking and receiving, and also, of course, the heart of receiving in mauna, is also advaita, because the heart of human communication witnesses to advaita, to the eternality of our jnanihood.

Oneness is not exclusive of play, the play of world-appearance or the play of human life in intricate communication and cooperation. The intensity of the play, its darker and more traumatic acts and scenes, often camouflage the underlying oneness of which the world and human life are a play or a display; but without the oneness, the play or display would be unintelligible and not only unbearable, rather it would be unbearable because essentially unintelligible. Two cannot play, they can only fight and destroy one another in gross or subtle ways. One alone can in play appear to be two and play the great game and unfold all the drama of recovery of self-knowledge.

V

Does the world or nature entirely only impinge upon us? And insofar as it does not overwhelm us with its causal power, is this failure to be attributed to some power of causal resistance in us? Are we to suppose that finite man has the causal power to resist the impinging causality of the infinite world? This would be an extreme fantasy, just as the view of a world benignly waking us to a perception of it as the prince awakens the sleeping beauty would be fantasy. The world is a passionate lover, a quiet as well as an insistent speaker, a disarmingly open as well as a deeply camouflaged partner in a play of hide-and-seek. But it is in play with us, quite simply because the only conceivable alternative to play would be our instant destruction. Kant's dictum that all our knowledge arises from experience but is not derived from it bears a communicative interpretation. The world as experienced disavows pure causal efficiency by only occasioning thought and belief, but not coercing it. The transformation of thought and belief—after their occasioning by experience—into insight and knowledge is the process of our more-or-less distorted reading and rendering of the message which the world communicates to us in its fundamental act of disavowing pure causal efficacy, in its act of pressing upon us but not overwhelming us with its power. In being there, the world is vibrantly dynamic, a *sthitaprajna muni*, or an instructing sage. In being there in this dynamic mode, the world says a hundred million different things as opposed to saying nothing, depending, analogously to the case of human communication, on the specific style and structure of disavowal, of causal efficacy which is our manifold experience of it; but abidingly it says also, *a priori*, that it is one with us in a way which becomes progressively clearer with the advance of insight and theory and imagination, with the advance of metaphysics and science and art. The world speaks to us, advaita its secret communication.

Postscript: What you confess to me in confidence, swearing me to secrecy, is logically strictly a private language, not because no one else can understand the secret words, but because they are unsharable unlimitedly with others without their ceasing to be secret words. Advaita is logically the most private word, impossible to communicate to *others*, there being no others. Rhetoric must not race beyond realisation.

VI

Apparent others, aspects of the world in their apparent otherness to myself, may occasion a stirring of myself to self-consciousness, but are not the mysterious operation of bestirring which has to remain my own, which has to be nothing but the rhythm of alertness of self-consciousness itself if we are talking about a subject's being stirred to self-consciousness unabsentmindedly in the sense of being moved to take a hold of himself/herself existentially reflexively. And yet apparent others do in communication, and in the vocative act which is at the heart of communication, stir me to self-consciousness by putting me in mind of the reflexive thoughts 'I' and 'me'. It would follow, then, that they can be none other than myself, witnessing to the many-centredness of self-consciousness, not to a plurality of selfhood. Communication is the many-centredness of self-consciousness, self-consciousness is not the internalisation of communication. Speaking and listening are the spanda of Shiva, *atmabodha*, illumined self-consciousness: Hermeneutics of Being.

Notes

[1] By 'advaita', in this chapter, I mean the non-duality of ultimate reality in all the coherent range of senses indicated in Upanishadic Mahavakyas and elsewhere at the heights of Indian metaphysical insightfulness, all the way down from antiquity to the witness of Ramana Maharshi and the innovativeness of Sri Aurobindo in our own times.

[2] Not a causal consequence of the noises, but the temporal realisation of the noise-sequence itself, our *uttering* of language.

[3] In uttering the words, 'I promise', in an appropriate context, I perform the illocutionary act of promising, according to Austin. But what do I *say* in so doing? Within the framework of Austin's theory of performative utterance, one would have to say in answer to this question *either* that I say nothing, I *do* something, that is, promise something, which most implausibly condemns a sophisticated linguistic act to semantic vacuity, *anartha*; *or* that the only saying involved here is the locutionary act of saying, uttering, the words

'I promise', which is an equally implausible reduction of a highly evolved cognitive and communicative action to automatism. Surely in addition to being the committing of the institutionally binding performative action which it is, my act of uttering the words 'I promise' is a massive *saying* of something, equal to the complete analysis of what promising is, filled out with the details of my specific promise. That analysis is what I inexplicitly say in doing the action describable as uttering certain words or as binding myself in a certain way.

[4]Two important clarificatory applications of the notion of saying something in doing something are: (a) Ethical judgement, invitation, commendation, etc., may be regarded as implying that certain actions and attitudes, or certain classes of action and attitude and other categories of things, are such that *in* doing or cultivating them, or seeking them, we *say* something which is necessary, metaphysical, non-trivial truth. To say that something is a virtue or a moral obligation, for example, is to imply that *in* cultivating or doing it, we *say* that we are not separatively other than what appear to be others, other beings, that is, to affirm necessary metaphysical non-trivial advaitin truth. Ethics becomes cognitive again. (b) All free action impliedly affirms its permittedness, no man being under a law of freedom apart from mankind. This truth illumines the theory of truth. A declarative utterance is an iteration of indicative words and, as such, an action impliedly affirms its permittedness, that is, the reiterability of the indicative words in question. Thus, when in affirmation of the truth of a declarative utterance we say, 'You can say that again', we only articulate the implied permission of the utterance itself. Language invites endorsement.

References

Austin, J. L. 1962. *How to Do Things with Words*. Oxford: Oxford University Press.

Gandhi, Ramchandra. 1974. *Presuppositions of Human Communication*. Delhi: Oxford University Press.

— twelve —

Philosophical Scepticism and Theistic Faith

Theistic Inquiry Cannot Be a Denial of Advaita, Only a Necessary Preparation for It[*]

What is it to doubt the reality of the (external) world? Does such doubt presuppose that one is not doubting the reality of the (internal) world? What does the external–internal contrast come to here? Possibly this: subjectivity (one's own) and its contents contrasted with that which is encountered as non-subjectivity. But aren't items of subjectivity also non-subjective? A particular feeling, sensation: Or, is it that items of subjectivity are also subjective, that is, have a dimension of inwardness? They are not objects barely encountered anyway. Their being gathered together within the matrix of one's own subjectivity frees them from the status of instances of encountered otherness.

What is it to doubt the reality of an item of one's own subjectivity? One can reject it as not-being-oneself. One can doubt its internality to oneself. There is yogic-meditative support for this. One can sustain an idea of oneself as other than every encountered item of one's own subjectivity. *Nairatmyavad* is the doctrine that

*Unpublished, University of Hyderabad, July 1980.

one doesn't encounter oneself as an item of one's own subjectivity. (Does one not ever? Suddenly in a mirror-reflection, or a snatch of voice, in a sharp self-image, is there not an encountered icon of oneself? Or is this delusive vanity?)

There might be also other ways of doubting the reality of items of one's own subjectivity. One might doubt the *truth* of every thought, feeling, sensation, etc. Pain is not pain, anger is cowardice, longing is not longing. The idea that items of one's own subjectivity are essentially misleading. Hunger is not hunger, pity is not pity. False movements, the unself-disclosing character of items of subjectivity, their essential camouflage of themselves, maya.

Wittgenstein: I can't deny that I am in pain. But can't I doubt the self-explanatoriness of pain? I can think that its inner meaning is something else, its opposite? (Items of subjectivity as false self-images, distorting mirror-reflections. The intensest iconoclasm is advaita's destruction of all self-images.)

Can I entertain the doubt that items of my own subjectivity perhaps have no meaning whatever? Yes, and here we are close to doubting the reality of the internal world. What is compelling about items of subjectivity appears to be their meaningfulness. A pain is meaningful because it has to do with *me*? I am in pain. Meaning as a characterisation of oneself? But doubt has a foothold here.

But is there not a more 'objective' meaning of items of subjectivity? Is a twinge in itself a *message*? Items of subjectivity are revelatory of and about *myself.* Percepts about something else. Is that the internal–external distinction? To sustain the *nairatmyavadi* doctrine, I have deliberately to reject items of subjectivity as not-being-myself. Not so with percepts. They do not even *prima facie* claim to be myself or parts of myself. One can make a special effort to see them as oneself or parts of oneself, but not without fantasy. (The world as my outreaching and dispersed body, mind, being.)

The Berkeleyan position reduces percepts to items of subjectivity. There is no *pressure* to reject percept, as not being myself or parts of myself. Am I thinking of colour exclusively here? What about touch? (I reject sensations. Percepts reject me?)

What is it to doubt the reality of percepts? To try and assimilate them to sensations (items of subjectivity) would be one way of doubting their reality. ('They do not point to the not-myself', one might maintain, complain.)

To stop doubting the reality of percepts is to stop assimilating them to sensations. What becomes of them then? Do they embody or constitute non-subjectivity? What about the percepts embodying another person? What do percepts embody? Nothing. Or can subjectivity be regarded as a something embodied by the perceptual contours of a human body, for instance? Percepts do point to the not-myself. But this not-myself turns out to be nothing. Because this not-myself is non-subjectivity. Finite subjectivity is haunted by an environing nothingness, the nothingness of matter.

But have I not so far totally ignored solidity? But the inner life even of solidity is incomprehensible. In fact, if the world were regarded exclusively phenomenalistically, it would be *something*, the being of percepts. But as something revealed by percepts, it is nothing. To refute phenomenalism is to affirm the nothingness of matter.

(The world of appearance and the appearance of the world.)

The nothingness of the world is the non-graspability of non-subjectivity. Phenomenalism is the fallacious attempt to deny non-subjectivity. A refusal to face nothingness. So philosophical scepticism about the world is really at bottom an affirmation of its nothingness. This nothingness can be seen as the 'place' of infinite creativity—the creativity of appearance. Maya and leela. The nothingness of maya is the possibility of leela.

Connected with the idea of the nothingness of the world is the thought that no given world-appearance exhausts the source of its creativity. The religious hope of novel kinds of world-environment is connected with this. But such hope is close to despair about nothingness. The thought that at death we become nothing is the fear that non-subjectivity is nothingness. (Becoming non-subjective. Participating in the infinite insentient creativity of appearance? Nirvana?)

The nothingness of non-subjectivity is not located in any one given material 'object'. What would it be for nothingness to be so confined? To submit to the world is to submit to its nothingness. Finite subjectivity is haunted by the thought of infinite environing nothingness. The play of appearance is the assurance of a miraculous distancing of nothingness.

What about the 'order' of the world of appearance? Order is what compensates nothingness. Order is a substitute for 'being'. In the world, we are not going to find 'being', only order, the shield against nothingness.

The most beautiful order is also a shield against nothingness. The grace of God in the world is appearance. The immanentist clings to appearance, not realising that appearance passes away, revealing nothingness. The clinging to the world of appearance is to be distinguished from a celebration of God's creativity.

The passage from consciousness to unconsciousness is indicative of the permanent possibility of appearance vanishing into nothingness.

Appearance is not an illusion. The argument from illusion is mistaken. But the fallaciousness of that argument substantiates only the 'order' of appearance. The non-subjectivity, and therefore nothingness, of whatever appearance points beyond itself towards is unassailed by the failure of the argument from illusion.

What I had, earlier on, described as the contrast between items of subjectivity and percepts calls for another look: What percepts point beyond themselves towards is non-subjectivity, nothingness. But what do items of subjectivity point to beyond themselves?

But let me first ask another question: What about percepts that delineate the boundary of a subjective being, its 'body'? Do they also point to nothingness? This can't be true! They 'house' subjectivity. They don't 'point' at all—is that the answer?

The body does not point to subjectivity, it appears to 'house' it. But for a different reason, it again seems to indicate nothingness. The appearance of the living body and the experience of the living body, its subjectivity—does the former 'point' to the latter?

Items of subjectivity do not reduplicate the appearance of the living body. A toothache does not have the 'shape' of a tooth. Or thought the shape of the brain. (Ignore fantastical interestingness here.)

The non-nothingness of subjectivity. The living human body (mine) is not related to me in the way in which the world of appearance is related to me. That world shields me from the nothingness, for example, non-subjectivity. But the living human body is different. How?

In 'inhabiting' the living human body, I am within, or so it looks, that which appearance points to beyond itself. I am within what could easily have been a non-subjective 'place'.

But I do not encounter nothingness. I encounter items of subjectivity. This is what it means to be saved from nothingness. To be subjective in a world of non-subjectivity is to be saved from nothingness. (Gandhiji: In the midst of death there is life.)

Subjectivity is comprehensible. It is the very meaning of comprehensibility. Non-subjectivity is indicated by appearance, and non-subjectivity is nothingness. Pan-psychism is the fallacy of generalising from the subjectivity of one's own living body to the subjectivity of every other 'place'. Why is the generalisation fallacious?

Because the world indicated by appearance demands to be understood as non-subjectivity, I can't, generalising from myself, ignore this demand. Finite subjectivity finds itself as a freak in a non-subjective world. But this need not be an experience of absurdity or despair.

One can say this: Whereas embodied in appearance—being a 'place' indicated by appearance—I should have been nothing, I am subjective, I *am*, I am not nothing.

There is ground here for hoping that when I die—when I most dramatically become a non-subjective place, I would be saved again. I am, therefore I will be saved from nothingness. Rather: I should have been nothing, but I am, I am subjective. So I can hope for the miracle of a rise of subjectivity beyond death.

Appearance shields us from nothingness, subjectivity saves us from it. The 'order' of appearance is what we find in the world as a substitute for nothingness. (And also, of course, vividness, generative of all the importance of that world within the world, appearance within the appearance, the works of man and the story of man.)

Subjectivity is not the 'order' of appearance. It is an intrusion into the nothingness of being. It can vanish without appearance vanishing. The environing nothingness can 'displace' it.

Mortality is the evanescence of subjectivity? Subjectivity is located *within* nothingness. It is the 'empty' place indicated by appearance. Subjectivity shares with nothingness its not-thingness. Nairatmyavad.

Modern writers (Sartre) have misunderstood the not-thingness of subjectivity and called it nothingness in contrast to the 'solidity' of matter. Being shielded and actually being saved from nothingness. Because this is miraculous, we can hope for post-mortem subjectivity. Otherwise, our generalisation would be a feeble one.

Subjectivity seems to be embodied. *This* person and *that* person. Is non-subjectivity also embodied—*this* material object and *that* material object? This is hard to grasp.

What are the limits of non-experience? Spatial metaphors deceive us here. Non-subjectivity is *totality*, the all-comprehending void, nothingness. Being finite seems to be a feature of subjectivity as we understand it. Being non-subjective is boundless. That is the terror of nothingness. Oblivion.

The notion of a bounded subjectivity is by no means a clear notion. My subjectivity does not have the shape of my body. Subjectivity over-reaches the body all the time. At any rate, in normalcy, in pain and suffering, there is a congealing of subjectivity. But is subjectivity infinite as we know it? The finitude of our subjectivity has to do with a victory over infinite nothingness.

As a sign of the ultimate non-supremacy of nothingness, finite subjectivity is enough. There is no vanity in the works of God. But subjectivity is evanescent. We die. What of this?

Because in the midst of nothingness there is subjectivity, and because this is strictly miraculous (creation out of nothing), there is ground for the hope that there will be a miraculous resuscitation of subjectivity beyond death.

The essential nothingness of non-subjectivity makes it possible to think this: innumerably different orders of world-appearance are possible. The appropriate order to sustain post-mortem subjectivity will be available.

I am now affirming a link between the world of appearance and subjectivity. What is this link? Subjectivity would be 'blind' if it lacked an environment of appearance. Worse, it would be self-centredness.

Between a given dimension of subjectivity and a given order of world-appearance, there is a pre-established harmony. (The connectedness of mystic self-transformations of subjectivity with 'visions' is explicable on this supposition.) There must be a connection between subjectivity and what shields it from the nothingness of non-subjectivity. (The relation between the centre and the boundaries.)

What I am doing is this: Explicating, to the extent this is possible, not only for me but generally, the structure of grace in *our* world-situation.

(Compare the religious orientation of such an exercise with the secular philosophical unearthing of the basic conceptual scheme which makes experience intelligible.) The general structure of salvation must already be given. (Compare: Moksha is not to be sought.)

What about the physical structure of the world? Does it not determine what is and what is not possible here, including the character and career of subjectivity and appearance here? The structure of the world is a measure of the *work*, the miraculous work of God in fashioning subjectivity out of and in the midst of nothingness. For this reason, physics is inexhaustible. And there must be possible an infinite variety of types of physics.

To posit the physical structure of the world *as* the ultimate reality is not just idolatrous. It is to see as fixed, finite, the infinite work of God. For the humblest mode of subjectivity is the consequence of Gods' infinite work.

What is the connection between what I have called the physical structure of the world and the nothingness of non-subjectivity of which I have spoken at such length? There is, on the one hand, the inexhaustible character of physical understanding. On the other hand, the terror of nothingness. No finite grasp of physical structure releases us from this terror. The structure is there—mathematically intelligible—to sharpen our sense of an environing nothingness.

Materiality seems to have a *character*. Why? Because appearance must have a structure and because ultimately materiality determines appearance? This way of regarding the matter fails to acknowledge the 'gap' between a condition, however elaborate, of material organisation and the appearance of appearance. What of this 'gap'? The phenomenalist wishing-away of this gap is as unsatisfactory as the materialist refusal to acknowledge its reality. How does one understand it? (This is not a phenomenon which calls for an explanation, but a riddle at the heart of the meaning of 'phenomenon' or 'appearance'.)

The order of materiality never *is* appearance because it is, as a given order, at an infinite distance from appearance, because nothingness is at an infinite distance from appearance. The order of materiality is a shadow of appearance. The order of materiality is the structure of evanescence as appearance fades into vacuity.

The fading of appearance into vacuity is more intelligible than the transformation of the order of materiality into appearance. The two movements are the same. Unconsciousness and death are persistent witnesses to the evanescence of appearance, its sinking into the nothingness of non-subjectivity. Also, the nothingness of a *given* (indicated) area of non-subjectivity is imaginatively always graspable—at any rate, it can be and is so acknowledged. (Whether or not there is life on the moon, there is no life *in* the moon, no subjectivity.) What does all this show? It augments the conviction that the order of materiality, however elaborate, does not detract from the nothingness of the non-subjectivity of materiality.

But how can something elaborately structured, like the order of materiality, be nothingness?

Any *given* order of materiality must infinitely fail to exhibit the work of God in fashioning appearance out of and in the midst of nothingness. Would an infinitely structured, and so described, an order of materiality *be* appearance? Would it 'exhibit' appearance? Would it close the gap between materiality and appearance?

Any *given* structure of appearance again does not exhibit God's creativity. But *the fact* of appearance, however abbreviated, is a sign of God's creativity. So we don't *need* to ask: Can an infinitely delineated order of materiality *be* appearance? *That* there is appearance, in the midst of nothingness, is a sign of the infinite work of God. The impossibility of an infinite physics does not preclude the possibility of our grasping the infinity of Gods' work.

What of subjectivity in all this? Subjectivity and appearance are not identical, I have not said they are. There is a *distance* between subjectivity and appearance. What is the character of this distance?

(Is there merely a non-identity between subjectivity and items of subjectivity, not amounting to distance?)

Items of subjectivity are a measure of the finitude of subjectivity. Subjectivity itself is a sign of the saving act of God. On the side of nothingness, but not nothing.

Although there is a non-identity between subjectivity (as it points to itself in self-consciousness in its most intimate form) and items of subjectivity, the two go together. Mystery and humility combine?

Subjectivity as it points to itself in self-consciousness has the character of a *sheerly given* and yet infinitely distant *someone*. Infinitely distant from items of subjectivity? Is this a yogic delusion?

Our condition of finitude means this: Items of subjectivity are *other than* me, but they are ascribable to me (true of me). As other-than items of my subjectivity, I am the eternally aloof purusha, but as the subject of which these items are true, I am finite, an ego.

My infinity is my subjecthood. My finitude is my subjectivity. The fashioning of appearance is the fashioning of predicates in the absence of subjecthood.

Nothingness is covered by appearance. (The many-veiled not-thingness of the holy of holies. Holiness and terror came together, fear of God.) But the predicates of appearance inescapably point to nothingness. (Away from subjecthood.)

Items of subjectivity are also predicates. But they point to someone, not to nothingness. Yet they fade like appearance. Subjectivity is evanescent. Measure of finitude. Being miraculous, though, subjectivity can *hope* for the miracle of resuscitation beyond death.

The world of appearance (any *given* world of appearance) does not exhaust me. My subjectivity is at an infinite distance from appearance. *This* distance is a sign of the eligibility of subjectivity for an infinite variety of world-appearances.

Does not this indicate some kind of perfection? The complete givenness of subjectivity (which is subjecthood)—is this perfection, a kind of perfection.

I am finite, infinitely distant from infinitude but complete. This is the *gift* of self-consciousness. Completeness is not absoluteness. Isn't a man in the making? Am I finished, complete?

The reality of grace is such that though I am infinitely distant from infinitude, nevertheless I *am*, in my completeness. (Though while a sinner, I am saved.)

Does not this misidentification of givenness, completeness, with absoluteness, infinitude, generate the misunderstood *aham-brahmasmi* [I am Brahman, the Absolute] of vulgar advaita?

Take appearance away and subjectivity confronts nothingness. Confrontation with nothingness and the absence of an environment of appearance. Aloneness, which is to be situated in a void. Hell? Alienation?

The distance between subjectivity and appearance is always a void-in-the-offing. Appearance shuts it out.

Am I primarily here thinking of visual appearance? No. Silence is always broken by a sound. I am not always touching things. Tactile appearance cancels the nothingness of placelessness.

I am always subjective, not always in the midst of appearance. The evanescence of subjectivity is not the same as the evanescence of appearance. Appearance is intermittent. Subjectivity is persistent. Appearance is recurrent protection against nothingness. Subjectivity is a *defeat* of nothingness.

Appearance is *for* a subject. Subjectivity is the condition of subjecthood. Items of subjectivity are not merely *for* me; they *qualify* me.

It makes sense to ask the Berkeleyan question: What is there when there is no appearance for a subject? Void. But it doesn't make sense to ask: What is there when there are no items of subjectivity for a subject? Items of subjectivity are *of* a subject, nor *for* it, merely.

The phenomenalist atomisation of subjectivity is fallacious because items of subjectivity do not relate to subjecthood in the way in which appearance relates to subjecthood.

There is besides the sheer givenness of subjecthood as the one who is myself, but this is not an *experience*.

The otherness of subjectivity from items of subjectivity is such that the evanescence of items of subjectivity does not begin to exhaust subjectivity (subjecthood) in the way in which the evanescence of appearance begins to exhaust the 'world'.

I use 'subjectivity' and 'subjecthood' interchangeably, or very nearly so.

The fear of death is the fear of nothingness. But is it the same as the fear of the evanescence of items of subjectivity? Appearance is not contingent, it is variable. *Subjectivity* is contingent. The fear of death is connected with the self-knowledge of subjectivity, that is, the knowledge of its contingency. The fear of death is the most passionate apprehension of one's contingency.

The fear of death is not the fear that something will happen to me (a new item of subjectivity will begin to qualify me). It is the fear that I will become *nothing*. This must be distinguished from the fear both of the evanescence of appearance and the evanescence of items of subjectivity.

The thought of the loss of appearance and experience in unconsciousness is not necessarily always a fear: it is often the longing of unhappiness (suicide). Total somnolescence is not death.

The sheer givenness of subjecthood—the eternal aloofness of the purusha—is no guarantee against the fear of death, and is no proof of immortality.

The fear of death is a form of doubt—it is the intensest scepticism. What is this doubt, this scepticism?

Subjectivity, being miraculous, is the permanent possibility of its own resurrection (resuscitation). The fear of death is the doubt that subjectivity is not miraculous. The idea of the contingent (not the variable) is the idea of the non-miraculous. The contingent as a thing, an object. But have I not said that the notion of a material object, a material thing, is the notion of a void, nothingness? To see oneself as contingent is to see oneself as an object, as essentially nothing, a vanishing appearance.

Items of subjectivity are assimilated to appearance, and subjectivity itself becomes, tends toward, an item of subjectivity. Terror. The loosening of the distinction between subjectivity (subjecthood) and items of subjectivity, and between items of subjectivity and appearance, this is loss of faith.

The sustenance of the distinctions which, in the grip of the fear of death, become blurred, *is* faith. Not to fear death is to *hold fast to faith*, it is not to repeat to oneself any proof of immortality. The sheer givenness of subjecthood, of the eternally aloof purusha, is this not the possession of a proof of immortality?

Subjectivity's essential structure or stance is *faith,* not knowledge. Doesn't this go contrary to the age-old identification of self-conscious subjectivity with the most luminous knowledge? Self-consciousness is a mode of being, not a mode of knowing.

Luminosity, in the case of self-conscious subjectivity, is internal to subjectivity, not an appearance for it of an item of subjectivity. It is coextensive with subjectivity. Self-conscious subjectivity is a condition of *being luminous*. The effortlessness of this luminosity of being is a *marvel,* a source of great *wonder*. It is not like appearance which harbours nothingness.

The sheer givenness of the self-luminous purusha. But at the heart of this luminous mode of being, on the other side of the marvel and the wonder, is *doubt, fear*. How can I continue to be? The self-sustenance of self-conscious subjectivity is the faith that this luminosity is the work of God. The faith that it is sustained by God.

Faith is grounded in the miraculous. There is the miracle of appearance, shutting out nothingness. There is the miracle of subjectivity which, although on the side of nothingness, is not nothingness. The inexplicable distance between subjecthood and appearance, which is the assurance—the promise—that I am suitable for an infinite variety of world-appearances.

Then there is the relationship between the eternally aloof purusha and items of subjectivity. Items of subjectivity are true of me, but they don't exhaust me. Herein is the assurance—the hope and the promise—that I am forgiven. Faith is grounded in this entire range of the miraculous. These are not 'facts' which are 'evidence' for belief in God. These are elements of the structure of grace.

You can see your situation differently. You can see contingency non-miraculously and despair over it. You can regard appearance as 'epiphenomenon', subjectivity itself as an epiphenomenal determination of material organisation. *You can lose faith in all the sions of the miraculous.*

The very search for the explanation in the realm of the order of material reality is an abandonment of appearance and subjectivity, that is, of revelation, the givenness of 'quality' as [Robert M.] Persig uses this expression in *Zen and the Art of Motorcycle Maintenance.*

Abandonment of faith is, paradoxically, connected with another form of faith, faith in the ultimacy of a *given* order of materiality. But any *given* order of materiality must always be tantamount to nothingness compared to appearance, quality. But can't one talk of the faith in question here as faith in a possible infinite order of materiality, infinitely delineated?

The nothingness of a given, that is, finite, order of materiality compared to appearance does not acquire substantiality by being sought to be conceived as infinite.

But we are here at loggerheads with the conviction that we can't exhibit, but only acknowledge, the infinite work of God in fashioning appearance and subjectivity.

Materialism seeks to reduce appearance and subjectivity to nothingness. Epiphenomenality is a euphemism for nothingness. This is the exact opposite of faith, which finds the order of materiality more deserving of the status of nothingness.

Am I proposing hypotheses and conjectures about the world? No. I am enquiring into the *ideas* of a world, of appearance, subjectivity, and so on. But is conceptional analysis all that I am trying to do?

The nature of the kind of inquiry I am undertaking can be understood by trying to understand what prompts it. It isn't ignorance or even conceptual confusion, nor is it a metaphysical urge to understand the world as a whole, or scientific curiosity about areas and aspects of the world. What is it then that prompts me to ask what subjectivity is, what appearance is, what is nothingness, and so on?

I could say this: What is existentially given is a deep sense of gratitude for being—there at all, and deep anxiety that the felicity of being—there is appearance, not reality. That there is a wider environing nothingness which will not only overcome oneself and one's situation, but that this environing nothingness is proof of the absurdity and vanity of oneself and one's situation. The fear of absurdity and vanity undermines gratitude and can make one cynically self-sufficient. The moral unsatisfactoriness of cynical self-sufficiency is another starting point.

But isn't one nothing, religiously? Is there only an environing nothingness, not also an inward hollowness? To hold fast to gratitude in the midst of fear, the fear of absurdity and vanity, is religious, more particularly, theistic faith.

The inward nothingness, hollowness, indicates the *scale* of gratitude. The *given* is a structure of grace, in the context of faith. To seek to exhibit the structure of grace is to engage in a central task of religious philosophy (theology).

Religious philosophy doesn't begin with assumptions, but with a *conviction*, the deepest possible conviction that one is the recipient of grace.

This is not to say that one begins from *within* religious language or discourse. One begins with the possibility—which is the conviction mentioned above—of participating in religious discourse.

Philosophical scepticism is one starting point. Doubting the reality of the external world involves one in making a distinction between subjectivity, items of subjectivity and appearance. Doubting the reality of appearance turns out on reflection to be an acknowledgement of the nothingness which appearance seems to point away from itself towards. This prompts a reflection about God and his creation of appearance in the midst of nothingness, to shield us from it. Here is one ground for gratitude. Reflection here is not an explanation of phenomena, but a mode of understanding the very meaning of 'phenomenon' or 'appearance'. Why is one constrained to see an appearance in this way? Because wherever we encounter nothingness, we encounter that from which we would wish to be saved. Appearance saves us from an encounter with nothingness. Theistic language alone can express this sense of being saved. Reflection upon subjectivity brings us to acknowledge the miracle of being saved from nothingness *in our being*, and not merely from an encounter with nothingness. Subjectivity is in the 'region'—(nothingness)—embodied or indicated by appearance, but is not nothingness. A deeper ground for gratitude. The various other things that I have tried so far to say about the subjecthood and its otherness and distance from items of subjectivity and appearance illustrate further the character of gratitude which constitutes our fundamental situation.

What about philosophical scepticism regarding one's own reality? Can this serve as a starting-point for religious inquiry? Or has Descartes finally banished such scepticism on logical grounds?

Am I real? What sense can we give to this question? What does the *cogito* achieve? This: Doubting one's own reality involves one inescapably in an encounter with something which can only be described as an item of one's subjectivity—that I am doubting, that I am thinking, imagining, etc. And the reality of oneself is the necessary presupposition of any encounter with an item of one's subjectivity.

But is my reality only a presupposition? Insofar as this is the case, I can always think this: I am at an infinite distance from myself. This is embarrassing. The necessity of acknowledging externality as that which appearance points beyond itself to, that is, nothingness, non-subjectivity. The necessity of acknowledging internality as the necessity of acknowledging the reality of that which items of subjectivity presuppose, that is, myself, but at an infinite distance from my subjectivity. Aren't nothingness and infinite distance analogously frustrating? (Too close to death, too far from God.)

Nairatmyavad not as a denial of the reality of the self but an affirmation of its infinite distance from items of subjectivity, leading to an abandonment of self-talk in favour of an exclusive items-of-subjectivity talk.

Appearance indicates nothingness; items of subjectivity dramatise inaccessibility. But haven't I talked of the sheer givenness of the eternally aloof purusha?

We are, subjectivity is, I have said, on the side of nothingness, but not nothingness. Perhaps the utter inaccessibility of the purusha has to do with subjectivity being on the side of nothingness, with how precariously close subjectivity is to nothingness.

So the self, purusha, the locus of subjectivity, remains a presupposition? Whose presupposition? What is the mode of givenness of the self as one, as the being, who presupposes his own reality? Doesn't this mode of givenness have the structure of faith? What looks like a simple, massive, sheer, givenness of oneself to oneself turns out to be faith. What is the nature of this faith?

I am given to myself as presupposing my own reality, and I have said that this mode of givenness is a form of faith. Faith that items of subjectivity do not exhaust me, that the evanescence of items of subjectivity does not entail my annihilation. Perhaps I should have said 'the evanescence of a *given* order of items of subjectivity'. There is, I had said a long time ago, an infinite distance between oneself and appearance, a distance which is the ground for hoping that one is suitable for an infinite variety of world-appearances. Perhaps I should also say in the present context that there is an infinite distance between myself and any given order of items of subjectivity, a distance which is the ground for hoping that one can be the subject of an infinitely varied order of items of subjectivity.

The givenness of oneself to oneself is just this faith. The luminosity of faith. Self-consciousness, I had said, is a luminous mode of being, not a mode of knowing. The faith I am now talking about displays itself as luminous. This contradicts the idea that faith is necessarily darkness, a mode of blindness.

The non-absorption of oneself in a given order of appearance and a given order of items of subjectivity is an intimation, though not a proof, of immortality. Well, it is the structure of the faith that one will not be annihilated.

This faith is the form of our deepest self-confidence. It is *given*, it is an element in the order of grace which is given. It is something we can give thanks for. It is a feature, possibly existentially the deepest feature, of the form of *gratitude* which is our fundamental *stance* in being-there at all.

Why is the non-absorption of oneself in appearance and items of subjectivity not a *proof* of immortality? Because of one's finitude? What does this mean?

We [are] seen to have a powerful predilection for *losing ourselves* in appearance and in the order of items of subjectivity which is given. This is loss of faith. This is absentmindedness. But because this is natural, its possibility militates against faith in immortality.

The possibility of a pantheistic attitude is both the source of a great immanentist joy and also of the fear of annihilation as appearance and items of subjectivity fade away.

Faith and fear go together. Self-consciousness oscillates between the sense of the aloofness of purusha and the sheer immanence of the ego.

Compare the faith: Fear contrasted with the knowledge–ignorance contrast. Our inquiry isn't into the structure of what we know and what we don't know. It is an inquiry into the given structure of salvation and grace and self-confidence.

When I have talked, and when I talk, of subjectivity without qualification, I have in mind the reality of oneself as contrasted with the reality of appearance and *items* of subjectivity. But sometimes also as a reality which carries along with it the given order of items of subjectivity.

What *is* the fundamental difference between appearance and items of subjectivity? Appearance points away from us, hinting at, and shielding us from, nothingness. Items of subjectivity point *towards* us, threatening to but failing to, engulf us.

What does philosophical scepticism about oneself then come to? To this: How do we know that the evanescence of appearance and items of subjectivity will not entail our annihilation? But this *fear* should be distinguished from the profoundly absentminded abandonment of self-talk, witness nairatmyavadi and Humean empiricism.

But isn't nairatmyavad noble? Where does its nobility derive from? From this, perhaps. If I saw myself as wholly constituted by items of my subjectivity—that is, by my thoughts, feelings, sentiments, impulses, and the like—I would, if I were ethically motivated, seek concertedly to fashion an ethically satisfactory *whole* out of my items of subjectivity. The effort would, of course, have to be absentminded, but it would nevertheless be morally impressive. I will reject evil thoughts, feelings, etc., and admit into my stream of subjectivity only edifying items. Whether such a self-control and self-management can be free from absentmindedness is a question we need not go into here. The nairatmyavad moralist's goal would be self-improvement, although this description would not be available to him. Well, if not self-improvement, we can say that the goal in question here would be the fashioning of ethically satisfactory conglomerations of items of subjectivity.

The nairatmyavad perfectionist can be very *impressive*. The nobility and majesty of the yogi's *stance*, *face*. Self-control and self-management, these are very impressive ethically and subliminally, even physically. (The temptress is tempted by the yogi.)

The nairatmyavadi moralist and a certain sort of immanentist pantheistic-aestheticist are close in their efforts. The latter too fashions a sublime and beautiful form of the inward life. But there would be in his case a greater abandonment to items of subjectivity, involving moral risks which the former wouldn't take. Both would accept mortality without despair. Nobility and beauty are not less worth cultivating and fashioning because they fade away. Mortality would even lend pathos to their lives.

The possibility of such control and management of subjectivity is to be acclaimed, but non-absentmindedly. What do I mean by this?

I have said that the locus of subjectivity, the self, purusha, is at an infinite distance from items of subjectivity. This realisation is the faith that I can be the subject of an infinite variety of orders of items of subjectivity. But this faith goes hand in hand with a terrible fear. I can always stumble in my effort at managing and controlling my inner life. Evil, destructive, base items of subjectivity can find their way into my consciousness. The infinite distance between myself as the purusha and items of subjectivity is the permanent possibility of this happening. What is to protect me from this possibility? The nairatmyavadi's inner life may suddenly be invaded by the fear of mortality, the dawning conviction that he has been absentminded in assimilating his subjectivity to items of his subjectivity. The aestheticist can also despair. How are we to face all this? Not by our own efforts, for the limits of such efforts are, just what we are investigating. The possibility of the invasion of our subjectivity by unacceptable and terrible items is the proof of our finitude. The infinite distance between oneself and items of one's subjectivity is no guarantee that such an invasion cannot or will not take place. In a certain sort of mood, this distance discloses itself as the permanent possibility of the invasion of our subjectivity by evil and terrible items.

Don't we need help? And insofar as our self-management and self-control have been successful, aren't we to give thanks? Isn't there here another ground for gratitude?

In what sense has my inquiry so far been an inquiry into the nature and structure of faith? I have talked about appearance shielding us from the nothingness of non-subjectivity. Is this knowledge or faith? The *clarity* of appearance *is* actual protection against an encounter with nothingness. Where, in relation to appearance, is faith then? Because appearance and its vividness are miraculous, they provide a ground for the faith that there will always be an environment of vividness and structure, that we will not be plunged into the darkness, nothingness, of non-subjectivity. Faith already fulfils. Appearance is its fulfilment here, and its permanent possibility the faith.

What about subjectivity? I mean various things here—the locus of subjectivity described variously as the purusha, the self, I, etc. Items of subjectivity—thoughts, feelings, emotions, impulses and the like, and the stream of one's consciousness, inwardness, internality, and so on. Well, what about subjectivity? The luminosity of self-consciousness is here the 'proof' of faith, the anticipatory blessing. Where is faith here [in] them? (a) I am on the *other* side of appearance, where nothingness should be, but I am not nothingness. But I find myself related to myself presuppositionally. There is an infinite distance between myself—the locus of subjectivity, the purusha—and items of subjectivity. This is the ground for hoping—and such hoping is the essence of faith—that I can be the subject of an infinite variety of orders of items of subjectivity, that the given order of items of subjectivity does not exhaust me. The infinite distance between myself and items of my subjectivity *is* the structure of the faith mentioned above. This faith too breaks through into the luminosity of self-consciousness. (b) The luminosity of self-consciousness harbours an infinite distance, so also does the vividness of appearance. The mode of givenness of my subjectivity is as environed by appearance and the possibility of appearance. There is here again an apprehension—a piece of self-awareness—that there is an infinite distance between oneself and the given order of appearance, furnishing ground for the faith that one is suitable for an infinite variety of world-appearances. (c) The givenness of items of subjectivity calls for a careful look, I have neglected this question so far. The refutation of the thought or the possibility symbolised by the words, 'I am or could be nothing!', would have at least two aspects. There would, to serve as a refutation, be first of all the sheer givenness of self-consciousness, encouraging a nirguna view of oneself. But there would also be a revelation of oneself as adjectival, as being-so-and-so, being-in-so-and-so-condition, etc. The *saguna* [manifestation of God in form] mode of the givenness of oneself would be a double-refutation of nothingness. The nirguna and saguna modes of giveness would go hand in hand, a refutation and a double-refutation of nothingness. Where is faith here? Here, in this thought, that we would always transcend any *given* order of items of subjectivity, and also that one would be immanent in the stream of one's subjectivity, that is, that we would be characterisable by items of subjectivity, that is, that these items would be true of one; that is, that one would be always—because one is, now, miraculously transcendent—immanent, that is, share in the Divine mode of being.

I do not merely observe the things I have mentioned above, if only because one's status as an observer itself demands understanding.

The faith that I have sought to describe above, is it theistic faith? Yes, if at the heart of the description, there is a description of gratitude.

Can't all that I have tried to describe as being the essence of faith be simply taken as what is *given*, calling for no gratitude? Such a view would be plausible if there were no fear of nothingness, of obscurity, no death. Besides, there is nothing *given*, period. Each acknowledgement of the given—in all its comprehensiveness—invites theistic reflection.

So far I have merely drawn attention to gratitude, to thankfulness. What are the things that threaten gratitude turn it into dismissive cynicism? I'll come back to this question.

Consider now scepticism about others. I have argued elsewhere ('Non-violence is the Law of Our Being'; see Raghuramaraju 2015: 218–38) that the 'overwhelming' character of subjectivity, morally and metaphysically, necessitates my acknowledgement of the possibility of there being other centres of subjectivity besides myself. *I* cannot exhaust the gift, the coming-down of subjectivity. This subjectivity, in its aspect of something which is coming-down, necessarily seeks a plurality of centres. When confronted with what looks like another person, I ask: How do I know he is real? I am displaying my self-centredness. I am claiming that subjectivity exhausts itself in me. But this is not how the problem of our knowledge of other minds has generally appeared in philosophy. What of its classic formulations?

In communication, in community, we inescapably acknowledge the reality of one another. There can be at this level no scepticism about other minds. The question is not: How do I know that there are others besides myself? I inescapably acknowledge the reality of other persons in community and communication. And our situation of communicative community is *given*, it is our form of life (Wittgenstein). The question at the back of the sceptical question is this: How can there *be* centres of self-conscious subjectivity other than myself? What is it to conceive of, envision, such centres? How can self-conscious subjectivity (let us not for the moment think of other forms of subjectivity) become embodied *elsewhere* too, is not merely *where* I am, but elsewhere too?

I have already indicated one kind of approach to these questions: if the structure of my subjectivity is infinite gratitude, and if I am finite (that I am is borne out by the thought that I could be, should be, nothing, but am not nothing, finitude sufficing for this defeat of nothingness), then it is the crassest self-centredness to suppose that I could be the only centre of subjectivity. But does this moral approach enable us to *envision* other centres of subjectivity? I think it does. The imagination needed is moral imagination—or at least moral imagination. To the extent I fail to see that you have as much metaphysical right to be a centre of subjectivity as I have, I do not fully conceive of your reality, I merely acknowledge it. Perhaps this is too moralistic an approach, consider another thought. At the heart of my subjectivity, I witness the miracle of being in the midst of nothingness, in the midst of the permanent possibility of nothingness. Given also, as the structure of my subjectivity, infinite gratitude and a sense of finitude, I am led fully to expect and encounter a many-centred manifestation of the miracle of subjectivity. Such 'expectation' is what constitutes the substance of adequate visualisation or envisioning of another.

But others die, go away, are at a distance from me. What of this? Isn't there an infinite distance between myself and others? In communication and community, three is a miraculous abridgement of this distance. The communal character of gratitude is what makes this acknowledgement possible. Our coming together is an expression of communal gratitude.

What ensures the possibility of human communication is the miracle of fellowship. The miracle of fellowship—the miraculous coming-together, being-together, of selves—is a proof and a promise that we will not be ultimately alone. Death, departure, these will not rob us of community, fellowship.

But isn't privacy important? Isn't an ultimate aloneness to be sought? Both distancing and communion are guaranteed in communication. We don't need to be alone, we often need to be *left* alone for refreshment.

Our communality is not an undermining of the unique character of each self-conscious centre of subjectivity, of the transcendental structure of each specific self-conscious centre of subjectivity.

We are both grateful for fellowship, and for the distance between one another, and also for the consequent transcendence of any *given* order of fellowship.

But aren't certain order of fellowship, families, friendships, meant to be eternal? Aren't lovers meant to be eternally together? Possibly, but don't they also need new forms of fellowship, friendship? Isn't it possible for the bonds of loyalty to combine with the adventure of novelty?

I have said elsewhere ('Non-violence is the Law of Our Being'; ibid.) that our love for one another can be unconditional, but never absolute. This is why we cannot hold anyone down. But because of the availability of absolute love—the transcendental structure of our subjectivity manifests such love—we need not despair over the finitude of our love for one another.

But all coming-together is not in love or fellowship. There is violence and torture and hatred. Not only is our love for one another not absolute, but it is also very rarely unconditional. So that while there is fellowship, there is also, quite pervasively, social and interpersonal chaos.

The miracle of fellowship makes it possible to hope that where there is chaos there will be fellowship (the multi-centredness of a miracle). But there is human work necessitated by all this. It must and can be motivated by the love of one another. But at its deepest level, if it does not flow from infinite gratitude for fellowship, and for the transcendental structure of our subjectivity, human transformative work would not be well-founded. The tyranny will be an inevitable consequence.

Can't there be infinite gratitude for others? For the miracle of centres of self-conscious subjectivity other than myself? I think there can. I do not fully adequately realise the miraculous character of my own subjectivity until I encounter subjectivity in others. The 'overwhelming' character of my own subjectivity receives 'confirmation' in such encounters. But this too does not necessitate absolute or even unconditional love.

Just as I am constantly slipping from the aloofness of the eternal purusha into identification with particular items and orders of items of my own subjectivity, I am also not able continuously to sustain my nirguna perception of another. I keep slipping here too. I identify you with your items of subjectivity, as expressed in relation to me and others in communication and community. I encounter you as an object, and not—I am not able to sustain this—as another transcendentally structured centre of subjectivity.

The 'problem of our knowledge of other minds' arises at this level of loss of perception. I can—in communication and community—*see* you as another transcendentally structured centre of subjectivity. But this perception of mine can falter and fail. How do I *then* recover my original nirguna vision of you? Again only by communicating attention and reflection on the necessarily multicentred manifestation of the miracle of subjectivity.

How can I infer mentality from mere behaviour? This is a moral–metaphysical problem, not an epistemological problem. Being able to see behaviour as the expression of mentality is an achievement of the moral imagination.

In all communal togetherness—and this what is given, our form of life—there is a minimum of unselfcentredness, and a proportionate ability on the part of each one of us to see a plurality of centres of subjectivity.

What sustains fellowship is not an imagined absolute love, which we do not have towards one another, but the unselfcentredness which is a vision of the subjectivity of others and the infinite gratitude implicit in such vision. Not infinite gratitude towards one another, but for the fact of subjectivity—transcendentally structured.

We can't think of behaviour without thinking of corporeality. What is our corporeality? I have / am a body. What does this thought come to?

On one level, I can regard my body as another order or structure of appearance, order and structure by means of which others perceptually identify me and by means of which I too perceptually identify myself.

But this structure of appearance and the possibility of appearance 'stays' with me in a way in which some other structure of appearance—say that wall over there—does not. What is the significance of this?

The elements which constitute the structure of my body-appearance do not merely point away beyond themselves to a 'nothingness' which they shield me from. Although I think they do this too. I find that I have arms, legs, a face, a heaviness and so on; I am not in a perceptual vacuum. But this can't be all. For instance, what do I mean by saying that I find I *have* an arm, a leg and so on? Perhaps one could say this. My encountering the reality of my body is an encounter with a structure of appearance whose elements have a function which is not exhaustively described by saying that they too, like any other appearance-structure, shield me from the nothingness of a perceptual vacuum. The elements of my body-appearance also indicate 'places', and my body-appearance as a whole indicates a 'place', which are animated by items of subjectivity, and which is (here I am thinking of my body-appearance as a whole) animated by self-consciousness itself, by subjectivity itself.

The notions of 'place' and 'places' which I have introduced above cannot be perceptually-spatially grasped.

'I have a pain in my tooth.' This can't be perceptually-spatially grasped. I will return to this set of questions later.

My living body—as it is 'appropriated' by me—is the substantiality, the being, of my subjectivity. Appearance shields us from perceptual nothingness. Our non-nothingness is a mode of being, the mode of being of the living human body illuminated by self-consciousness.

Here we must think of self-consciousness not merely as a sharp centre of selfhood, but also as animation, which is the empowered living human body.

A corpse would be non-subjective nothingness, so would our mere anatomy, and so on. The non-nothingness, the substantiality, that I am thinking of is of the living human body appropriated by self-consciousness.

We not only find that we are not nothing, we find that we have the power to structure and restructure items of appearance and generate possibilities of items of appearance and subjectivity. Our embodiment is evidence both of our power and our vulnerability.

In what sense do we inhabit the world? The perceptual identifiability of ourselves is our immanence in world-appearance. This is why the *other* appears to us as part of the world. The limits of our power of structuring and restricting world-appearance is proof not only of our finitude, but of our finitude in relation to the totality of world-appearance which is the work of God.

We don't create items of appearance, we only structure and restructure them within limits. Our subjectivity and our items of subjectivity are our autonomy. World-appearance is not contiguous with subjectivity and items of subjectivity. The appropriated living human body is the autonomy and finitude of subjectivity and items of subjectivity situated in world-appearance.

But if subjectivity and appearance are not contiguous or continuous, how can the former be situated in an order of the latter? Is there here a surrealist juxtaposition?

Why does the human body look like an object in the world? Yes, but not the living, appropriated, a human body. Does percipience require embodiment?

Our primary experience of not-being-nothing is our experience of the self-situatedness of self-consciousness, the self-consciousness of the eternally aloof purusha. The thought, 'I am', is a dispeller of the fear of nothingness, also a disproof of it.

But is bare self-situated self-consciousness—which *is* the thought 'I am'—sufficient for me, the being, the one, who is self-situated in self-consciousness? I want to say 'no', although I realise that in not saying 'no', I appear to be going against a whole tradition of mystic teaching.

My being able to think of myself as self-situated self-consciousness is essential for my grasping the infinite *distance* between self-consciousness and given items and orders of subjectivity. And the grasping of this distance—the truth of this distance—is essential for my faith in the possibility of a limitless development of subjectivity.

But if I *were* bare self-situated self-consciousness, would I be *subjective* in the human sense?

I see myself as the centre of a massive luminosity of self-consciousness. And in so seeing myself, I see myself not merely as one who *is*—although this bare existential nirguna self-description is available to me. In seeking myself as the centre of a massive luminosity of self-consciousness, I see myself as one who *is* or *is not* afraid, who *is* or *is not* fulfilled, who *is* or *is not* alone, and so on, that is, I see myself as self-situated self-consciousness qualified by items of subjectivity.

Bare self-situated self-consciousness would not be full human subjectivity. Bare self-situated self-consciousness is my ultimate refuge against death. But if items of subjectivity do not reappear, there would be no *survival*.

My present condition of self-conscious subjectivity is *itself* a condition of being-saved, from a nothingness which I fear without being able to characterise as the absence, the negation, of this or that.

If the transcendental structure of my subjectivity is a promise of survival, *this sense of being saved*, which requires the qualification of self-consciousness by items of subjectivity, must be preserved.

Talk of survival is there not essential. If *now*, I tried to see myself as bare self-situated self-consciousness, I would fail. I would not be able to think of myself as myself at all. (Isn't this why, in mystic thought, when bare self-situated self-consciousness is seen in a profoundly deepened form—as self-realisation—there is *no* thought of *myself* at all? Such self-realisation as a higher goal, or condition of being is a topic I have not touched at all so far.)

So my innermost conviction or 'perception' that I am not-nothing is a vision of myself as qualified by items of subjectivity.

Self-conscious subjectivity is the miracle, of being there at all, and the miracle of being characterised by some item of other of subjectivity. The *that* as well as the *what* of 'I am'.

But mere self-conscious subjectivity, although it isn't as deprived-looking a condition as the condition of bare self-situated self-consciousness, is nevertheless a condition of deprivation. Because it is a condition of 'unsituatedness'. The 'where' of 'I am' is missing.

A 'perceptual environment' fulfils this want. It overcomes the 'blindness' of mere self-conscious subjectivity. Our perceptual environment is also a measure of our finitude. The threat of nothingness, the nothingness of non-subjectivity, is not totally removed, it is held in check, abeyance.

Thus, our perceptual environment serves a double function. It overcomes the 'blindness', 'unsituatedness', of mere self-conscious subjectivity. But not in a way which makes self-conscious subjectivity forgetful of its finitude.

The non-subjectivity of 'matter', its nothingness, always hovers over the perceptual environment.

Our finitude is our vulnerability. And we are vulnerable in countless ways, ways which register as unacceptable items of subjectivity. There is also the sheer fear of death, of being reduced to the nothingness of non-subjectivity.

The structure of our perceptual environment is a measure of our current finitude, vulnerability. And the 'reality', the 'nothingness' of matter which it reveals is the reality of the fear of death.

That which is non-living must be the picture of death.

Our motor capacities are a complex revelation of our finitude, of our non-nothingness (that is, our limited capacity for 'management' in an environment which threatens us, and assists us, in complex ways, and also of the *incapacity* inherent in motor abilities).

I am trying here to express something like the following thought: Our embodied condition in a perceptual environment is a full revelation—as something *there*—of our finitude. It is not to be understood as the mere arrangement in the nature of natural objects.

But our embodied condition in a perceptual environment also has a structure of salvation. We do have *some* motor capacities, we are not 'unsituated' (we have a perceptual environment). There is also a general 'fittingness' here. This is the basis of pantheism and even materialism.

What materialism and naturalism take to be the nature of things is merely a revelation of the structure of salvation. Of our being *given* a condition of being which is such that it can be 'accepted' with gratitude, not as the most perfect condition conceivable, but as a condition which is not at all inappropriate to our condition of spiritual development.

This harmony between ourselves and our condition of being—the objective layout of it—is what I think the theory of *karma* is getting at.

I am not sure if this harmony is so perfectly 'individuated' that we could say that each one of us has the condition of being which he deserves.

There is, though, at the back of the specificities of our condition of being, a structure of givenness which we can't complain about, to put it negatively. It also calls for gratitude.

'The reality of our material environment forces itself upon us': Can this thought be phenomenalistically understood, as I seem to have tried to? Or are we to say: 'There is, in and for itself, a material world, in which we find ourselves.' I don't know what such an utterance could come to unless it was the acknowledgement of the overwhelming dimension of non-subjectivity, the nothingness of this non-subjectivity, which haunts our experience.

But what about the 'inherent geometry' of the world? There is a disposition of material realities, and there is a microcosmic structure of material reality. Are you denying all this? Isn't there the world, a structured place? Isn't there *already* such a world? Isn't materiality *something*?

But is my body *something*? I can't talk of my body but only of my embodiment. Is my embodiment one thing, and my situatedness in the world another thing? They are the same. My embodiment is the clearest proof that I need an environment, that finite spirit needs a supportive environment.

Being alive. Embodiment is *being alive*. *Being alive* is the reality, the possibility, the permissibility, of finitude, the revelation of limited capacity, and the infinite labour which makes this possible. My motor-perceptual capacities are proof of my power. What about my intellectual capacities?

They are a measure of the distance between myself and any given order of world-appearance, and any given scale of motor-perceptual capacity. Not a proof of my infinitude, but of my transcendence of any given set of world-limitations.

The material world overwhelms me. But I 'distance' it by means of my perceptual capacities, and I 'ride' it by means of my motor capacities.

The living human body is the *limited* appropriation of nothingness which is self-conscious animation. What about the anatomical-physiological intricacies of the human body?

Individuality has a structure because there is, has to be, a plurality of individualities. The overwhelming character of subjectivity necessitates the acknowledgement of the possibility of plurality. And the 'given' discloses a plural form of life. Hence, the structured character of individuality. If there were no plurality, there would be no structure.

Am I talking merely about a plurality of centres of self-conscious subjectivity? There is the plurality of centres of non-human subjectivity and percipience. They too must be structured in virtue of their plurality.

But what about the plurality of material, non-living, realities? Do they not reveal structure? But on deeper reflection, they reduce, don't they, to a continuum? The *possibility* of percipience and subjectivity. The laws of physics, to the extent they are fundamental, are the laws of the possibility of percipience and subjectivity and motor-perceptual intellectual capacity.

The law-governed character of our nature, and of the nature of things, is a measure of God's labour in fashioning subjectivity, and the permanent possibility of subjectivity, out of nothingness. God's labour is both infinite and *not labour at all*.

The structure of the world is thus both infinitely intricate and a nothingness, *shunya*. Order is nothingness *overcome*. The nothingness of the world as, for example, proclaimed in Buddhism and advaita vedanta is the self-sufficiency of God.

There are now: (a) Self-situatedness in self-consciousness, the conviction of this, of oneself as the eternally aloof purusha. (b) Items of subjectivity—feelings, emotions, sensations, moods, etc. These are essential for self-situated self-consciousness to be *subjectivity:* for there to be *inwardness*. (c) Appearance, or world-appearance, or a perceptual environment. (d) Motor-perceptual intellectual capacities. The overcoming of nothingness, which is one's subjective reality, is not merely an overcoming of 'blindness' but also of 'impotence'. The living human body reveals itself as self-conscious animation and finite power.

The material layout of the world is then, on this interpretation, a complex structure of appearance and the possibility of appearance. This structure has stability, but not ultimacy. No given order of world-appearance has ultimacy.

Our embodiment is the harmony between ourselves and any given order of world-appearance. The causal connection between subjectivity (and its items) and the course of world-appearance is proof of this.

We can say this: We are not merely self-situated in self-consciousness. We are also situated in an environment which matches our spiritual development. This is what the theories of karma and reincarnation come to.

If there is a solution to the problem of evil at all, it must be this—that we and our environment are not ill-matched, that fundamentally, not in this or that specific respect, we not only deserve our condition, we ought to be grateful for it. This is hard, but anything less hard would be sentimentality.

A theory of karma and a theory of reincarnation, which would be *generalised* theories of the human condition, and not theories restricted to the private careers of individuals, would be profoundly illuminating.

Reference

Raghuramaraju, A. (ed.). 2015. *Seven Sages: Selected Essays by Ramchandra Gandhi*. New Delhi: Penguin.

— thirteen —

Ethics, Ecology and Enlightenment*

Chandan Gowda: What are some of your current intellectual preoccupations?

Ramchandra Gandhi: They are what they have been for many years. The truth of advaita vedanta is my chief passion. The formulation of this, as I understand it, in clearer terms, and exploring its relevance to our times is an exciting, endless task.

I have also been looking closely at our epics, the Ramayana and Mahabharata, some of the Upanishads, and continue to study the teachings of the sages of modern India, their potential to change the course of history.

CG: In an earlier conversation, you said that you were not interested in the Right or the Left but in the truth. 'People want the truth,' you said. What did you mean by this?

RG: Ignoring questions about the meaning and purpose of life, politics in our times has merely championed the cause of exclusive identities: caste, religious, socio-economic, nationalist.

*Originally published in *Lankesh Patrike*, 21 September 2003. Reprinted in *The Hindu*, 18 November 2007.

Never contemplating the possibility that these identities might be falsehoods, false answers to questions, 'Who am I?' and 'Who are we?', which concern us most deeply. Pitting us against one another and all of us against non-human life, nature and nothingness, the politics of exclusive identities has understandably failed to deliver on its promises of justice, freedom or happiness. Truth matters. Selfhood might be non-dual, we might be all things and nothingness too. Each one of us. Empowerment and humility can be like gifts only if exclusive identity and its agenda of limitless compassion and love and joy.

CG: Could you illustrate the failure of exclusivist politics with an example?

RG: Let us look at Gujarat. After Godhra, Gujarat was witness to a dance of vengeful destruction. All Muslims were projected as 'Other' and hostile to Hinduism. And Hindus sought to be defined exclusively as communally, as a collectivity of believers threatened by all Muslims. Middle-class Hindu youths sought empowerment in murder and rape and loot. If some of them were to ask Hindutva leadership the question: Are we only Hindus? Are we not also trustees of all cultures and faiths? Is the slaughter of innocent men, women and children evidence of power? Is organised, murderous retaliation likely to be a resolution of Hindu–Muslim differences? There would be no answers forthcoming from Hindutva leadership to these fundamental questions. Imitating Islamic separatism that created Pakistan, Hindutva politics seeks Hindu hegemonism in India, forgetting that a hegemonism is a form of separation, as all exclusivism is.

CG: You have pointed to the dangers of thinking in narrow terms of 'self' and 'other'.

RG: Yes. The experience of sympathy is very important in life. In your very mode of thinking, if you have established a strict 'self' and 'other' distinction, in a moment of crisis you won't have sympathy, which alone will prevent you from harming others.

CG: What would Gandhi have done in Gujarat?

RG: Gandhi would have tried to convert the adversity of Godhra into a spiritual advantage by initiating a wide-ranging enquiry and debate in Gujarat and the rest of India: 'Who are we?'

CG: What are some of the weaknesses of the secularist imagination?

RG: The implicit anthropocentrism of the secularist imagination, even more than its explicit Eurocentrism, is its chief weakness. Anthropocentrism makes it impossible for secularism to be ecologically sensitive. Licensed to plunder nature, secularism, becomes the ideology of those who are most capable of plundering nature: the industrialised, scientifically and technologically advanced societies of Europe, and their imitators and servitors around the world.

CG: Are there corresponding weaknesses of the religious imagination?

RG: In politics, certainly. Politically, religions define themselves demographically and anthropocentrically no less dogmatically than secular collectivities: as collectivities of believers pitted against one another and secular societies. Religious politics, like secularist politics, acquires an annihilationist agenda, a license to hate 'others' till doomsday. This is the naked truth underlying the ongoing wars between Islamic militancy and Western hegemony, Pakistan and India, Sinhala majoritarianism and Tamil separatism in Sri Lanka, for instance. This is a tragedy especially for Hinduism and Buddhism, both spiritual traditions which do not legitimise anthropocentrism. Political dualism lures even these traditions away from the goals of inclusive life.

CG: You pointed earlier to the dangers of dualist thinking in terms of 'self' and 'other'. How does one overcome dualist thinking?

RG: Each time we think of apparent others as really only variant images of ourselves and that is what is involved in ethical behaviour, we widen self-awareness. And, when we think of non-human life and non-living matter also as constituting variant images of ourselves, that is, when we live ecologically sensitively and non-anthropocentrically, self-awareness is further and greatly widened. However, in the face of death and irretrievable loss and unbearable agony, we confront the spectre of nothingness and our consciousness congeals in fear. Self-awareness stops flowering. Our reality loses its plasticity, vitality. We recover this vitality when we are able to see nothingness also as our own form (symbolising our not being something as opposed to something else, teaching central to vedanta and Buddhism).

This revolutionary widening of self-awareness, essential for the practise of non-violence, is possible only in individual contemplativeness. In their anthropocentric and collectivist forms, secularism and religion do not encourage such contemplativeness. They deprive us of enlightenment. Ethics and ecology are insufficiently empowering without enlightenment. The traditional three 'Rs' of education (reading, writing and arithmetic) may widen our knowledge. But self-awareness, our deepest reality, can only be widened and deepened by the three 'Es': ethics, ecology and enlightenment.

CG: What do you think must be done at the site of [the] demolished Babri Masjid?

RG: The status quo should be preserved. The debris, the rubble, representing the hardness of our hearts and the shallowness of our minds, is more sacred as a confession of our unregenerateness than an aggressive, avenging, construction of a Ram temple at the site can ever be. Or a legalistic reconstruction of the demolished mosque.

At the deepest level, no new Ram temple can in all conscience be constructed at the site until the questions of Sita's banishment and the killing of Shudraka by Ram in the Ramayana are satisfactorily resolved by a more self-questioning Hinduism than Hindutva can ever be.

Without atonement for the miseries heaped upon women and the 'lower' castes as a result of an uncritical acceptance of the authenticity of these episodes in the Ramayana, it would be an insult to Sita and Ram to build a new temple at the site of arrogance and vengefulness in Ayodhya, whether or not it is the site of Ram's birth.

CG: In discussions on culture, the market often drops out of view. I know you are not an economist. But, have you thought about what the neo-liberal economic reforms have done to the country?

RG: I don't grudge the middle-classes the widening of consumerist consciousness, which these reforms have facilitated! But the further impoverishment of the poor, which has occurred, is unforgivable. The gap between rich and poor has widened. The agenda of ethics, ecology and enlightenment has been largely damaged.

CG: What has it meant to be Gandhi's grandson?

RG: The relationship evokes both kindness and unkindness. One is treated with undeserved special respect and affection. And with undeserved special chastisement if one does anything insufficiently saintly. Beyond both is an urgent invitation to inquire into the meaning of truth and non-violence which the relationship holds out. I cling to that blessing and ignore the discomforts of special attention.

— *fourteen* —

In Conversation with Ramchandra Gandhi*

Rajiv Mehrotra: Hello! And welcome to my series of conservations with men and women whose ideas, vision, philosophy define our contemporary world. My guest today is one of India's distinguished philosophers. I am deeply honoured and delighted to welcome a former teacher in more ways than one to this programme. He has PhDs from Delhi and Oxford and [a] distinguished career as a teacher, philosopher and writer. Delighted to welcome, Professor Ramchandra Gandhi.

Ramchandra Gandhi: Rajiv, I am so happy to be here and very nervous.

RM: Well you know, you were sort of, I was having this conversation with you, and you were talking about how philosophy as an issue first came up for you as a space between home and school. When you asked yourself the question, 'Who am I.' Who are you, Ramu Bhai?

RG: Well, let me tell you what exactly happened. I used to live in the old Hindustan Times at Connaught Place and my school was Modern School at Barakhamba Road. I used to walk from home to school. One day while I was walking to my school from

*Originally from *In Conversation with Rajiv Mehrotra* for Doordarshan, New Delhi, date unknown.

home, I must have been about 12, I think, I remember stopping suddenly in the middle and asking myself the question, 'Who am I', and I didn't know what the answer was but the question seemed to me the most important question one could ask. So I went to the school and read my books and went back home and I had all the love and affection, but neither love nor affection, nor schooling could answer that question satisfactorily.

RM: So what sort of life's journey has answered for you that question?

RG: Well, this is a large question; and I think it deserves a considered answer. After I had studied, and I was very fortunate to have studied in good colleges, both in India and abroad, when I came back I was in great doubt about two or three things. One, whether the philosophy that I had learned, European philosophy, was really adequate to the task of life. Two, why should I go on living? What is the meaning of life? And three, is there another direction in philosophy and life for me and I didn't know the answers to them? But slowly, through contacts with people who knew about Sri Ramana Maharshi, I came across books by him and on him and over the years my sense of Ramana Maharshi being quite right on that point about who am I, and not that I fully understand the tradition of advaita, but I think I have a sense of the truth of it and a relationship of trust is grown between him—he is not in his body now—and me, his teachings with me, which has not robbed be of my philosophical independence. That is the last thing I would like to be ...

RM: [I am] sitting in front of you, who am I?

RG: [Laughs] Who am I! No, when I ask myself that question, 'Who am I?', I know that I am here in the studio talking to you, so that is not what I want to know, but what is this awareness, which at this moment makes for itself this image of a person who is being interviewed. For a little while ago it was in a car that brought me here and before that, but that remains the same, circumstances change, appearances change. Now that I cannot then be limited to merely these pictures of my life but it must include all that I see, including apparent others, and not only apparent other human beings, but other life and not only other life but also matter, and not only a matter and nature but also that vast emptiness, the circus tent which surrounds everything. This consciousness reaches out to all that becomes one with it and nearly one point of it.

RM: You have talked about the sacredness of nature and the sense of balance in it and how in nature there isn't pointed destruction, motivated destruction.

RG: Yes, yes. That is, I think a very important discovery that everyone can make for themselves. There is the sheer power and violence of the tiger, but, never beyond necessity does the tiger destroy life. Non-human life observes this ecological discipline perfectly and I would like to think of it as being in a state of permanent nirvana or moksha. From this must emerge respect for nature and our ecological responsibility will then be more easily carried out. But if we don't think of nature as in itself something realised, and we alone amongst the living are not able to do this, but then there will be hope for us, because we are surrounded by a self-realisation, by wisdom inherent in life, in the matter, in sheer obedience to laws. The tsunami comes, but it doesn't target a particular category of human beings. Most do, violence does.

RM: You are a philosopher by training, by vocation, and [a] journey started really in response to a personal question that we discussed. What do you think is the larger public vocation, public role, the obligations of a philosopher?

RG: I think one must begin with self-knowledge, there is no other ... you can't discover what anything else is if you haven't made an effort to discover yourself. So like everything else, self-knowledge also begins with yourself and this could be a variety of things, I don't mean by this biographical information, autobiographical information, whatever, but being quiet and allowing all the good and the bad that's happening to you, to flow through you, and to touch that point of stillness in our consciousness which everyone is aware of, but from which we fall away easily, but the touch that, to stay there, and to allow consciousness to grow around it, become very wide in its embrace of other things and that could involve energetic action that could involve contemplative isolation that could involve everything but the style of doing things would be different.

RM: Is there a formal sadhana or a practice that you follow in this journey towards becoming aware of this process of consciousness.

RG: Yes, this has been taught by sages and one can follow the sadhana of being quiet and close to the sense of I within us. Not the sense of I am Ramchandra Gandhi, I am a man, I am happy—not that, but just that sense of I, that is, one sadhana, and to hold it and that leads to a sense of its source which is a groundswell of consciousness, which includes not only your personality but all life, that is one sadhana. Or, if one has found a guru, living or no longer living, then do love that guru as a true shishya. If you have found a true guru, you have to be a true shishya, a true seeker, to love him, to address him with affection because he is not only your teacher, he is the teacher of everything, he is that source of consciousness in a human form and that also takes one to that centre.

RM: Ramu Bhai, has being a Gandhi, the heritage, what has that meant to you? Has that been a difficult standard to live up to?

RG: Yes indeed, but it's also been a privilege and also a responsibility. Since you are a television and film person besides so many other things, I think what really enabled me to confront the issue that you have raised, I was looking at some old footage of Gandhiji, on 31 January, the day after he was killed, his body lay on top of the military vehicle and there was a crowd, surrounding the vehicle and I was watching this, and I had taken a friend with me to watch this, and there in the crowd I saw myself, that I was there and that [a] little boy was looking at this old man and saying, 'How did you get there?' I think at least two things, how did you deal with the Gandhi heritage, and have you dealt with the question of death. How can you become an adult without doing good these things and so I had to do that.

And dealing with the legacy, when people ask me, 'Are you the grandson of Mahatma Gandhi, I am now inclined to say, "No". Then they look confused, and I say, "Oh! I am indeed the grandson of Mohandas Karamchand Gandhi and from him, I have inherited a lot of stubbornness, but I am not the grandson of Mahatma, because the Mahatma has no grandchildren specifically of his own—all are his children or none."' That roughly sums up the way in which I have been able to deal with that, both love him and admire him without being possessive of him, or without that legacy possessing me.

RM: There is also, it being genetic, hereditary in terms of the Mahatma aspect of the legacy—you were obviously inspired by Gandhiji, you have done a film on him, and you have written extensively, much of your philosophy is guided by his vision. What is that guiding vision for you? I know that this is sort of, in some ways, an impossible question to encapsulate a life, to encapsulate the Mahatma, in a few minutes of a television programme, but if you were to attempt that, what would you say?

RG: I think I would say that the chief problem of the twentieth century was racism. The idea that race is superior to another, we haven't quite got rid of this, but Gandhi gave this tremendous fight. He wasn't only fighting for Indian independence. India not being independent was, under the domination of a racist idea, that the British race was superior, and he wanted, I think, to break this idea. And we know that Hitler in the heart of the twentieth century represented racism in its fullest horror, but by giving it battle throughout his life, I think, he has weakened the power of racism—this I can see very, very clearly. In fact, I think Gandhi's battle against British imperialism was a very British thing to do. It was a way of helping the British understand that this was wrong. And when they were suddenly threatened by Hitler, I think, Gandhi's challenge must have helped them to take on Hitler.

RM: You have been one of the people instrumental in organising the ritual ceremony on Gandhiji's death anniversary at his samadhi each year. What is the message that you are sending out, that you are reaching out for an event like that, what is it saying to people? What is it reminding people about Gandhiji?

RG: That he was not being merely sentimental when he said that he was a Hindu, a Muslim, a Buddhist, a Christian and everything because I think he believed, and I believe—and I think everyone would believe—that when a baby is born, he or she has inherited the totality of spiritual traditions of humanity, so there is no room for division in respect of child and this inheritance, but the other thing is that religion is not the only sacred dimension of life, that the search for truth in all dimensions of life, not only in the dimension which science deals with, but every book of life, in every day, every event, every moment of life, the search for truth and this cannot be conducted without what he called *sanmati*, which means goodwill, the goodwill towards all and, hereby all I don't think he meant only human beings, but all life, all nature, all reality.

RM: You have written and talked extensively about the agony of partition, the agony for Gandhiji and have on occasions called for rituals of atonement for the millions of people who died on both sides. What are you calling out for there?

RG: Well, Rajiv, you have asked me this question which troubles me continuously, but which also brings me a certain measure of hope, because I think, the people of this subcontinent, or the erstwhile subcontinent, are a religious people, and it does matter to them if the last ceremonies of their dead have been performed or not. And I maintain that these two million who were slaughtered were not Indians or Pakistanis. They belonged to the Indian subcontinent, they didn't have Indian passports or Pakistani passports and we are responsible for their slaughter because we accepted the partition in one way or another. So in no law can the murderer perform the last ceremonies of the murdered. So we haven't performed the last ceremonies for the two million, including Gandhi, who perished, and I think there is, therefore, a curse upon us, there is a guilt within our hearts, we only have to ask one another: We have built these nuclear bombs, what are they? They are, if you look carefully at them, they are confessions, they are not deterrents, they are a way of confessing to one another, look, we have hated each other so much that we have wanted to wipe each other out, loot and perish, this knowledge, this bitter self-knowledge, and the knowledge that we have not performed the last rites can bring our countries together again on a spiritual basis. This is my conviction and Kashmir is an area which is still sort of both here and there, neither here nor there, it's fortunately ambiguous for such an experiment in atonement to be carried out. Just think about it, Rajiv, if there were a cultural parliament in the whole of Jammu and Kashmir, and I am not speaking as a politician, I don't know what the latest talks are about. For a long time, I have felt the need in Kashmir especially, a cultural assembly to which people should be elected from the whole subcontinent, not as rulers but as servants of every stone, every rock, every river, every brook, every shrine, every masjid, every mandir, and nature. The first students, the first members of this should be demobilised *jihadis* and the military of both sides. If we do this, we would have done atonement and the two million dead who are thirsty would be able to touch our water and slake their thirst and then depart to wherever they were meant to go, and we would be an example for [the] people of Tibet, for Palestine, for Sri Lanka and all other places where religion is a factor in conflict. I firmly believe this Rajiv, but I don't know how many people take me seriously when I talk about it.

RM: Ramu Bhai, you have talked about Ramana Maharshi's being the great influence on you. Who were some of the living gurus or teachers that you engage with, that you identify with, that inspire you and move you, you are a teacher yourself?

RG: Rajiv, when you found somebody you can call a guru from the inmost part of your being, it's like finding a parent. You don't go around looking for another parent, with due respect to other parents. I have the profoundest love for Sri Ramakrishna Paramahansa, but those who are still living, in my view a sage one who has realised the limitlessness of his or her selfhood, he is not dead, was never born, he or she was always there.

So for me Sri Ramakrishna Paramahansa, Swami Vivekananda, Sri Aurobindo, Mahatma Gandhi and my own *sadguru* [real teacher] Sri Ramana Maharshi are always there in no hierarchy but in kind of togetherness, which leaves us free to pursue our own path, they don't impose anything upon us. So I would not be able to comment on those who are living, because I don't think it is right, it is not spiritually wise to say that. It reminds me of an interesting story, Raja Rao, the great Indian novelist and a devotee of Ramana Maharshi and other teachers of advaita, was here. Would you believe, Rajiv, I did an interview with him, that is one television interview I had done, I am not really as competent as you, Rajiv, but I did during that interview take Raja Rao to Raj Ghat, and I said, 'Raja Rao, we are sending out so many gurus to the world, some of them are fake, does this bother you as a devotee and somebody who has a guru?' Raja Rao turned to me and said, 'Ramu, it is better to be a fake guru than a fake doctor!' What he meant was that those who are in search of a spiritual truth will be able to see through a fake guru, because this knowledge is with us, but we know nothing about science. If a fake doctor comes along, brings medicines about which we know nothing, we wouldn't be able to seek truth, but that was a good way of saying, 'Well, look for the true guru, don't blame the fake guru.' And I think when you have found a guru, and you can't find a guru without very hard examination of everything that he has written, his whole life, then you find that you have really examined yourself. When you do that, you are not troubled by the failings or the attainments of anybody because your mind is at rest, you are a *shishya* of all, fake and genuine. The true guru says that you must first understand what a shishya is.

RM: What is a good shishya? Who is a good shishya?

RG: Shishya is the Sanskrit word for which the colloquial term in Punjabi is Sikh. In fact the whole of the Sikh faith to my mind has redefined humanity in a way which inaugurates a true renaissance. Aristotle said, famously, that human beings are rational and social animals. I think he is completely wrong. As the history of our times shows, we are social and we are horribly anti-social too. We are rational and we are insanely irrational. But at all times when we are social or not, whether we are rational or not, we are seeking something, we are seeking meaning, we are seeking self-knowledge. So to be a shishya is to be a human being.

RM: As a philosopher, you are a man of ideas of the large, the expansive, when you bring your vision to bear on contemporary predicaments and contemporary society, what is it that most anguishes you?

RG: The sense of limitedness, the collective limitedness which we hide behind when we talk about us Indians, or us Americans, or us Muslims, or us Hindus, this us, and we, these are terribly limited notions, far worse than the I, the ego, because the I can be shamefaced more easily than the us, because there are so many *Is* that hide behind the we, so this is what troubles me the most.

I read a recent book by Professor [Samuel] Huntington, the great American scholar, who has written this book about the conflicts of civilisations. It is a book whose title is *Who Are We?* Then I turned to it hoping that he would be addressing the question about who we human beings are? No, he only wanted to ask who Americans were. This is a very limited exercise, who am I, is a much wider question, a question which includes all others and I think that is not egoism, or individualism, it is self-knowledge, it is the knowledge of the heart, the centre of all things, including yourself, the movement away from this either in the direction of egoistic individualism, we don't care about anything here, or of hardhearted collectivism, of one kind or the other, I know that we have strayed.

RM: You have been a man of many parts, you know, teacher, writer you know, a philosopher both sort of by profession and by your living being, you have written a novel *Munia's Light*, soon to be released and published. What prompted this foray into fiction, or is it fiction?

RG: It is fiction, but I won't call it a novel because it is more like a *katha* [story]. A novel brings to mind various ideas of contemporary writing, it is a bit like that but it is more like a contemporary story about teacher and the pupil but within that story are many stories from the Ramayana and the Mahabharata. What prompted me to do this? I felt that though I was a devotee, I am a devotee of Sri Ramana Maharshi and the teachings of advaita become clearer and clearer every day, doesn't make me sectarian at all. But there is a question in my heart, there was, [what do] we do with this tremendous heritage of advaita for instance, non-duality, no difference between genders, why do we in India treat the girl-child so horribly? So I wanted to write a story of a man who has grown old in search of this answer and who is confronted by this question.

RM: How autobiographical it is?

RG: No, this was happening to me, but I made it, no, I kept myself out and created a character who has the features of all sadhakas, including myself, who has his very distinctive Uttar Pradesh identity, who is not a Brahmin, who is a Kayastha, so I wanted to break this idea, that who can decide that only the Brahmin can teach, and the pupil, a young woman, who is graduating from an American university is a Brahmin. She seeks instruction from this man who has been struggling with this question and they talk about [it]. When I started writing about it, I discovered that I wasn't writing about myself, but fictionally, in order to answer this question. It's very important to invoke stories from the Ramayana and the Mahabharata and to make it easier for young Indians to understand these questions.

RM: You are both a shishya and a guru. You go to several people and the thousands that you have taught in classrooms and workshops and in formal conversations, what would Ramu Gandhi, the guru, say to Ramu Gandhi, the shishya? What does he say to himself?

RG: I think the more silent I am in relation to myself, the more I say anything worthwhile, having to say something then something which is only apparently more important or interesting, something else comes up when I am completely quiet, then whatever is required would occur to me, this is experience. But when I am not, when I am obsessed with some one aspect of my life only, then what I say to myself is coloured by that, but when I am not so obsessed, I am simply aware of this vibrant thing called self-awareness, consciousness, and aware of the fact that this is not limited to my body but it includes all bodies, all life and that speaks for itself, you don't have to have words for it, because look at the rest of life, they don't speak, this is not a limitation, a failure of evolution, this is wisdom, they don't need words, they can do with silence. It doesn't affect their intelligence, birds chatter, birds' chatter sounds like Sanskrit *slokas* [couplets of Sanskrit verse] to me and that's a Veda of its own, and the silence of the sky, that's saying something, when you are quiet with yourself, you hear all that. When you are obsessed with something which will happen only in your life, you lose this very easily. But you had asked me earlier on, Rajiv, what sadhana was, it is not confined only to what has been laid down by tradition of gurus. There is a sadhana of everyday life when we meet a friend and address him when I say, 'Rajiv, hello!', I am not giving you a piece of information that your name is Rajiv, you could turn around and say, 'Ramu, thank you very much, but I know my name is Rajiv', that is not what you think of me doing, but when I say, 'Rajiv', without any desire to convey any information to you, you and I both realise that I am studying both you and me to self-awareness.

RM: Well, Ramu Bhai, that's exactly what you have done during this programme to me and the audience certainly. Thank you very much, this has been a great privilege.

RG: Thank you so much.

— *fifteen* —

CONFUSION AND COMMUNICATION*

Indian morale was most cruelly assaulted in recent months by two things: the unsightly panic which seized thousands of people from Kanyakumari to Kashmir during the last days of the Skylab, and the paralysis of will during the last days of Janata rule of a nation which had dislodged tyranny only two-and-a-half years ago as evidenced by the crazy, desperate, defensive manoeuvres undertaken in relation to an impending small-scale accident beyond human control, and fatalist helplessness witnessed in relation to what may well turn out to be the deliberate unmaking of Indian democracy by its recent inheritors and vociferous custodians.

Lust for Power

I am not suggesting that Skylab called for no response. Panic ought to have yielded to a fighting resolve on the part of thousands of people, both in India and abroad, to defy the might of a civilisation of runaway greed not confined to any nation or continent now, of which Skylab was merely a symptom, by a readiness through *satyagraha* [passive political resistance] to fill prisons in America or

*Originally published in *Swarajya*, 30 December 1979, pp. 35–37.

Russia or China or wherever in the name of utopia; the lust for power over the lives of human beings commits the world dangerously, unavoidably to slavery and destruction, including of course, India, where in the name of tradition or modernity, callousness and cruelty are practised on a scale unprecedented in history. But if we had been capable of making such a response to what Skylab symbolises, and one day soon we must or else forsake our claim to being a civilisation, we would also have been able, through mass-mobilisation aided by mass media, to end the folly and knavery in Parliament, which has made allies of lepers and enemies of saviours, humiliating and cancelling the verdict of the electorate of March 1977.

What could we have done? Mass media ought to have been entrusted by their patrons, that is, the public, to constitute a panel of uncompromised inquirers into the details of the truth, the bitter truth of betrayal of national responsibility underlying recent political happenings. Listeners, viewers, readers, would have had every right—and I don't mean merely a moral right—to summon before such a panel all the major characters involved in the drama of demolition that was being played out in Parliament. (Was the plot of the play dreamt at Chikmagalur? I recall Madhu Limaye's pathetically feeble criticism of Mrs Gandhi in a public speech there. Had she apologised for what she had done and felt some contrition, he, Limaye, would have welcomed her at Chikmagalur—this is what the unforgiving socialist had declared.) Satyagraha could have compelled Morarjibhai, Chaudhary Charan Singh, Babu Jagjivan Ram, George Fernandes, Atal Behari Vajpayee and others—do you remember the pantheon of early Janata posters?—to answer a series of searching questions, for example:

Morarjibhai: Your main charge against many of your difficult and defecting former colleagues was that they are position-hungry and power-crazy. Would you, as proof of your having overcome the lust for position or power, be prepared to serve the next Lok Sabha indefinitely as a non–office holding ordinary MP who had more or less scraped through to victory at the last general elections? This is more difficult than wanting to opt out of power politics, and a surer test of sincerity.

Suspicion and Resentment

Chaudhary Charan Singh: Your passion for communal harmony is laudable. But your failure as a caste Hindu to work hand in hand with Babu Jagjivan Ram, a Harijan, is poor encouragement to Hindus and Muslims caught in the tragedy of suspiciousness and resentment. Are you prepared to relinquish your political ambitions and assume total charge of Gandhiji's unfinished mission of love in India and Pakistan? If you cannot, would you consider advising your chief supporters and destroyers, Shri Raj Narain and Mrs Gandhi, to emigrate to Iran and Argentina, respectively?

Babu Jagjivan Ram: It is well known that you command great respect among the ranks and officers of our fighting forces. Your part in the victorious Bangladesh war has not at all been adequately appreciated. Would you turn the magic of your ability and popularity to the problems underlying the widespread breakdown of law and order in our country, and allay the anxieties of citizens who cannot in broad daylight walk without fear? Would you do this even if it meant sacrificing or postponing your strong claims to the highest political office in the country, a claim you would further strengthen by the offer of such a sacrifice? Would you do this for the sake of Harijans and other ill-protected communities who symbolise the pervasive insecurity of life in our country? Our nation turns its lonely eyes to you.

Comrade Fernandes: Persuasive nationaliser that you are, would you please help nationalise resentment against the decay of authority and the resurgence of authoritarian voices in our George-forsaken land? Such was the trust you enjoyed that in relation to possibilities one could have said: 'In the beginning was the word. The word was with George. The word was George.' Such has been the end and the irony that a soft drink called '77' is all that is left of the word you spoke, a tribute not to the revolution of that year, but to the prohibitionist dreams of your erstwhile leader.

Shortsightedness

We are a forgiving nation. If many have already forgiven Mrs Gandhi, millions more will forgive your brief but costly lapse into the politics of shortsightedness. All you have to do, for instance, is set up a people's university on rails, a far-flung collaboration between railway workers and unemployed youth in the communication not only of goods and people, but also of revolutionary ideas and ideals across our land. The goodwill this will generate will more than meet the just demands of the brave workers you wish to lead once again. Think about it. But you will have to shelve your political aspirations for a while. Become, like Gandhiji, a mobile revolutionary and collect not only funds, as he did, but also lasting goodwill, not brief infatuation. Will you?

Vajpayeeji: Many who admired your initiatives in foreign affairs will sympathise with the sadness you expressed at leaving a delicate task unfinished. But there is a greater task, hardly begun, which you alone can initiate: the task of deepening and updating, not diluting, the Hinduism of organisations like the RSS. You owe it to the thousands of young members of such organisations, whose heart bleeds for their motherland, to tell them fully what somebody like Gandhiji has meant in the evolution of Hinduism, what Islam and Christianity have meant in the rediscovery of Hinduism by Hindus. Gandhiji had said, 'Make God your Guru,' implying at the same time the thought, 'Don't make you Guru God.'

No Greatness without Love

It is vital for Hindus, indeed all Indians, to face this hard but unalterable truth, both individually and organisationally. It is the failure of many Hindu organisations to teach and live this truth adequately that prevents them from playing a greater part in the development of our nation, not conspiracy or treachery on the part of others. The starting of newspapers, more representative of the pains and triumphs of Hindu sensibility than the ones you recently took to task, is your clear duty and opportunity, a far greater task than merely securing working political arrangements and equations.

Orator, will you decide to write thousands of postcards to Hindus and Muslims and Christians, as Gandhiji did? There is no greatness without love.

The panel ought, of course, also to have invited Mrs Gandhi to participate in its deliberations. In this year of the centenary of the birth of Rajaji, many will ponder the meaning of Gandhiji's words: 'Not Rajaji but Jawaharlal will be my successor.' Mrs Gandhi could also enigmatically declare, 'Not Sanjay but Stephen will be my successor', although comparisons would be nonsensical here. And Shri Raj Narain, such is his creative opposition to Mrs Gandhi that he may well contradict her and say, 'Not Stephen but Sanjay will be my successor.' More seriously, both Mrs Gandhi and Shri Raj Narain could be asked why the nation should pay the slightest attention to either of them considering how utterly destructive of credibility their partnership has been, how costly to the nation.

I write needlessly in the language of what would have been done. A panel of inquiry can still be set up. Mass mobilisation can still compel our leaders who say they are fashioning the destiny of our nation to speak to us, answer our questions, allay our anxieties about their intentions if they can, seek our advice and not merely our support. If we cannot conduct such an inquiry before further dangerous and deep political developments take shape invisibly and inaudibly, the midterm poll will at best yield the results of confusion, not the fruits of communication. Or is that now a foregone conclusion? We crawl in our response even to manifest danger.

— *sixteen* —

Testing Times*

India and Pakistan were justified in conducting nuclear weapons tests if only as a gesture of protest against the iniquity and irrationality of the nuclear weapons limitation and test-ban treaties sought to be imposed upon them and other nations by the big nuclear powers, and not only because of the demands of their national security perceptions. They cannot, however, escape the charge that by increasing the probability of another nuclear assault on life and civilisation on Earth, their nuclear-armament exercises contribute to the cumulative humiliation of the victims of the Hiroshima and Nagasaki carnage: whose only redemption lies in the possibility that what happened to them would not ever happen to any group of human beings again. And there is more bad news for those in India and Pakistan who would heed the voice of conscience and refrain from denying the possibility of redemption to victims of unthinkable evil.

Pakistan rests its claim to the territory of Jammu and Kashmir on the consideration that Muslims constitute the majority of the state's population, invoking one of the explicit principles on which the partition of India was based. Invoking another explicit

*Unpublished essay, undated.

principle of partition, India bases its claim to the same territory on the consideration that the erstwhile ruler of Jammu and Kashmir, Maharaja Hari Singh, had acceded to India, not Pakistan, the only two options he was allowed by the partition plan. The time has come to acknowledge the unavailability of these principles today as morally acceptable guidelines for resolving the explosive (in the special sense which that word has now acquired) question of Jammu and Kashmir.

At the time when partition was being negotiated, religious minorities (Muslim, Hindu, and others) existed, and had done so for centuries, all over the subcontinent. It was this reality of roots, and not numbers alone or at all, which constituted the right of religious minorities to remain in their existing habitats. This right was undermined by the majoritarian logic of the partition plan. Had this logic been followed to its conclusion, there would have had to be arranged a wholesale exchange of religious minorities between India and Pakistan: a morally bizarre exercise mercifully, although inconsistently, not undertaken as a corollary of partition by its presiding deity, Lord Mountbatten. But the idea of such an exchange was strongly enough suggested by the demographic insanity of the split-India scheme. Legitimising lust for territories and presenting an opportunity for the free play of historical and communal hatred, partition caused the expulsion of millions of human beings from their ancestral homelands, and the sacrifice of at least one million lives at its altar. If only as a gesture of compassion towards the spirits of these dead and uprooted masses of humanity, India and Pakistan should address the question of Jammu and Kashmir with the aid of principles that are morally superior to the bullying power of majoritarianism, religious or secular, and the whims of hereditary rulers of states.

Pakistan is a theocratic, Islamic, state today, which it was not at the time of its formation; indeed, even the possibility of Pakistan becoming a theocratic state by the sheer momentum of its majoritarian origin was not discussed during the partition negotiations. Thus, the claim of a theocratic Pakistan to the territory of Jammu and Kashmir today is not the original, merely majoritarian, claim of the sovereign state that came into being on 14 August 1947. So that if Jammu and Kashmir were formally incorporated within the Islamic state of Pakistan, religions of the region other than Islam would not enjoy equality of status with Islam; nor would the non-Islamic sacred sites and places of worship scattered throughout the territory enjoy the same status as Islamic sacred sites and places of worship.

With due respect to the theocratic constitution of contemporary Pakistan, it must be pointed out that the religious diversity of Jammu and Kashmir rules out any morally acceptable subsumption of the area within Pakistan.

India, since its independence, has refused to become a theocratic state, refused to follow the example of Pakistan in this respect, and remains constitutionally a secular and spiritual democracy, committed to equal respect for all religious traditions, and respect also for the right of non-religious traditions to profess their points of view. This openness and accommodatingness of its Constitution is what confers upon India the right to view Jammu and Kashmir as an integral part of its national life; but only so long as the ground rules and realities of that life are not allowed to be distorted by hegemonist Hindu demands. Such as the demand that a Sri Ram Mandir be established at the self-same site where the demolished Babri Masjid stood, and that a mosque in Mathura and another in Varanasi be demolished or relocated to accommodate Hindu temples at their sites. For the Indian state to yield to such demands would be for it to function as a *de facto* Hindu theocratic state, nullifying its claim to Jammu and Kashmir. The integrity of India demands the renunciation of historical vengefulness.

Renouncing their claims to the whole territory of Jammu and Kashmir, and accepting the present division of the area as mirroring both the reality and tragedy of the partition of undivided India, India and Pakistan, Hindus and Muslims and others, could seek to do that which alone can bring some consolation to the victims of partition, that is, participate as reconciled brothers and sisters in the service of the unique gift of God to them which is the land of Jammu and Kashmir. For this purpose, a cultural parliament could be inaugurated in the area to which members would be elected and nominated from the subcontinent as a whole. This is just one thought. A deluge of constructive suggestions would overwhelm us once the barriers of hate and suspicion, pride and prestige, are overcome. And when the killing stops.

It would then also become possible for India and Pakistan to do something together for the violated of Hiroshima and Nagasaki, and with a special empathy. As survivors of an explosion themselves, the explosion which was the ill-thought-through partition of India, Indians and Pakistanis could together wage irresistible satyagraha towards global nuclear disarmament. Our acquisition of nuclear-weapons capability could become a blessing in disguise. We now have nuclear weapons to renounce, of course at the same pace as the rest of the nuclear powers! But this is not the end of the news. Good and bad.

All nuclear weapons in existence would have been tested against the Hiroshima and Nagasaki scale, for there is no other way of determining their destructive power against human life and its environment with precision. Thus, knowledge of the devastation of Hiroshima and Nagasaki is built into nuclear weapons, along with the threat of the shame, as opposed to mere destruction and mutilation, which awaits the targets of a nuclear attack: shame similar to what was experienced by the victims of Hiroshima and Nagasaki by reason of the fact that they were the unique targets of a weapon fashioned by the abuse of the most advanced science of our times, that is, nuclear physics, and that the genetic damage suffered by survivors could harm their descendants till eternity. The experience of this intensity of shame is so far confined to the survivors of Hiroshima and Nagasaki. It is their intellectual property, for moral experience, such as of shame or gratitude, is undeniably a form of knowledge, whatever Western philosophy may have been saying on the subject.

It follows that the possession of nuclear weapons, let alone their threatened use, involves theft of intellectual property. As would, for instance, the possession of gas chambers built to Auschwitz and Belsen specifications.

The shame experienced by survivors of the holocaust of India's partition is also singular, for they were victims of the subversion of one of the most morally evolved forms of political struggle:

the Indian struggle for freedom and unity. Each time India and Pakistan threaten to go to war against one another, they desecrate the memory of that struggle and its martyrs. Nuclear disarmament and the disarmament of India–Pakistan, Hindu–Muslim, hate are alarmingly similar and urgent duties. Have we tested nuclear weapons, or are nuclear weapons–testing our humanity and reminding us of our duty towards it? These are indeed testing times.

— seventeen —

Towards Nuclear Non-violence*

There is surely something grossly absentminded about a peace measure, such as the CTBT [Comprehensive Nuclear Test–ban Treaty] proposal, which seeks to ban all nuclear test explosions except what would be the most ban-worthy instances of these, that is, explosions caused by military or otherwise violent deployments of nuclear weapons or devices. Unleashing mass murder like their Hiroshima and Nagasaki ancestors, these explosions would nevertheless also be strictly scientific demonstrations of the extreme vulnerability of life to nuclear violation.

Modern idolatry of science obscures the dark truth that there is nothing inherent in the idea of a scientific experiment which requires that it be non-violent. The scope of nuclear tests cannot, except self-deceivingly and arbitrarily, be restricted to non-military test explosions. Besides, it should not be forgotten that nuclear weapons are monster weapons which cannot be fully tested until the willingness of human beings to use them monstrously has also been tested. There is an unbroken line of continuity between non-military nuclear tests and nuclear apocalypse.

*Unpublished essay, 10 September 1996.

It would also be self-deceiving to think that violent nuclear explosions are implicitly covered by CTBT's general category of a nuclear explosion. Had this been the case, the proposed treaty would have been obliged to prohibit the possession of nuclear weapons, each and every existing nuclear weapon being a holocaust project, a satanic experiment-in-the-offing, which is as close to actualisation as an intended non-military nuclear test explosion is to its occurrence. Instructively, a ban on the possession of nuclear weapons is not perceived by CTBT advocates as a necessary consequence of the treaty's premises.

Nuclear disarmament, global and total, is an imperative which is internal to the idea of outlawing hubris-ridden explorations of the holocaust power of nuclear explosions; it is not an additional or merely closely connected issue which calls for separate negotiations with nuclear powers. India's case against the present form of the CTBT proposal would gain sharpness and strength if this corollary of it were more aggressively highlighted by our negotiators for nuclear parity and sanity.

Extending the scope of the notion of a nuclear test along the lines suggested above, India could launch a counter CTBT initiative, proposing a simultaneous but synchronised ban on nuclear tests and weapons, so as to ensure that no country arrives prematurely and vulnerably at a condition of nuclear defencelessness in relation to a nuclear power; and to ensure a democratically simultaneous attainment of global nuclear harmlessness.

To avoid the ecological hazardousness of nuclear test explosions, the technology of computer-simulated tests could be made available to nuclear-vulnerable countries under international supervision; alternatively, already tested nuclear weapons could perhaps be loaned to them. International supervision could also ensure a rapid and irreversible pace of elimination of all nuclear weapons.

It is likely that such a proposal would be sneeringly rejected by nuclear powers and their allies; but it would at least expose the hypocrisy of their self-serving delimitation of the notion of a nuclear test, calculated to conceal the violent experimental designs embodied in existing nuclear weapons and their threatened deployment.

Asian countries were the first—and have, so far, been the only—target of nuclear violence. Also an Asian, Mahatma Gandhi, was the first world leader to condemn the Hiroshima and Nagasaki outrages on strictly moral grounds. The victims of those outrages, and Gandhi, have bequeathed a moral capital to Asian countries which they should not squander in deluded pursuit of nuclear violence. Nor should they let it remain idle in the face of big power bullying and hypocrisy.

The proposal sketched above of an alternative Indian CTBT initiative could mark a democratic middle path towards nuclear non-violence, avoiding the unrealistic extreme of unilateral nuclear renunciation and also the unacceptable extreme of competitive nuclear armament.

Meanwhile, nuclear and economic powers are likely to put unworthy pressure on India to sign flawed test-ban treaties, demanding to know just who we think we are. Delving deep into the sources of our civilisation, and echoing the late British comedian Peter Sellers, we should respond with the *mahavakya* [great or wise sentence], 'In India we don't think who we are, we know who we are!' And do what we think is right.

— *eighteen* —

Private Knives, Hives*

Hijacker Gajendar Singh is reported to have grumbled to a grinning but unbelieving Zia that acid Hinduism could not be neutralised by the Alkali Dal alone; that the unfolding of Asian Drama as prophesied by that eminent Sikh in Swedish disguise, Myrnal Gurdyal, urgently needs the supplanting of the mystic vegetarian motto, 'Peas that passeth all understanding', by the fruity Nihang call, '*Raj karega Phalsa*'; that the private knives of *des* Panjabis should be left well alone by public policy, putting an end to air-hostesses who ask such rhetorical questions as '*Kaisa kaan khaiyega, meetha ya saada*?' Still grinning, but not compassionately, Zia is reported to have muttered that it was Pakistan's hoary pre-Aryan, and not hoary Hindu past that inspired him to give his special secret service for gobbling up all dissent, the evocative name 'Harappa'; that all obscene modern military dancing will be ended in Pakistan, especially no khan-khan dancers of humiliating memory will be left with any legs to stand on; that only the punitive, and not the pacifist, interpretation of Hemingway's novel *A Farewell to Arms* will be permitted in martial law 'hands out'; that far more acute than Gandhi's was Iqbal's critique of Western civilisation in such

*Originally published in *Himmat* 17 (23), 1 November 1981: p. 40.

suppressed (by Bhutto) works of his as 'Maan na Maan, Main Tera Thomas Mann', 'Upar Nahin, Nietzsche', and 'Sigmund Fraud'; that whatever Hindu historians might say, Taj Mahal is made of marble and not of Oak; that so long as Bharat prefers CPM to IBM, CPI to CBI, he and Indira Gandhi cannot CIA to IA with one another. 'AI AI, Sir', said the young frightened pirate with dreams of international flight, his entourage being reduced from a *kirpan* to a *kirtan mandali*, thank God!

Meanwhile in Canberra thunders Indira that the Tihar *andolan* under Sobhraj will be as brutally suppressed as the Bihar andolan under Jayaprakash of a bygone era; that trusts-worthy aides of hers like Antulay will never eat humble pie, Vij or Non-Vij, in prison. Hailing Antulay as amass-leader in her own image, she struck a deep chord of sympathy in the hearts of the assembled third-underworld elite as she invoked the infectious principle, 'Leave the private hives of leaders well alone'. 'We missed you in Watergate, Indira', lamented a ruined former Nixon aide now 'down under' playing hive-and-seek. Rumour has it, however, that when Mrs Indira Gandhi presented a miniature Apple to Ramphal, the latter inaudibly and yet grinningly queried 'Buddha or *yuddha*, Gandhi or *aandhi*?'

For more details of cynical world machinations, see 'Makhiyan-wali Gali', late Lala Jagat Narain, Amritsar Arya Press, forthcoming.

— *nineteen* —

A Sense of Rumour*

It is rumoured that the Charan Singh government had received a proposal from the famous French anthropologist [Claude] Lévi-Strauss entitled 'towards a plural religious consciousness'. The Lok Dal manifesto, however, announced the proposal under the heading, 'towards a rural religious consciousness', causing, it is feared, a rift between Lévi-Strauss and Charan Singh. The French always put *des*-cartes before *des* heart, complained a bitter Mani Ram Bagri.

It is feared that get-ahead politicians belonging to the 'formers lobby', that is, the lobby of former members of all political parties and programmes, not Sharad Joshi's 'farmers lobby', are about to present a volume of tributes to our President entitled, 'Reddy, steddy go'.

It is held that Babu Jagjivan Ram received a message from Mrs Indira Gandhi on the eve of the last general elections, which said, roughly, this: '*Chunav jorgaram, Babuji, mein layee majedar chunav jorgaram. Mera chunav bada hai ala, isme dala Nagarvala chunav jorgaram*'. It is postulated that 'with a few reservations', Babuji would now be open to a variety of political opportunities, although he is

*Originally published in *Himmat* 17 (14), 15 June 1981: p. 47.

said hotly to have denied that President Regan's scepticism regarding our country derives from his perception of it as an Indian reservation.

It is feared that Mr Chandra Shekhar will soon appeal to all of us to give the Janata Party the benefit of the rout.

It has been claimed that succumbing to her passion for the automatic as opposed to the democratic aspects of Indian life, the prime minister will shortly propose a switch to the providential form of government.

It is suspected that the radical, pro-bomb wing of the Bharat Sant Samaj will slightly modify the Gayatri Mantra and offer the nation the new motto: '*Om bourgeois svaha, tat savitururanium.*'

They say George Fernandes hotly denies that the effect of the railway strike of 1974 on railway workers has been such that if you gave them an inch they would take a yard.

It is being whispered that all manner of electoral malpractices are being traced by blasphemous elements to the rig-Veda.

The blasphemous are also tracing the decline of slow-bowling in the West to Christ's words, 'Behold the lilies of the field, they toil not, neither do they spin', and the decline of fast-blowling in the East to certain Quranic *surras*.

More hope-giving than some of the above news is the report that P. V. Narasimha Rao's current favourite film song is '*Zia Milan ko jana*', and that he has recommended to the Third World the motto of the Barbers' Association of India, that is, 'Friendship towards all, *malish* towards none.'

No less encouraging is the fabrication that when asked to recount their favourite spiritual words, a large number of our uninformed policemen said, 'We have eyes, but see not' and 'He makes the dumb to speak', although when Kedar Pande asked them out of the blue to name their favourite train, they blurted out 'Indian Express'.

But to end on a more cautiously realistic note, it is strongly surmised that the Chinese pull-back from our doorstep in 1962 was caused by President Radhakrishnan's thunderous declaration on All India Radio that Dharma was on our side. Thinking that Burma, a new ally, was on our side, the Chinese wisely withdrew.

— *twenty* —

Stephen Lila*

Dr D. C. Ghose, modern Hanuman in red velvet underwear and nothing else, pipe in mouth and upholding on the palm of left hand the hill of St Stephen's (brick and stone and lawn and gravel and corridors that activate even now memory-pictures of perfect illusory happiness, slow-motion montages of cricket and non-alignment and good manners and cigarette-smoke set in a winter afternoon after lazy lunch and Coffee House coffee) intermittently illuminating the multi-coloured bulb-adorned structure with sharp short cries of '*Do* you see?', '*Do* you see?'

II

The Kayastha community of Delhi insisting that St Stephen's was the first Christian Mathur.

III

'Knock and it shall be opened unto you', says Jesus. Radicalism.

'Don't knock on anybody's door more than three times; it is rude', says Mr Walker. Revisionism.

*Originally published in *The Stephanian*, St Stephen's College, date unknown.

'Behold Vinoo Mankad (in his later fat years), he is like the lilies of the field. He toils not, neither does he *spin*', does Balbir say this? Cynicism.

'Sikkim and you shall find him', says mountaineer Bamzai. *Pun*ditry.

'I shall give you living waters', says Morarji Desai. The deluge.

'*Chunav jorgaram, chunav jorgarm, Babuji, mein layee majedar chunav jorgaram*', says Indira Gandhi to Jagjivan Ram on the eve of the general elections. But are she and her father one? After the deluge, Me!

IV

When, as head of the hazardous college climbing expedition to the Leaning Tower of Misa, Balbir failed to get reservations on the Janata Express, he dropped his haversack full of the *Collected Works of Wittgenstein* and *Frankenstein* on the unsuspecting toes of T. T. Rajpal, who thundered, 'Admit it, admit that you are A (B) SURD!' Balbir's cunning reply was, 'I will, I will, with a few reservations.' Balbir got his reservations, and the haver SACK!

V

Notice on College Café wall during Emergency: '*Batein cum! Chay zyada*!'

All India Coffee Board's dastardly propaganda that [K. L.] Sehgal's hit song was '*Chay barbad karegi hamein maloom natha*!'.

All India Tea Board recommends a permanent mobile sculptural show of Bose Saheb, Dr Ghose, and Colonel Pierson dancing the Cha! Cha! Cha! on the lawn in Andrews' Court, advertising three eternal choices: Plato or Aristotle, Tea or Coffee, St Stephen's or Hindu College. Inspired by the topsy-turvy-ness of the final outcome of the world-process as prophesied by Jesus, yogiji issues the following inversions and conversions:

'*Garam khet mein, naram khet mein, sub neta yuyutsavaha khanmakhan pandavashchaiva, kya gurbathai, Sanjaya?*' (from 'Epistle to Dhritarashtra').

The Law of Old said, '*Sau chuhe kha ke billi haj ko chali*', whereas I say, '*Sau billi kha ke chuha haj ko chala*' (from 'Requiem for Billimaran').

Yesterday it was said, '*Jiski lathi uski bhains*'; today I say, '*Jiski bhains uski lathi!*' (from 'Tribute to Charan Singh').

Don't say '*Aham brahmasmi*', '*Tat tvam asi*' and '*Sarvam khalvidam brahma*'; say now, '*Aham garam admi*', '*Dhat tvam teri aisi ki taisi*', '*Sarvam kha jaoonga mein*', you do not deserve to say anything else! (from 'Mein Mao Se Tung Hoon').

VI

St Stephen's College Ravana Society (a) demands that the names of two popular films be changed: *Savan ko Ane Do* to be changed to *Ravan ko Ane Do*, and *Solva Savan* to be changed to *Solva Ravan*, (b) adopts the motto '*Langoor khatte hein!*', (c) offers its members a choice of two principal foods: *aloo mater dhobi* or *ganwar ki phali*, and (d) proposes that the ancient scripture Isa Upanishad, that is, Isopanishad, be supplanted by the new Misa Upanishad, that is, Misopanishad, if not by the even newer Ghoonsa Upanishad, that is, Ghoonsopanishad, and Bhoosa Upanishad, that is, Bhoosopanishad, a free rendering of the first line of the new refrain being: 'We live and move and have our being in *misa*, *ghoonsa* and *ghoosa*.'

VII

In gratitude for the fact that although grace is no longer said before dinner in college, the name of the college was not changed to Mr Stephen's College, especially after the last elections, and that the college is not likely to make its political cheques payable to (VAJ) Payee's account only, I dedicate the above longing for an absurdist martyrdom to the feet of the Lord.

Ramchandra Gandhi, 1954–59, 1961–74

Born 1937. Old student, 1954–59; B.Sc. (Hons.). Physics and M.A. (Philosophy).

Later obtained D.Phil. (Oxon.). Lecturer in Philosophy, 1961–74 (with minor breaks). Subsequently, Reader in Philosophy at Rajasthan and Delhi; at present, Professor of Philosophy at the University of Hyderabad.

Index